Study Guide
to accompany

ECONOMICS TODAY
The Micro View
Twelfth Edition

Roger LeRoy Miller
Institute for University Studies,
Arlington, Texas

David VanHoose
Baylor University

Reproduced by Pearson Addison-Wesley from Microsoft® Word files supplied by the author.

Copyright © 2004 Pearson Education, Inc.
Publishing as Pearson Addison-Wesley, 75 Arlington Street, Boston MA 02116

All rights reserved. Printed in the United States of America.

ISBN   0-321-19424-1

3 4 5 6 CRS 06 05 04

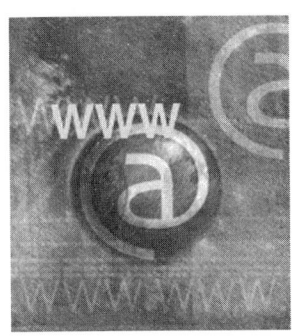

TABLE OF CONTENTS

Preface: To the Student v

Chapter 1: The Nature of Economics 1

Chapter 2: Scarcity and the World of Trade-offs 8

Chapter 3: Demand and Supply 19

Chapter 4: Extensions of Demand and Supply Analysis 33

Chapter 5: The Public Sector and Public Choice 43

Chapter 6: Taxes, Transfers, and Public Spending 59

Chapter 19: Consumer Choice 71

Appendix E: More Advanced Consumer Choice Theory 80

Chapter 20: Demand and Supply Elasticity 88

Chapter 21: Rents, Profits, and the Financial Environment of Business 98

Chapter 22: The Firm: Cost and Output Determination 111

Chapter 23: Perfect Competition 124

Chapter 24: Monopoly 136

Chapter 25: Monopolistic Competition 146

Chapter 26: Oligopoly and Strategic Behavior 157

Chapter 27: Regulation and Antitrust Policy in a Globalized Economy 168

Chapter 28: Labor Demand and Supply 177

Chapter 29: Unions and Labor Market Monopoly Power 187

Chapter 30: Income, Poverty, and Health Care 197
Chapter 31: Environmental Economics 209
Chapter 32: Comparative Advantage and the Open Economy 219
Chapter 33: Exchange Rates and the Balance of Payments 228

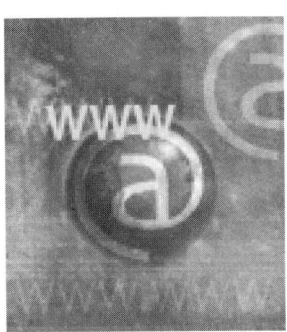

PREFACE TO THE STUDENT

This *Study Guide* is designed to help you read and understand *Economics Today*, 12th Edition. Lesson one in economics is that nothing is free; a price must be paid for every activity that is performed and for every good or service that is obtained. The price that you must pay to learn economics certainly includes the course tuition and the costs of your textbook and this *Study Guide*. The price for learning economics also includes the time and effort that it will take you to read and think about this discipline. But the benefits are, potentially, enormous.

If you really learn economics you will achieve your immediate objective, which is (presumably) to make a good grade. More importantly—for the long run—if you learn to think like an economist, you will gain some very crucial insights into human behavior. You should never forget that economics is, first and foremost, a study of human behavior. An understanding of human behavior is a necessary prerequisite to attaining your personal goals and to fulfilling any goals that you might have of helping other people. Good intentions are not enough; if you really want to help people you must understand how they are likely to respond to specific policies. And economics has proven to be an invaluable aid in understanding human motivation.

HOW THIS *STUDY GUIDE* CAN HELP YOU

This student guide can help you to maximize your learning, subject to constraints on the amount of time that you can allot to this course. There are at least five specific ways in which you can benefit from this guide.

1. The *Study Guide* can help you decide what topics are the most important. Because there are so many topics analyzed in each chapter (in *all* principles of economics textbooks) many students become confused about what is essential and what is not. You can't learn everything; the *Study Guide* can help you concentrate on the crucial topics in each chapter.

2. If you are forced to miss a class or two (we strongly recommend that you attend class regularly, but we realize that emergencies do arise), you can use this *Study Guide* to help you learn the material discussed in your absence.

3. There is a good chance that the questions you are required to answer in this *Study Guide* are representative of the types of questions that you will be asked during examinations.

4. You can use this *Study Guide* to help you review for exams.

5. Finally, this *Study Guide* can help you decide whether you really do understand the material. Don't wait until exam time to find out!

Ultimately, the way to learn economics is by reading your textbook and *thinking about the theories*. You should try to express the analysis in your own words and to apply the theory to real world circumstances. This *Study Guide* can't teach you to think like an economist—you'll have to learn to do that on your own. It can, however, provide feedback on your progress; if you can answer the questions and solve the problems, then you will know that you are on the right path.

THE CONTENTS OF THE *STUDY GUIDE*

Economics is considered to be a rather difficult subject because (a) it is theoretical in nature, (b) it uses a specialized jargon, or vocabulary, and (c) it takes (most people) much time and effort to learn. We who are economists, however, believe that our discipline is exciting and provides tremendous insights into human behavior. Your text and this *Study Guide* have been written for the precise purpose of helping you to learn economics. We always try to keep you, the student, in mind.

Before we indicate to you how we think you can best utilize this *Study Guide* to achieve your goals we want to indicate to you what it contains. Most chapters include the following sections.

1. Learning Objectives

Here we list approximately ten things that you should be able to do after you have completed the chapter.

2. Chapter Outline

This section presents a sentence outline for the chapter; it provides you with a quick overview of the contents of the chapter and it includes only the most important topics.

3. Key Terms

This section provides a list of the most important terms used in the text chapter; these terms are crucial to your understanding and each is defined in the glossary at the end of its *Study Guide* chapter.

4. Key Concepts

This is a list of the most important theoretical concepts used in the chapter; these too are explained in the end-of-chapter glossary.

5. Completion Questions

This set of short answer "fill-in-the-blank" questions is intended to test your knowledge of key terms, key concepts, and facts. Some will require an application of the theoretical concepts contained in the text.

6. True-False Questions

This is another objective test to help you see if you understand the main issues in the chapter. We also explain what is wrong with each false statement. We believe that this will be very helpful to you.

7. Multiple-Choice Questions

The numerous multiple-choice questions in each chapter are another objective test to help you decide whether or not you need to spend more time and effort on the chapter at hand.

8. Working with Graphs

Because graphs are so central to the study of economics, we decided to allocate an entire section (in those chapters where applicable) devoted to helping you interpret graphs. We believe that if you can master graphical analysis, the rest of economics will follow easily. The questions appearing in this section are the actual questions that we pose to our students in the classroom; teachers know that if students cannot answer such questions there is no point in moving on.

9. Problems

This section requires you to take a pencil in hand and solve specific problems that depend on your knowledge of the chapter's contents. Often students believe that they understand certain concepts, but then they cannot solve related problems. By working on these questions you will see the concepts in another light, and a deeper understanding will emerge.

10. Answers

We have placed the answers to the *Study Guide* at the end of each chapter, and not at the end of the book. We believe that you will find this convenient.

11. Chapter Glossary

Because economics vocabulary is so important, we decided to add it to the student guide. And we have placed it where it is the most useful: at the end of the relevant chapter, not at the end of the book.

HOW TO USE THIS STUDY GUIDE

What follows is a recommended strategy for improving your grade. It may seem like an awful lot of work, but the payoffs will be high. Try the whole program for the first three or four chapters. If you feel you can skip some steps safely, then try doing so and see what happens. After all, only you can know your capabilities and individual circumstances. We do urge you, however, to give this approach a chance.

For each chapter we recommend that you follow the sequence of steps below.

1. Read the introduction, the learning objectives, the sentence outline, and the lists of key terms and concepts in this *Study Guide*; follow any study suggestions offered in the introduction.

2. Read the Chapter Summary in your text at the end of the chapter.

3. Read about half the textbook chapter (unless it is very long), being sure to underline only the most important points which you should be able to recognize after having read two chapter outlines. Put a check mark by that material that you don't understand.

4. If you find the textbook chapter easy to understand, you might want to finish reading it. Otherwise, rest for a sufficient period (you can be the judge of how long it takes you to be refreshed) before you read the second half of the chapter. Again be sure to underline only the most important points and to put a checkmark by the material you find difficult to understand.

5. After you have completed the entire textbook chapter, take a break. Then read only what *you* have underlined, throughout the entire chapter.

6. Now concentrate on the difficult material, by which you have left checkmarks. Reread this material and *think about it*; you will find that it is very exciting to figure out difficult material on your own.

7. Read each of the chapter preview questions in the textbook and write out your answer. After you have finished, compare your answers to the answers to those questions provided by your author at the end of the chapter.

8. Find the comparable chapter in this *Study Guide* and answer the completion questions, the true-false questions, the multiple-choice questions, the problems, and the working with graphs questions. Compare your answers with the answers provided at the back of the *Study Guide* chapter. Make a note of the questions you have missed and find the page(s) in your textbook upon which these *Study Guide* questions are based. If you still don't understand—ask your teacher or your student teaching assistant. (If you decided that our answers are wrong, then by all means write and tell us.)

9. Re-read the learning objectives in this *Study Guide* and decide if you are able to achieve each of these objectives.

10. Before your examination, study your class notes. Reread the *Study Guide* outline, then re-do the completion questions, the true-false questions, the multiple-choice questions, and the problems. Compare your answer with the answer at the back of the appropriate chapter in this guide. Identify your problem areas and re-read the relevant pages in the book. Think through the answers on your own. If you still can't understand the analysis, ask your teacher or your student teaching assistant for help. (Be sure to let your teacher know that you have tried to answer the questions on your own.)

If you have followed the strategy outlined above, you should feel sufficiently confident and be relaxed to do well on your exam.

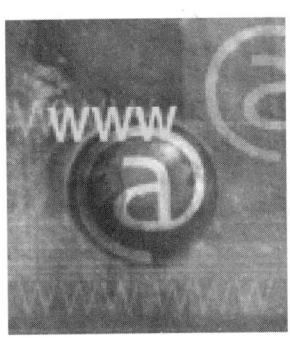

CHAPTER 1
THE NATURE OF ECONOMICS

LEARNING OBJECTIVES

After you have read this chapter, you should be able to

1. define economics;

2. distinguish between microeconomics and macroeconomics;

3. recognize the rationality assumption;

4. recognize elements of an economic model, or theory;

5. recognize that economics is ultimately concerned with human behavior;

6. define resource;

7. distinguish between positive economics and normative economics, and be able to classify specific statements under each category.

CHAPTER OUTLINE

1. Economics, a social science, is defined as the study of how people make choices to satisfy their wants.
    a. Wants are all the things that people would consume if they had unlimited income.
    b. Because wants are unlimited and people cannot satisfy all their wants, individuals are forced to make choices about how to spend their income and how to allocate their time.

2. Economics is broadly divided into microeconomics and macroeconomics.
    a. Microeconomics studies decision making undertaken by individuals (or households) and by firms.
    b. Macroeconomics studies the behavior of the economy taken as a whole; it deals with such economy-wide phenomena as unemployment, the price level, and national income.

3. Economists assume that individuals are motivated by self-interest and respond predictably to opportunities for gain.

a. The rationality assumption is that individuals act *as if* they were rational.
b. Self-interest often means a desire for material well-being, but it can also be defined broadly enough to incorporate goals relating to love, friendship, prestige, power, and other human characteristics.
c. By assuming that people act in a rational, self-interested way, economists can generate testable theories concerning human behavior.

4. Economics is a social science.
   a. Economists develop models, or theories, which are simplified representations of the real world.
   b. Such models help economists to understand, explain, and predict economic phenomena in the real world.
   c. Like other social scientists, economists usually do not perform laboratory experiments; they typically examine what already has occurred in order to test their theories.
   d. Economic theories, like all scientific theories, are simplifications—and in that sense they are "unrealistic."
   e. Economists, as do all scientists, employ assumptions; one important economic assumption is "all other things being equal."
   f. Models or theories are evaluated on their ability to predict, and not on the realism of the assumptions employed.
   g. Economic models relate to behavior, not thought processes.

5. Economists maintain that the unit of analysis is the individual; members of a group are assumed to pursue their own goals rather than the group's objectives.

6. Positive economics is objective and scientific in nature, and deals with testable *if this, then that* hypotheses.

7. Normative economics is subjective and deals with value judgments, or with what *ought* to be.

KEY TERMS
Aggregates
Ceteris paribus
 (other things being equal)
Economics
Empirical
Incentives
Macroeconomics
Microeconomics
Models (or theories)
Resource
Wants

KEY CONCEPTS
Normative economics
Positive economics
Rationality assumption

COMPLETION QUESTIONS
Fill in the blank, or circle the correct term.

1. Because it is impossible to have all that we want, people are forced to make _____.

2. Economics is a (natural, social) science.

3. Economics is the study of how people make _____ to satisfy their _____.

4. Microeconomics deals with (individual units, the whole economy).

5. A nation's unemployment level is analyzed in (microeconomics, macroeconomics).

6. (Macroeconomics, Microeconomics) studies the causes and effects of inflation.

7. Economists maintain that a member of a group usually attempts to make decisions that are in (her own, the group's) interest.

8. The rationality assumption is that individuals (believe, act as if) they are rational.

9. Economic models are (simplified, realistic) representations of the real world.

10. The *ceteris paribus* assumption enables economists to consider (one thing at a time, everything at once).

11. Married men are more likely to earn higher incomes if their wives work (inside, outside) the home.

12. Economists maintain that incentives (are, are not) important to decision making.

13. Economists define self-interest (narrowly, broadly).

14. Economists take the (individual, group) as the unit of analysis.

15. Economic statements that are testable and are of an "if/then" nature are (positive, normative).

TRUE-FALSE QUESTIONS
Circle the **T** if the statement is true, the **F** if it is false. Explain to yourself why a statement is false.

T F 1. Economics is the study of how people think about economic phenomena.

T F 2. The economists' definition of self-interest includes only the pursuit of material goods.

T F 3. Macroeconomics deals with aggregates, or totals, of economic variables.

T F 4. When economists attempt to predict the number of workers a firm will employ, they are studying macroeconomics.

T F 5. Economists maintain that people respond in a predictable way to economic incentives.

T F 6. The rationality assumption is that individuals attempt, quite consciously, to make rational economic decisions, and will admit to it.

T F 7. It is justifiable to criticize theories on the realism of the assumptions employed.

T F 8. Households cannot be thought of as producers.

T F 9. Because economics is a science, economists do not make normative statements.

T F 10. Medical issues such as what form of treatment to use for kidney dialysis patients are outside the scope of economics.

CHAPTER 1: THE NATURE OF ECONOMICS

MULTIPLE CHOICE QUESTIONS
Circle the letter that corresponds to the best answer.

1. Economics is
   a. a natural science.
   b. nonscientific.
   c. a social science.
   d. usually studied through lab experiments.

2. Wants include desires for
   a. material possessions.
   b. love.
   c. power.
   d. All of the above

3. Which of the following areas of study is concerned, primarily, with microeconomics?
   a. the steel industry
   b. inflation
   c. the national unemployment rate
   d. national income determination

4. Macroeconomic analysis deals with
   a. the steel industry.
   b. how individuals respond to an increase in the price of gasoline.
   c. inflation.
   d. how a change in the price of energy affects a family.

5. Economists maintain that Mr. Smith will usually make decisions that promote the interests of
   a. his colleagues at work.
   b. himself.
   c. his class.
   d. his race.

6. Economic models
   a. use unrealistic assumptions.
   b. are seldom tested in laboratories.
   c. are concerned with how people behave, not with how they think.
   d. All of the above

7. An economic model is justifiably criticized if
   a. its assumptions are not realistic.
   b. it cannot be tested in a controlled, laboratory experiment.
   c. it fails to predict.
   d. All of the above

8. Which of the following is true of the "marriage premium"?
   a. It amounts to about 20 percent of women's earnings and about 10 percent of men's earnings.
   b. It results from one spouse handling the bulk of household management tasks.
   c. Both married men and married women earn equal marriage premiums.
   d. It is most commonly observed among women instead of men.

9. Economics
   a. is a natural science.
   b. is concerned with how people respond to incentives.
   c. is unconcerned with value judgments.
   d. deals with assumptions and therefore is unrealistic.

10. As is true of a road map showing how a traveler can move about a geographic region, a model of economic behavior typically
    a. omits trivial details and emphasizes factors most relevant to the problem under consideration.
    b. makes no simplifying assumptions, so that every feature of a problem is taken into account.
    c. must be rejected if it leaves out some information, even if it makes correct predictions.
    d. includes each and every element of a problem confronting an individual or group.

11. Which of the following is a normative economics statement?
    a. If price rises, people will buy less.
    b. If price rises, people will buy more.
    c. If price rises the poor will be injured; therefore price should not be permitted to rise.
    d. If price rises people will buy less; therefore we ought to observe that quantity demanded falls.

12. Which of the following is a positive economics statement?
    a. Full employment policies should be pursued.
    b. If minimum wage rates rise, then unemployment will rise.
    c. We should take from the rich and give to the poor.
    d. The government should help the homeless.

13. Normative economics statements
    a. are testable hypotheses.
    b. are value-free.
    c. are subjective, value judgments.
    d. can be scientifically established.

MATCHING
Choose the item in Column (2) that best matches an item in Column (1).

(1)	(2)
a. normative economics	f. nonscientific value judgments
b. macroeconomics	g. objective, scientific hypotheses
c. self-interest	h. study of individual behavior
d. positive economics	i. study of economic aggregates
e. microeconomics	j. rational behavior

ANSWERS TO CHAPTER 1

COMPLETION QUESTIONS

1. choices
2. social
3. choices; wants
4. individual units
5. macroeconomics
6. macroeconomics
7. her own
8. act as if
9. simplified
10. one thing at a time
11. inside
12. are
13. broadly
14. individual
15. positive

TRUE-FALSE QUESTIONS

1. F Economics is the study of how people make choices to satisfy their wants.
2. F Economists have a broader definition of self-interest; wants include power, friendship, love, and so on.
3. T
4. F The example is about microeconomics.
5. T
6. F That assumption is merely that people act *as if* they are rational.
7. F All theories employ unrealistic assumptions; what matters is how well they predict.
8. F Households can be thought of as combining goods and time to produce outputs such as meals.
9. F Economists, like other scientists, can and do make normative statements.
10. F Choices of all types, including among alternative medical treatments, can be subjected to economic analysis.

MULTIPLE CHOICE QUESTIONS

1.c; 2.d; 3.a; 4.c; 5.b; 6.d; 7.c; 8.b; 9.b; 10.a;
11.c; 12.b; 13.c.

MATCHING

a and f; b and i; c and j; d and g; e and h

GLOSSARY TO CHAPTER 1

Aggregates Total amounts or quantities; aggregate demand, for example, is total planned expenditures throughout a nation.

***Ceteris paribus* assumption** The assumption that nothing changes except the factor or factors being studied.

Economics The study of how people allocate their limited resources to satisfy their unlimited wants.

Empirical Relying on real-world data in evaluating the usefulness of a model.

Incentives Rewards for engaging in a particular activity.

Macroeconomics The study of the behavior of the economy as a whole, including such economywide phenomena as unemployment, the price level, and national income.

Microeconomics The study of decision making undertaken by individuals (or households) and by firms.

Models, or theories Simplified representations of the real world used as the basis for predictions or explanations.

Normative economics Analysis involving value judgments about economic policies; relates to whether things are good or bad. A statement of what *ought to* be.

Positive economics Analysis that is *strictly* limited to making either purely descriptive statements or scientific predictions; for example, "If A, then B." A statement of *what is*.

Rationality assumption The assumption that people do not intentionally make decisions that would leave them worse off.

Resources Things used to produce other things to satisfy people's wants.

Wants What people would buy if their incomes were unlimited.

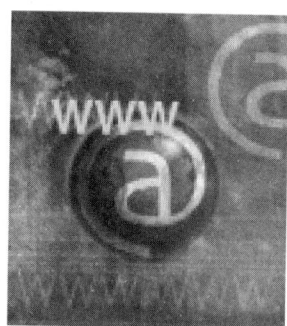

CHAPTER 2
SCARCITY AND THE WORLD OF TRADE-OFFS

LEARNING OBJECTIVES

After you have studied this chapter, you should be able to

1. define production, scarcity, resources, land, labor, human and physical capital, entrepreneurship, goods, services, opportunity costs, production possibilities curve, technology, efficiency, inefficient point, law of increasing relative costs, specialization, absolute advantage, comparative advantage, and division of labor;

2. distinguish between a free good and an economic good;

3. determine the opportunity cost of an activity, when given sufficient information;

4. draw production possibilities curves under varying assumptions, and recognize efficient and inefficient points relating to such curves;

5. understand the difference between a person's or nation's absolute advantage and comparative advantage.

CHAPTER OUTLINE

1. Because individuals or communities do not have the resources to satisfy all their wants, scarcity exists.
    a. If society can get all that it wants of good A when the price of good A is zero, good A is not scarce.
    b. If the price of good B is zero, and society cannot get all that it wants of good B, then B is scarce.
    c. Because resources, or factors of production, are scarce, the outputs they produce are scarce.
        i. Land, the natural resource, includes all the gifts of nature.
        ii. Labor, the human resource, includes all productive contributions made by individuals who work.
        iii. Physical capital, the man-made resource, includes the machines, buildings, and tools used to produce other goods and services.
        iv. Human capital includes the education and training of workers.

v. Entrepreneurship includes the functions of organizing, managing, assembling, and risk-taking necessary for business ventures.
d. Goods include anything from which people derive satisfaction, or happiness.
   i. Economic goods are scarce.
   ii. Noneconomic goods are not scarce.
   iii. Services are intangible goods.
e. Economists distinguish between wants and needs; the latter are objectively undefinable.

2. Because of scarcity, choice and opportunity costs arise.
   a. Due to scarcity, people trade off options.
   b. The production possibilities curve (PPC) is a graph of the trade-offs inherent in a decision.
      i. When the amount of one resource or good that must be given up to produce an additional units of another resource or good remains constant, the PPC is a straight line.
      ii. When the amount of one resource or good that must be given up to produce an additional unit of another resource or good rises, the PPC is bowed outward.
      iii. A point on a PPC is an efficient point; points inside a PPC are inefficient; points outside the PPC are unattainable (impossible), by definition.
   c. People have an economic incentive to specialize in that endeavor for which they have a comparative advantage.
   d. The process of division of labor increases output and permits specialization.

3. Economic growth can be depicted through PPCs.
   a. There is a trade-off between present consumption and future consumption.
   b. If a nation produces fewer consumer goods and more capital goods now, then it can consume more goods in the future than would otherwise be the case.

4. Opportunity costs are important determinants of voter turnouts for elections.
   a. Instead of spending time going to and from a polling site and waiting in line to cast a ballot, an individual can be earning income or engaging in leisure activities, so every individual who casts a ballot incurs an opportunity cost of voting.
   b. Voter turnout at elections would be higher if society found ways to reduce the time commitment required to cast ballots.

KEY TERMS
Land
Labor
Physical capital
Human capital
Consumption
Economic goods

Goods
Services
Entrepreneurship
Technology
Production possibilities curve

Division of labor
Inefficient point
Scarcity
Production
Specialization

KEY CONCEPTS
Efficiency
Absolute advantage

Opportunity cost
Comparative advantage

Law of increasing relative cost

COMPLETION QUESTIONS
Fill in the blank, or circle the correct term.

1. The factors of production include _____, _____, _____, _____, and _____.

2. People tend to specialize in those activities for which they have (a comparative, an absolute) advantage.

3. When people choose jobs that maximize their income, they are specializing according to their _____ advantage.

4. If at a zero price quantity demanded exceeds quantity supplied for a good, that good is a(n) _____; if at a zero price quantity supplied exceeds quantity demanded for a good, that good is a(n) _____.

5. The _____ of good A is the highest-valued alternative that must be sacrificed to attain it.

6. If the opportunity cost of additional units of a good remains constant, the production possibilities curve will be (linear, bowed outward); if the opportunity cost of additional units of a good rises, the production possibilities curve will be (linear, bowed outward).

7. Because specialized resources are more suited to specific tasks, the opportunity cost of producing additional units of a specific good will (rise, fall).

8. If an economy is inefficient, its actual output combination will lie (inside, outside) the production possibilities curve.

TRUE-FALSE QUESTIONS
Circle the **T** if the statement is true, the **F** if it is false. Explain to yourself why a statement is false.

T F 1. Most individuals' needs exceed their wants.

T F 2. Because resources are scarce, the goods that they produce are also scarce.

T F 3. For most activities no opportunity cost exists.

T F 4. If a production possibilities curve is linear, the opportunity cost of producing additional units of a good rises.

T F 5. At any given moment in time, it is impossible for an economy to be inside its production possibilities curve.

T F 6. The cost to society of lowering the speed limit is zero.

T F 7. People have little incentive to specialize in jobs for which they have a comparative advantage.

T F 8. Economic growth shifts the production possibilities curve outward.

T F 9. If the price to a specific user is zero, the good must be a noneconomic good.

T F 10. The opportunity cost of casting ballots in elections is likely to be almost the same for all voters.

MULTIPLE CHOICE QUESTIONS

Circle the letter that corresponds to the best answer.

1. Because of scarcity
    a. people are forced to make choices.
    b. opportunity costs exist.
    c. people face trade-offs.
    d. All of the above

2. Which of the following is **NOT** considered to be "land"?
    a. bodies of water
    b. fertility of soil
    c. capital
    d. climate

3. Which of the following words does **NOT** belong with the others?
    a. opportunity cost
    b. economic bad
    c. scarcity
    d. economic good

4. Which statement concerning a production possibilities curve is **NOT** true?
    a. A trade-off exists along such a curve.
    b. It is usually linear.
    c. Points inside it indicate inefficiency.
    d. A point outside it is currently impossible to attain.

5. The production possibilities curve is bowed outward because
    a. the relative cost of producing a good rises.
    b. of the law of decreasing relative cost.
    c. all resources are equally suited to the production of any good.
    d. All of the above

6. When nations and individuals specialize,
    a. overall living standards rise.
    b. trade and exchange increase.
    c. people become more vulnerable to changes in tastes and technology.
    d. All of the above

7. When a nation expands its capital stock, it is usually true that
    a. it must forego output of some consumer goods in the present.
    b. the human capital stock must decline.
    c. fewer consumer goods will be available in the future.
    d. no opportunity cost exists for doing so.

8. Ms. Boulware is the best lawyer and the best secretary in town.
    a. She has a comparative advantage in both jobs.
    b. She has an absolute advantage in both jobs.
    c. She has a comparative advantage in being a secretary.
    d. All of the above

9. From 2:00 to 4:00 on a Thursday afternoon, Mr. Stapleton, a fast-food worker who earns the minimum wage, waits while his daughter is examined at a pediatrician's office. Ms. Black, a successful marketing consultant who normally charges a fee of $100 per hour and who recently has turned down several potential clients, spends exactly the same amount of time waiting for her own daughter to be examined. The pediatrician charges Mr. Stapleton $100 for the office visit. Ms. Black also pays the pediatrician $100. We may conclude that during this two-hour period,
   a. both parents incurred identical child-raising costs.
   b. from an economic standpoint, it was irrational for Ms. Black to wait while the pediatrician examined her child.
   c. Ms. Black incurred a higher child-raising cost, because she otherwise could have been earning consulting fees during this time.
   d. Mr. Stapleton incurred a higher child-raising cost, because he otherwise could have been looking for a higher-paying job during this time.

MATCHING
Choose the item in Column (2) that best matches an item in Column (1).

	(1)		(2)
a.	absolute advantage	i.	production possibilities curve
b.	efficiency	j.	specialization
c.	trade-offs	k.	capital
d.	comparative advantage	l.	ability to produce at a lower unit cost
e.	resource	m.	specializing in one's comparative advantage
f.	economic good	n.	society cannot get all it wants at a zero price
g.	inefficiency	o.	highest-valued foregone alternative
h.	opportunity cost	p.	inside PPC

WORKING WITH GRAPHS

1. Given the following information, graph the production possibilities curve in the space provided and then use the graph to answer the questions that follow.

Combination (points)	Autos (100,000 per year)	Wheat (100,000 tons per year)
A	16	0
B	14	4
C	12	7
D	9	10
E	5	12
F	0	13

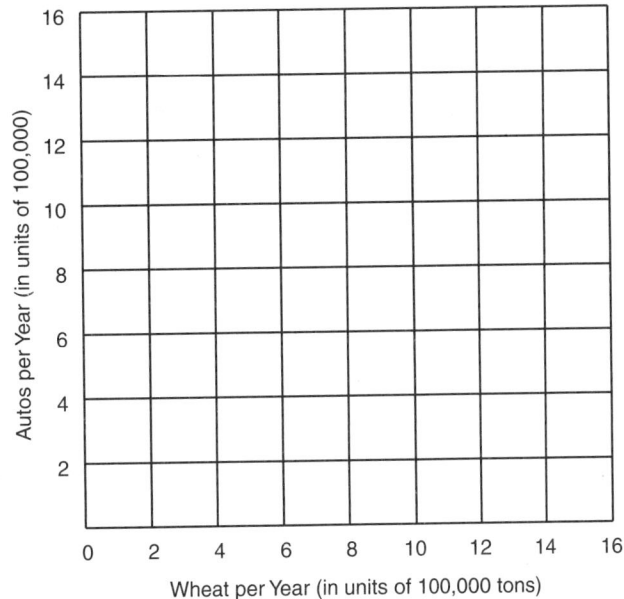

a. If the economy is currently operating at point C, what is the opportunity cost of moving to point D? to point B?

b. Suppose that the economy is currently producing 1,200,000 autos and 200,000 tons of wheat per year. Label this point in your graph with the letter G. At point G the economy would be suffering from what? At point G we can see that it is possible to produce more wheat without giving up any auto production, or produce more autos without giving up any wheat production, or produce more of both. Label this region in your graph. This region appears to contradict the definition of a production possibilities curve. What is the explanation for this result?

c. Suppose a new fertilizer compound is developed that will allow the economy to produce an additional 150,000 tons of wheat per year if no autos are produced. Sketch in a likely representation of the effect of this discovery, assuming all else remains constant.

d. What sort of impact (overall) will this discovery have on the opportunity cost of more wheat production at an arbitrary point on the new production possibilities curve, as compared to a point representing the same level of output of wheat on the original curve?

2. Consider the graphs below, then answer the questions that follow.

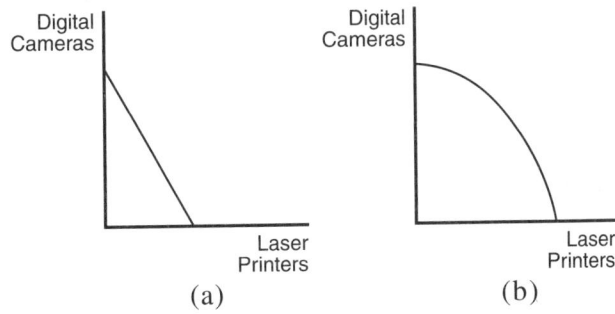

a. Which graph, a or b, shows constant relative costs of producing additional laser printers? Why?

b. Which graph, a or b, shows increasing relative costs of producing additional laser printers? Why?

c. Which graph seems more realistic, a or b? Why?

3. Graph the probable relationship between
   a. income and the amount of money spent on housing;
   b. annual rainfall in New York City and the annual value of ice cream sales in New Orleans;
   c. number of vegetarians per 10,000 people and meat sales per 10,000 people.

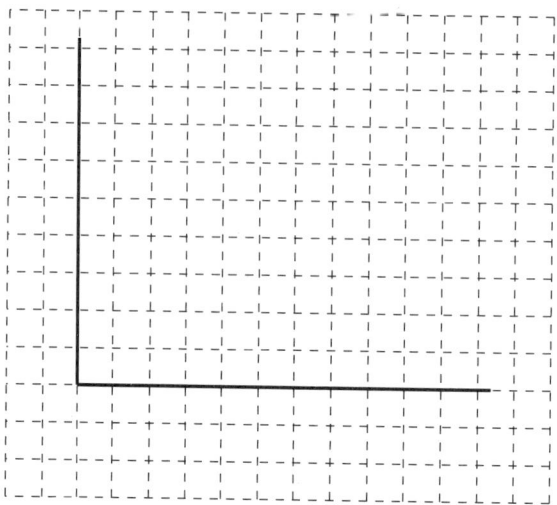

PROBLEMS

1. If a *nation* wants to increase its future consumption, it must forego some present consumption because it must allocate some resources to the production of capital goods. Suppose *you* want to increase your future consumption. Given a fixed lifetime income, what can you do?

2. Assume that Ms. Gentile values her time at $150 per hour because she has the opportunity to do consulting, and that Joe College values his time at $6 per hour. Assume that it costs $400 to fly from their hometown to San Francisco, and that the flight takes 6 hours. Assume that it costs $200 to take a bus, and that the bus trip takes 24 hours.
   a. What is the cheaper way to get to San Francisco for Ms. Gentile? Why?
   b. Which transportation is cheaper for Joe College? Why?

3. Suppose you have a friend currently working as a salesperson in a local computer store that sells personal computers. This friend is thinking about going back to school full-time to finish up work on her computer science degree. She explains to you that she earns $45,000 (after taxes) per year in her current job and that she estimates tuition will cost $4,800 per year. In addition she estimates fees, supplies, books, and miscellaneous expenses associated with attending school will run $2,400 per year. She wants to attend a university that is located directly across the street from the store where she currently works. She claims that she pays $1,050 per month for rent and utilities and that she spends about $600 per month on food, clothing, and related expenses.

Using what you have learned, calculate and explain to your friend the opportunity cost to her of another year back at school.

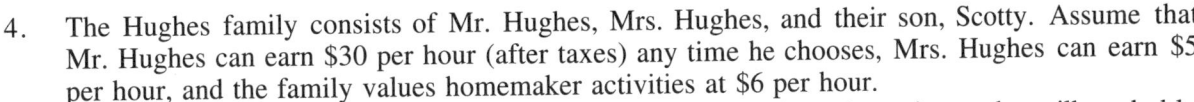

4. The Hughes family consists of Mr. Hughes, Mrs. Hughes, and their son, Scotty. Assume that Mr. Hughes can earn $30 per hour (after taxes) any time he chooses, Mrs. Hughes can earn $5 per hour, and the family values homemaker activities at $6 per hour.
   a. Because the family requires income to purchase goods and services, who will probably work in the marketplace?
   b. Who will probably do the housework?
   c. If the family must pay $3 per hour to have its lawn mowed, who will be assigned that work?
   d. If Scotty can now earn $4 per hour on a job, who now might mow the grass?
   e. If wage rates in the marketplace for Mrs. Hughes rise to $7 per hour, what is the family likely to do?

ANSWERS TO CHAPTER 2

COMPLETION QUESTIONS

1. land, labor, physical capital, human capital, entrepreneurship
2. a comparative
3. comparative
4. economic good; economic "bad"
5. opportunity cost
6. linear; bowed outward
7. rise
8. inside

TRUE-FALSE QUESTIONS

1. F Wants vastly exceed needs (which can't be defined anyway) for everyone.
2. T
3. F An opportunity cost exists for all activities.
4. F A linear PPC implies a constant cost of production.
5. F All an economy need be is inefficient to be inside the PPC.
6. F If people drive more slowly, they suffer opportunity costs for their time.
7. F People can earn more income in jobs for which they have a comparative advantage.
8. T
9. F An individual user *may* pay a zero price for a good, but that doesn't necessarily mean it's a noneconomic good.
10. F A fundamental component of the opportunity cost of casting ballots is wages that a voter foregoes by devoting time to this activity, and wages vary considerably across individuals.

MULTIPLE CHOICE QUESTIONS

1.d;   2.c;   3.b;   4.b;   5.a;   6.d;   7.a;   8.b;   9.c.

MATCHING

a and l; b and m; c and i; d and j; e and k; f and n; g and p; h and o

WORKING WITH GRAPHS

1. See the following graph.

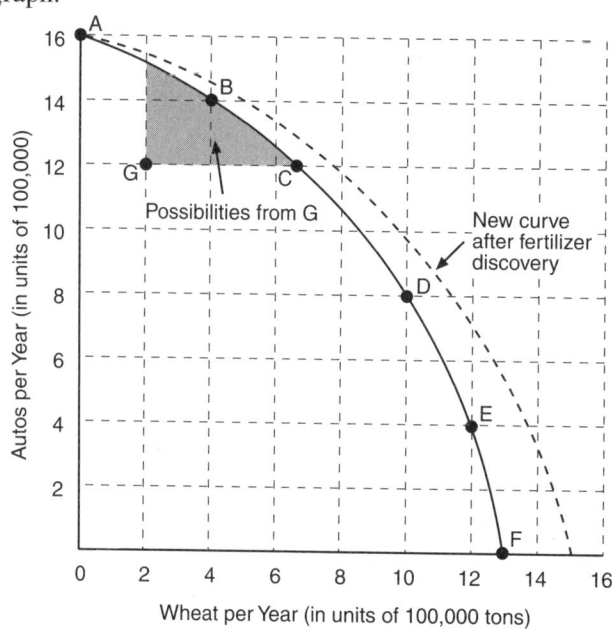

   a. The move from C to D "costs" 300,000 autos—that is, the economy must give up 300,000 autos (1,200,000 - 900,000) to make such a move. The move from C to B "costs" 300,000 tons of wheat. Notice that in both cases there are gains (C to D involves 300,000 more tons of wheat, and C to B means 200,000 more autos are produced), but we measure opportunity costs in terms of movements along a production possibilities curve and what has to be given up to make the choice reflected in the move.
   b. See the preceding graph. Remember, the production possibilities curve shows all possible combinations of two goods that an economy can produce by the efficient use of all available resources in a specified period of time. Since point G is not on the production possibilities curve, the statement contained in this portion of the question does not contradict the definition of the curve. Point G is inside the curve, which implies available resources are not being used efficiently.
   c. See the preceding graph.
   d. It will lower the opportunity cost of additional wheat production.

2. a. Graph a shows constant relative costs because the PPC is linear.
   b. Graph b shows increasing costs because the PPC is bowed out.
   c. Graph b is more realistic because it is likely that the production of laser printers and digital cameras requires specialized resources.

3. a. The graph should be upward sloping from left to right.
   b. There should be no systematic relationship between these two variables.
   c. The graph should be downward sloping from left to right.

PROBLEMS

1. If you want to increase your future consumption—for retirement, say—then you will have to save more out of your current income. The principal and interest that accrue will permit you to purchase more goods in the future than you otherwise would have been able to. Note that by doing so you—as an individual—must forego some present consumption in order to increase your future consumption. In that sense, what is true for the nation is also true for an individual.

2. a. plane; flying costs her $400 plus 6 hours times $150 per hour, or $1,300, while taking a bus would cost her $200 plus 24 hours times $150 per hour, or $3,800.
   b. bus; taking the bus costs him a total of $344, while his total cost of flying is $436.

3. The opportunity cost of another year back at school for your friend is as follows:

Foregone after-tax salary	$45,000
Tuition costs	4,800
Expenses associated with school	2,400
Total opportunity costs	$52,200

4. a. Mr. Hughes
   b. Mrs. Hughes or Scotty
   c. Scotty
   d. The family (or perhaps Scotty) will hire someone to mow the lawn.
   e. Mrs. Hughes may enter the labor force and the family may hire someone to do housework.

GLOSSARY TO CHAPTER 2

Absolute advantage The ability to produce more units of a good or service using a given quantity of labor or resource inputs. Equivalently, the ability to produce the same quantity of a good or service using fewer units of labor or resource inputs.

Comparative advantage The ability to produce a good or service at a lower opportunity cost compared to other producers.

Consumption The use of goods or services for personal satisfaction.

Division of labor The segregation of a resource into different specific tasks; for example, one automobile worker puts on bumpers, another doors, and so on.

Economic goods Goods that are scarce, for which the quantity demanded exceeds the quantity supplied at a zero price.

Efficiency The case in which a given level of inputs is used to produce the maximum output possible. Alternatively, the situation in which a given output is produced at minimum cost.

Entrepreneurship The factor of production involving human resources that perform the functions of raising capital, organizing, managing, assembling other factors of production, and making basic business policy decisions. The entrepreneur is a risk taker.

Goods All things from which individuals derive satisfaction or happiness.

Human capital The accumulated training and education of workers.

Inefficient point Any point below the production possibilities frontier, at which resources are being used inefficiently.

Labor Productive contributions of humans who work, involving both mental and physical activities.

Land The natural resources that are available from nature. Land as a resource includes location, original fertility and mineral deposits, topography, climate, water, and vegetation.

Law of increasing relative cost The observation that the opportunity cost of additional units of a good generally increases as society attempts to produce more of that good. This accounts for the bowed-out shape of the production possibilities curve.

Opportunity cost The highest-valued, next-best alternative that must be sacrificed to attain something or to satisfy a want.

Physical capital All manufactured resources, including buildings, equipment, machines, and improvements to land that is used for production.

Production Any activity that results in the conversion of resources into products that can be used in consumption.

Production possibilities curve (PPC) A curve representing all possible combinations of total output that could be produced assuming (1) a fixed amount of productive resources of a given quality and (b) the efficient use of those resources.

Scarcity A situation in which the ingredients for producing the things that people desire are insufficient to satisfy all wants.

Services Mental or physical labor or help purchased by consumers. Examples are the assistance of physicians, lawyers, dentists, repair personnel, housecleaners, educators, retailers, and wholesalers; things purchased or used by consumers that do not have physical characteristics.

Specialization The division of productive activities among persons and regions so that no one individual or one area is totally self-sufficient. An individual may specialize, for example, in law or medicine. A nation may specialize in the production of coffee, computers, or cameras.

Technology Society's pool of applied knowledge concerning how goods and services can be produced.

CHAPTER 3
DEMAND AND SUPPLY

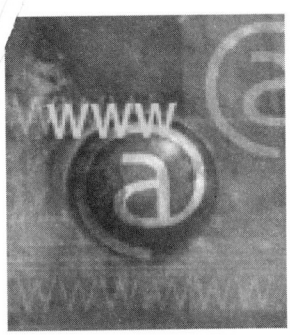

LEARNING OBJECTIVES

After you have studied this chapter, you should be able to

1. define demand schedule, quantity demanded, supply schedule, quantity supplied, equilibrium, shortage, and surplus;

2. graph demand and supply curves from demand and supply schedules;

3. state the law of demand and state two reasons why we observe the law of demand;

4. enumerate five *ceteris paribus* conditions determining demand and five *ceteris paribus* conditions determining supply;

5. predict the effects of a change in the price of one good on the demand for (a) a substitute good, and (b) a complementary good;

6. recognize, from graphs, the difference between a change in demand and a change in quantity demanded, and the difference between a change in supply and a change in quantity supplied;

7. determine from a supply curve and a demand curve what the equilibrium price and the equilibrium quantity will be;

8. explain how markets eliminate surpluses and shortages.

CHAPTER OUTLINE

1. The law of demand states that at higher prices a lower quantity will be demanded than at lower prices, other things being equal.
   a. For simplicity, things other than the price of the good itself are held constant.
   b. Buyers respond to changes in relative, not absolute, prices.

2. The demand schedule for a good is a set of pairs of numbers showing various possible prices and the quantity demanded at each price, for some time period.
   a. Demand must be conceived of as being measured in constant-quality units.
   b. A demand curve is a graphic representation of the demand schedule and it is negatively sloped, reflecting the law of demand.
   c. A market demand curve for a particular good or service is derived by summing all the individual demand curves for that product.

3. The determinants of demand include all factors (other than the good's own price) that influence the quantity purchased.
   a. When deriving a demand curve, other determinants of demand are held constant. When such *ceteris paribus* conditions affecting demand do change, the original demand curve shifts to the left or to the right.
   b. The major determinants of demand are consumers' income, tastes and preferences; changes in their expectations about future relative prices; the price of substitutes and complements for the good in question; and number of buyers.
   c. A change in demand is a shift in the demand curve, whereas a change in quantity demanded is a movement along a given demand curve.

4. Supply is the relationship between price and the quantity supplied, other things being equal.
   a. The law of supply posits generally a direct, or positive, relationship between price and quantity supplied.
      i. As the relative price of a good rises, producers have an incentive to produce more of it.
      ii. As a firm produces greater quantities in the short run, a firm often requires a higher relative price before it will increase output.
   b. A supply schedule is a set of numbers showing prices and the quantity supplied at those various prices.
   c. A supply curve is the graphic representation of the supply schedule; it is positively sloped.
   d. By summing individual supply curves for a particular good or service we derive that good or service's market supply curve.
   e. The major determinants of supply are the prices of resources (inputs) used to produce the product; technology; taxes and subsidies; price expectations of producers; and the number of firms in an industry.
   f. Any change in the determinants of supply (listed in part e) causes a change in supply and therefore leads to a shift in the supply curve.
   g. A change in price, holding the determinants of supply constant, causes a movement along—but not a shift in—the supply curve.

5. By graphing demand and supply on the same coordinate system, we can find equilibrium at the intersection of the two curves.
   a. Equilibrium is a situation in which the plans of buyers and of sellers exactly coincide, so that there is neither excess quantity supplied nor excess quantity demanded; at the equilibrium price, quantity supplied equals quantity demanded.
   b. At a price below the equilibrium price, quantity demanded exceeds quantity supplied, and *excess quantity demanded*, or a shortage, exists.
   c. At a price above the equilibrium price, quantity supplied exceeds quantity demanded, and an *excess quantity supplied*, or a surplus, exists.
   d. Seller competition forces price down and eliminates a surplus.
   e. Buyer competition forces price up and eliminates a shortage.

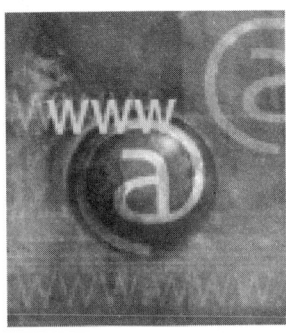

CHAPTER 3
DEMAND AND SUPPLY

LEARNING OBJECTIVES

After you have studied this chapter, you should be able to

1. define demand schedule, quantity demanded, supply schedule, quantity supplied, equilibrium, shortage, and surplus;

2. graph demand and supply curves from demand and supply schedules;

3. state the law of demand and state two reasons why we observe the law of demand;

4. enumerate five *ceteris paribus* conditions determining demand and five *ceteris paribus* conditions determining supply;

5. predict the effects of a change in the price of one good on the demand for (a) a substitute good, and (b) a complementary good;

6. recognize, from graphs, the difference between a change in demand and a change in quantity demanded, and the difference between a change in supply and a change in quantity supplied;

7. determine from a supply curve and a demand curve what the equilibrium price and the equilibrium quantity will be;

8. explain how markets eliminate surpluses and shortages.

CHAPTER OUTLINE

1. The law of demand states that at higher prices a lower quantity will be demanded than at lower prices, other things being equal.
    a. For simplicity, things other than the price of the good itself are held constant.
    b. Buyers respond to changes in relative, not absolute, prices.

2. The demand schedule for a good is a set of pairs of numbers showing various possible prices and the quantity demanded at each price, for some time period.
   a. Demand must be conceived of as being measured in constant-quality units.
   b. A demand curve is a graphic representation of the demand schedule and it is negatively sloped, reflecting the law of demand.
   c. A market demand curve for a particular good or service is derived by summing all the individual demand curves for that product.

3. The determinants of demand include all factors (other than the good's own price) that influence the quantity purchased.
   a. When deriving a demand curve, other determinants of demand are held constant. When such *ceteris paribus* conditions affecting demand do change, the original demand curve shifts to the left or to the right.
   b. The major determinants of demand are consumers' income, tastes and preferences; changes in their expectations about future relative prices; the price of substitutes and complements for the good in question; and number of buyers.
   c. A change in demand is a shift in the demand curve, whereas a change in quantity demanded is a movement along a given demand curve.

4. Supply is the relationship between price and the quantity supplied, other things being equal.
   a. The law of supply posits generally a direct, or positive, relationship between price and quantity supplied.
      i. As the relative price of a good rises, producers have an incentive to produce more of it.
      ii. As a firm produces greater quantities in the short run, a firm often requires a higher relative price before it will increase output.
   b. A supply schedule is a set of numbers showing prices and the quantity supplied at those various prices.
   c. A supply curve is the graphic representation of the supply schedule; it is positively sloped.
   d. By summing individual supply curves for a particular good or service we derive that good or service's market supply curve.
   e. The major determinants of supply are the prices of resources (inputs) used to produce the product; technology; taxes and subsidies; price expectations of producers; and the number of firms in an industry.
   f. Any change in the determinants of supply (listed in part e) causes a change in supply and therefore leads to a shift in the supply curve.
   g. A change in price, holding the determinants of supply constant, causes a movement along—but not a shift in—the supply curve.

5. By graphing demand and supply on the same coordinate system, we can find equilibrium at the intersection of the two curves.
   a. Equilibrium is a situation in which the plans of buyers and of sellers exactly coincide, so that there is neither excess quantity supplied nor excess quantity demanded; at the equilibrium price, quantity supplied equals quantity demanded.
   b. At a price below the equilibrium price, quantity demanded exceeds quantity supplied, and *excess quantity demanded*, or a shortage, exists.
   c. At a price above the equilibrium price, quantity supplied exceeds quantity demanded, and an *excess quantity supplied*, or a surplus, exists.
   d. Seller competition forces price down and eliminates a surplus.
   e. Buyer competition forces price up and eliminates a shortage.

10. When the determinants of supply change, the entire supply curve will shift; five major determinants of supply are _____, _____, _____, _____, and _____.

11. Videocassettes and videocassette players are (substitutes, complements); if the price of videocassette players rises, then the demand for videocassettes will _____ .

12. When the price of peaches rises, the demand for pears rises; peaches and pears are (substitutes, complements).

13. *Analogy*: An excess quantity supplied is to a surplus as a(n) _____ is to a shortage.

14. A rise in demand causes the demand curve to shift to the (left, right); an increase in quantity demanded occurs when there is a movement (up, down) the demand curve.

15. By convention, economists plot (price, quantity) on the vertical axis and (price, quantity) on the horizontal axis.

TRUE-FALSE QUESTIONS
Circle the **T** if the statement is true, the **F** if it is false. Explain to yourself why a statement is false.

T F 1. A demand schedule relates quantity demanded to quantity supplied, other things being constant.

T F 2. A change in the quantity demanded of cigarettes results from a change in the price of cigarettes.

T F 3. A graphical representation of a demand curve is called a demand schedule.

T F 4. An increase in price leads to a leftward shift in demand and a rightward shift in supply.

T F 5. An increase in the price of CDs causes a rise in the supply of CDs.

T F 6. Buyers are concerned with absolute, not relative, prices.

T F 7. As producers increase output in the short run, the cost of additional units of output tends to rise.

T F 8. If the price of tennis racquets rises, the demand for tennis balls will tend to rise also.

T F 9. If the price of butter rises, the demand for margarine will rise.

T F 10. If price is below the equilibrium price, a shortage exists.

CHAPTER 3: DEMAND AND SUPPLY

KEY TERMS
Demand schedule
Demand curve
Supply schedule
Supply curve
Market price
Market demand
Market
Money price

KEY CONCEPTS
Relative price
Law of demand
Normal goods
Inferior goods
Substitutes
Subsidy
Complements
Law of supply
Equilibrium
Shortage, or excess quantity demanded
Surplus, or excess quantity supplied

COMPLETION QUESTIONS
Fill in the blank, or circle the correct term.

1. A(n) _____ relates various possible prices to the quantities demanded at each price, and a(n) _____ relates various prices to the quantities supplied at each price.

2. A change in quantity demanded is a (movement along, shift in) the demand curve; and a change in demand is a(n) _____ the demand curve.

3. At the intersection of the supply and demand curves, the quantity supplied equals the quantity demanded, and at that price a(n) _____ exists; at a price above that intersection, quantity supplied exceeds quantity demanded and a(n) _____ exists; at a price below that intersection, quantity demanded exceeds quantity supplied, and a(n) _____ exists.

4. The law of demand states that, other things being equal, more is bought at a (lower, higher) price and less is bought at a(n) _____ price.

5. There is (a direct, an inverse) relationship between price and quantity demanded, and demand curves will be (positively, negatively) sloped.

6. When the other determinants of demand change, the entire demand curve shifts; the five major *ceteris paribus* conditions affecting demand are _____, _____, _____, _____, and _____ .

7. If the demand for pizza rises, given the supply, then the equilibrium price of pizza will (rise, fall) and the equilibrium quantity will _____.

8. The law of supply relates prices to quantities supplied; in general, as price rises, quantity supplied _____ . Therefore (a direct, an inverse) relationship exists, and the supply curve is (positively, negatively) sloped.

9. The supply curve is positively sloped because as price rises, producers have an incentive to produce (less, more).

CHAPTER 3: DEMAND AND SUPPLY 23

MULTIPLE CHOICE QUESTIONS
Circle the letter that corresponds to the best answer.

1. A demand schedule
    a. relates price to quantity supplied.
    b. when graphed, is a demand curve.
    c. cannot change.
    d. shows a direct relationship between price and quantity demanded.

2. If the price of milk rises, other things being constant,
    a. buyers will drink less milk.
    b. buyers will substitute milk for other beverages.
    c. the demand for milk will fall.
    d. the demand for cola drinks will fall.

3. Which of the following will **NOT** occur if the price of hamburger meat falls, other things being constant?
    a. The demand for hamburger buns will increase.
    b. People will substitute hamburgers for hot dogs.
    c. The demand for hot dogs will rise.
    d. The quantity of hamburgers demanded will increase.

4. If the price of good A rises and the demand for good B rises, then A and B are
    a. substitutes.
    b. complements.
    c. not related goods.
    d. not scarce goods.

5. Several years ago some cities in North Carolina passed a law that limited showers to 4 minutes, with a possible 30-day jail sentence for violators. Which of the following statements is probably true for those cities?
    a. A surplus of water existed.
    b. The price of water was too high.
    c. A shortage of water would exist regardless of how high its price got.
    d. The price of water was below the equilibrium price.

6. If the supply of gasoline rises, with a given demand, then
    a. the relative price of gasoline will rise.
    b. the equilibrium price of gasoline will rise.
    c. the equilibrium quantity of gasoline will increase.
    d. the equilibrium price and equilibrium quantity of gasoline will increase.

7. If income falls and the demand for steak falls, then steak is a(n)
    a. substitute good.
    b. complement good.
    c. normal good.
    d. inferior good.

Consider the graphs below when answering questions 8 and 9.

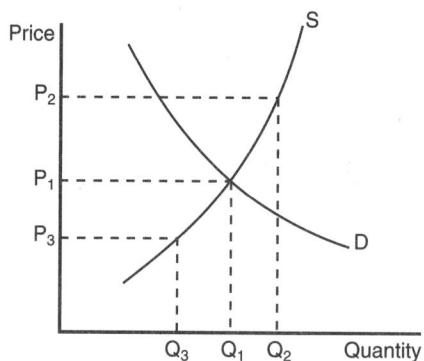

8. Given the figure above,
   a. the equilibrium price is P_1, and the equilibrium quantity is P_2.
   b. the equilibrium quantity is P_1.
   c. the equilibrium price is P_3, and the equilibrium quantity is Q_1.
   d. the equilibrium quantity is Q_1, and the equilibrium price is P_1.

9. Which of the following is **NOT** true?
   a. A shortage exists at P_2.
   b. The equilibrium price is P_1.
   c. An excess quantity demanded exists at P_3.
   d. The market-clearing price is P_1.

10. If the demand for hamburgers rises, with a given supply, then
    a. the supply of hamburgers will rise because price rises.
    b. the equilibrium price of hamburgers will fall and the equilibrium quantity will rise.
    c. the equilibrium quantity and the equilibrium price of hamburgers will rise.
    d. the quantity supplied of hamburgers will decrease.

11. If a shortage exists at some price, then
    a. sellers can sell all they desire to sell at that price.
    b. sellers have an incentive to raise the price.
    c. buyers cannot get all they want at that price.
    d. All of the above

12. Which of the following will lead to a rise in supply?
    a. an increase in the price of the good in question.
    b. a technological improvement in the production of the good in question.
    c. an increase in the price of labor used to produce the good in question.
    d. All of the above

13. Which of the following probably will **NOT** lead to a fall in the demand for hamburgers?
    a. a decrease in income.
    b. an expectation that the price of hamburgers will rise in the future.
    c. a decrease in the price of hot dogs.
    d. a change in tastes away from hamburgers.

14. When a demand curve is derived,
    a. quantity is in constant-quality units.
    b. the price of the good is held constant.
    c. money income changes.
    d. consumer tastes change.

15. If a surplus exists at some price, then
    a. sellers have an incentive to raise the price.
    b. buyers have an incentive to offer a higher price.
    c. sellers cannot sell all they wish to at that price.
    d. seller inventories are falling.

MATCHING
Choose the item in Column (2) that best matches an item in Column (1).

(1)

a. excess quantity demanded
b. supply curve
c. demand curve
d. bread and butter
e. eyeglasses and contact lenses
f. demand shifts to the left
g. supply shifts to the left
h. equilibrium price
i. equilibrium quantity rises
j. excess quantity supplied

(2)

k. relation between price and quantity demanded
l. law of supply
m. population increases
n. raw material prices rise
o. community money income falls
p. market clearing price
q. surplus
r. complements
s. substitutes
t. shortage

WORKING WITH GRAPHS

1. Use the demand schedule below to plot the demand curve on the following coordinate system. Be sure to label each axis correctly.

Price per bottle of shampoo	Quantity demanded of bottles of shampoo per week (in thousands)
$6	8
$5	10
$4	12
$3	14
$2	16
$1	18

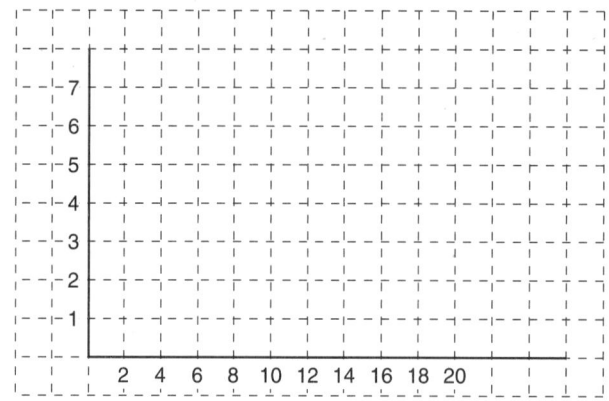

2. Use the supply schedule below to plot the supply curve on the coordinate system in problem 1.

Price per bottle of shampoo	Quantity supplied of bottles of shampoo per week (in thousands)
$6	18
$5	15
$4	12
$3	9
$2	6
$1	3

3. Using the graphs from problems 1 and 2, indicate on the graph the equilibrium price and the equilibrium quantity for bottles of shampoo. What is the equilibrium price? The equilibrium quantity?

4. Continuing with the same example, assume that the government mandates that shampoo cannot be sold for more that $3 per bottle. What is the quantity demanded at that price? The quantity supplied? Does a surplus or a shortage exist at that price?

5. Consider the two graphs below, in panels a and b. Which panel shows an increase in quantity demanded? Which shows a rise in demand?

6. Distinguish between a fall in supply and a decrease in quantity supplied, graphically, using the space below. Use two panels.

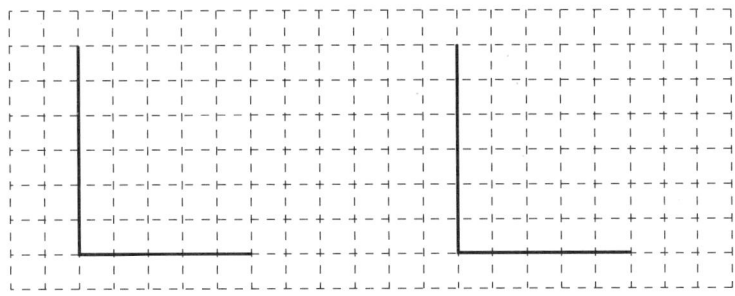

7. Consider the graphs below in panel (a). Then show, in panel (b), the new equilibrium price (label it P_1) and the new equilibrium quantity (label it Q_1) that result due to a change in tastes in favor of the good in question.

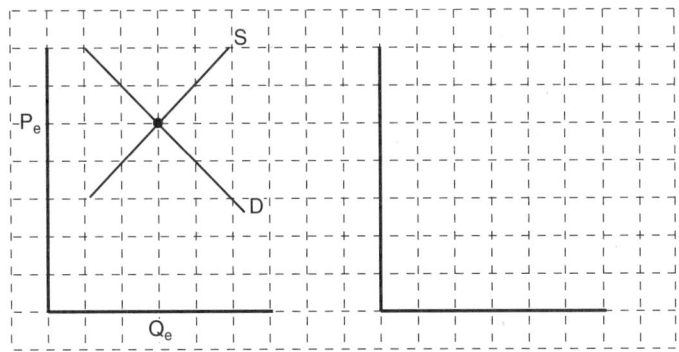

PROBLEMS

1. In the table below, monthly demand schedules for turkey are indicated. Assume that column 2 represents quantities demanded in October, column 3 represents November, and column 4 represents December.

(1) Price per pound	(2) Q_d	(3) Q_d	(4) Q_d
5 cents	10,000		16,000
10 cents	8,000		14,000
15 cents	6,000		12,000
20 cents	4,000		10,000
25 cents	2,000		8,000

   Fill in column 3 yourself. What happens to the demand for turkey in November relative to October and December? Why?

2. List the kinds of changes in the *ceteris paribus* conditions of demand that will lead to a decrease in demand. Be specific.

CHAPTER 3: DEMAND AND SUPPLY

3. List the kinds of changes in the *ceteris paribus* conditions of supply that will lead to a rise in supply. Be specific.

4. Concerning oranges, indicate whether each event leads to (i) a rightward shift in demand, (ii) a leftward shift in demand, (iii) an increase in quantity demanded, (iv) a decrease in quantity demanded, (v) a rightward shift in supply, (vi) a leftward shift in supply, (vii) an increase in quantity supplied, (viii) a decrease in quantity supplied.

   (Note: some events may lead to more than one of the above.)

   _____ a) An early frost in Florida destroys some orange groves.
   _____ b) Migrant workers organize a union and raise wage rates.
   _____ c) The price of oranges rises.
   _____ d) The price of oranges falls.
   _____ e) The Federal government lowers the price of oranges below equilibrium and freezes the price at the lower level.
   _____ f) Orange growers leave the industry.
   _____ g) Lemons (but not oranges) are demonstrated to cause cancer in lab rats.
   _____ h) The government subsidizes orange growers at 3 cents per orange.
   _____ i) News is released that the government forecast is for a poor orange crop this year.
   _____ j) The price of lemons rises (assume now that orange growers can also grow lemons).

5. For each of the statements (a) through (j) in the previous question, decide whether the market clearing *(equilibrium)* price will rise, fall, or be unaffected.

   a) _____   f) _____
   b) _____   g) _____
   c) _____   h) _____
   d) _____   i) _____
   e) _____   j) _____

ANSWERS TO CHAPTER 3

COMPLETION QUESTIONS

1. demand curve or schedule; supply curve or schedule
2. movement along; shift in
3. equilibrium; surplus; shortage
4. lower; higher
5. inverse; negatively
6. income, tastes and preferences, prices of related goods, expectations about future relative prices, number of buyers
7. rise; rise
8. increases; direct; positively
9. more
10. prices of inputs, technology, taxes and subsidies, price expectations, number of firms in industry
11. complements; fall
12. substitutes
13. excess quantity demanded
14. right; down
15. price; quantity

TRUE-FALSE QUESTIONS

1. F A demand schedule relates quantity demanded to price.
2. T
3. F A graphical representation of a demand schedule is a demand curve.
4. F An increase in price leads to a decrease in quantity demanded and an increase in quantity supplied.
5. F It increases the quantity of CDs supplied, which is a movement along the supply curve, not a shift in the curve.
6. F Buyers respond to changes in relative prices.
7. T
8. F The demand for tennis balls will tend to *fall*, because they are complements.
9. T
10. T

MULTIPLE CHOICE QUESTIONS

1.b;   2.a;   3.c;   4.a;   5.d;   6.c;   7.c;   8.d;   9.a;   10.c;
11.d; 12.b; 13.b; 14.a; 15.c.

MATCHING

a and t; b and l; c and k; d and r; e and s; f and o; g and n; h and p;
i and m; j and q

WORKING WITH GRAPHS

1. See graphs.
2. See graphs.

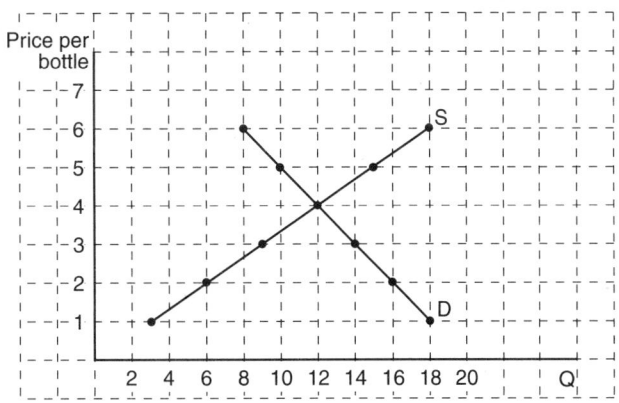

3. $4; 12,000 bottles
4. 14,000 bottles; 9,000 bottles; shortage
5. Panel (a); Panel (b)

6.

(a) A decrease in supply

(b) A decrease in quantity supplied

7.

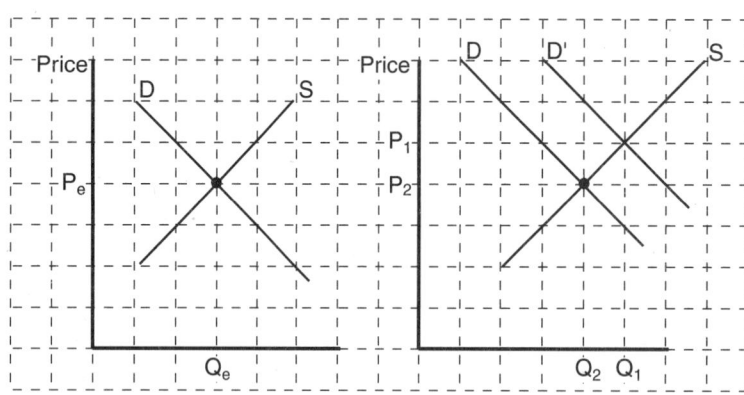

PROBLEMS

1. Due to Thanksgiving, rises significantly relative to October, and (perhaps) slightly relative to December.
2. Income falls for a normal good; change in tastes occurs away from the good; price of a substitute falls or price of a complement rises; expectations exist that the good's future relative price will fall; decrease in the number of buyers occurs.
3. Reduction in the price of inputs; technological advances; decrease in a sales tax on the good or increase in the (per unit) subsidy of the good; expectation that the future relative price will fall; increase in the number of firms in the industry.

4.
a. vi and iv
b. vi and iv
c. iv and vii
d. iii and viii
e. iii and viii
f. vi and iv
g. i and vii
h. v and iii
i. i
j. i and vi

5.
a. rise
b. rise
c. be unaffected
d. be unaffected
e. be unaffected
f. rise
g. rise
h. fall
i. rise
j. rise

GLOSSARY TO CHAPTER 3

Ceteris paribus **conditions**   Determinants of the relationship between price and quantity that are unchanged along a curve; changes in these factors cause the curve to shift.

Complements   Two goods are complements if both are used together for consumption or enjoyment—for example, coffee and cream. The more you buy of one, the more you buy of the other. For complements, a change in the price of one causes an opposite shift in the demand for the other.

Demand   A schedule of how much of a good or service people will purchase at any price during a specified time period, other things being constant.

Demand curve   A graphical representation of the demand schedule; a negatively sloped line showing the inverse relationship between the price and the quantity demanded (other things being equal).

Equilibrium   The situation when quantity supplied equals quantity demanded at a particular price.

Inferior goods   Goods for which demand falls as income rises.

Law of demand   The observation that there is a negative, or inverse, relationship between the price of any good or service and the quantity demanded, holding other factors constant.

Law of supply   The observation that the higher the price of a good, the more of that good sellers will make available over a specified time period, other things being equal.

Market   All of the arrangements that individuals have for exchanging with one another. Thus we can speak of the labor market, the automobile market, and the credit market.

Market clearing, or equilibrium, price The price that clears the market, at which quantity demanded equals quantity supplied; the price where the demand curve intersects the supply curve.

Market demand The demand of all consumers in the marketplace for a particular good or service. The summing at each price of the quantity demanded by each individual.

Money price That price that we observe today in terms of today's dollars; also called the *absolute*, *nominal*, or *current* price.

Normal goods Goods for which demand rises as income rises. Most goods are normal goods.

Relative price The price of one commodity divided by the price of another commodity; the number of units of one commodity that must be sacrificed to purchase one unit of another commodity.

Shortage A situation in which quantity demanded is greater than quantity supplied at a price below the market clearing price.

Subsidy A negative tax; a payment to a producer from the government, usually in the form of a cash grant.

Substitutes Two goods are substitutes when either one can be used for consumption to satisfy a similar want—for example, coffee and tea. The more you buy of one, the less you buy of the other. For substitutes, the change in the price of one causes a shift in demand for the other in the same direction as the price change.

Supply A schedule showing the relationship between price and quantity supplied for a specified period of time, other things being equal.

Supply curve The graphical representation of the supply schedule; a line (curve) showing the supply schedule, which generally slopes upward (has a positive slope), other things being equal.

Surplus A situation in which quantity supplied is greater than quantity demanded at a price above the market clearing price.

CHAPTER 4
EXTENSIONS OF DEMAND AND SUPPLY ANALYSIS

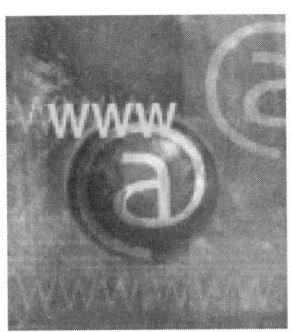

LEARNING OBJECTIVES

After you have studied this chapter, you should be able to

1. define price system, voluntary exchange, terms of exchange, transactions costs, price controls, price ceiling, price floor, nonprice rationing devices, black market, rent control, minimum wage, and import quota;

2. predict what happens to equilibrium price and equilibrium quantity when supply increases or decreases relative to demand, and when demand increases or decreases relative to supply;

3. predict what happens to the relative price of a good or resource if it becomes more or less scarce;

4. differentiate between the causes of short-run and long-run (prolonged) shortages;

5. recognize various methods of rationing goods and services;

6. recognize, from graphs, how a black market emerges;

7. enumerate several consequences of rent control;

8. recognize several consequences of government quantity restrictions;

9. recognize the consequences of price floors and the causes of prolonged surpluses.

CHAPTER OUTLINE

1. In a price system (free enterprise) voluntary exchange typically determines price; buyers and sellers transact with a minimum amount of governmental interference.
   a. Under a system of voluntary exchange, the terms of exchange (the terms, usually price, under which trade takes place) are set by the forces of supply and demand.
   b. Markets reduce transactions costs (all the costs associated with exchanging, including such costs associated with gathering information and enforcing contracts).

33

c. Under voluntary exchange *both* buyers and sellers are presumed to benefit—otherwise the transactions would not continue.

2. Changes in demand and/or supply lead to changes in the equilibrium price and the equilibrium quantity.
    a. If demand shifts to the right (left), given supply, then the equilibrium price rises (falls) and the equilibrium quantity rises (falls).
    b. If supply shifts to the right (left), given demand, then the equilibrium price falls (rises) and the equilibrium quantity rises (falls).
    c. When both supply and demand change, it is not always possible to predict the effects on the equilibrium price and the equilibrium quantity.

3. Prices are not always perfectly flexible.
    a. If prices are inflexible, published prices will not change very much, but such hidden price rises as a quality reduction might occur.
    b. Markets do not always move to equilibrium (given a change in demand or supply) immediately; hence shortages can emerge in the short run.

4. Price reflects relative scarcity and performs a rationing function.
    a. If an input or output becomes less scarce (more scarce), its relative price will fall (rise).
    b. If governments prevent prices from rising to their equilibrium level, via a price control or ceiling, then goods cannot (legally) be allocated to the highest bidders and prolonged shortages result; other forms of rationing emerge.
    c. During prolonged shortages, such nonprice rationing devices as cheating, long lines, first-come first-served, political power, physical force, and other nonmarket forces arise.
    d. Governments also interfere in markets by putting price floors on price; for example, governments impose minimum wage rates, and they have put price floors on agricultural goods, which have caused surpluses.

5. Rent controls are governmentally imposed price ceilings on rental apartments, which lead to predictable results; nonprice rationing for apartments results.

6. The government has put price floors in several markets.
    a. For many years, price supports created minimum prices for agricultural goods.
    b. When the government sets minimum wages above the equilibrium, some unemployment is created.
    c. Governments sometimes restrict quantity directly through import quotas, which prohibit the importation of more than a specified quantity of a particular good in a one-year period.

KEY TERMS
Price ceiling
Transactions costs

Price floor
Minimum wage

Black market
Import quota

KEY CONCEPTS
Price controls
Voluntary exchange

Rent control
Terms of exchange

Price system
Nonprice rationing devices

COMPLETION QUESTIONS
Fill in the blank, or circle the correct term.

1. Resources are scarce; therefore we cannot have all we want at a (zero, positive) price and there will be various ways in which people will _____ for resources.

2. If demand shifts to the left, given supply, then the equilibrium price will (rise, fall) and the equilibrium quantity will _____.

3. If supply shifts to the right, given demand, then the equilibrium price will _____ and the equilibrium quantity will _____.

4. If both demand and supply shift to the right, then the equilibrium price (will rise, will fall, is indeterminate) and the equilibrium quantity (will rise, will fall, is indeterminate).

5. If both demand and supply shift to the left, then the equilibrium price (will rise, will fall, is indeterminate), and the equilibrium quantity (will rise, will fall, is indeterminate).

6. If the demand for good A or resource A rises relative to its supply, A has become relatively (less scarce, more scarce) and its relative price will (rise, fall); if the demand for good B or resource B falls relative to its supply, then B has become relatively _____, and its relative price will _____.

7. If the published price of good A remains constant, but its quality falls, then its relative price has actually (risen, fallen). If the published price of good A remains constant, but people have to wait in line to get it, then the relative price of good A has actually _____, because people have an opportunity cost for their _____.

8. If the demand for a good rises relative to its supply, that good becomes (less scarce, more scarce) and its relative price will (rise, fall); this leads to (a decrease, an increase) in the quantity of the good supplied by producers of the item.

9. Price performs a(n) _____ function; inputs or outputs go to the _____ bidders, if people are free to exchange voluntarily in markets. If such economic freedoms do not exist, then other (price, nonprice) determinants will allocate goods and services.

10. Price controls that put a price ceiling on goods and services create (surpluses, shortages); and price floors create (surpluses, shortages).

11. If governments place price (floors, ceilings) on goods, then black markets might emerge.

12. Rent control is a form of price (floor, ceiling); rent control (increases, reduces) the future supply of apartment construction, (increases, reduces) tenant mobility, (improves, causes a deterioration in) the quality of the existing stock of apartments, and hurts _____.

13. By prohibiting the sale and use of tobacco products, the government would cause the supply of cigarettes to shift to the (left, right), make cigarettes (more, less) scarce, and cause their relative price to (rise, fall).

14. Import quotas, licensing arrangements, and outright bans on specific goods are forms of government (price, quantity) restrictions.

15. An import quota tends to (lower, raise) price to consumers.

16. If governments put price floors on agricultural goods, a (shortage, surplus) will result.

TRUE-FALSE QUESTIONS

Circle the **T** if the statement is true, the **F** if it is false. Explain to yourself why a statement is false.

T F 1. If supply shifts to the left, given demand, then the equilibrium price and the equilibrium quantity will rise.

T F 2. If demand shifts to the left, given supply, then the equilibrium price and the equilibrium quantity will fall.

T F 3. If both supply and demand shift to the right, then equilibrium price and equilibrium quantity are indeterminate.

T F 4. If the supply of good A increases relative to its demand, then good A is now more scarce, and its relative price will rise.

T F 5. If the published price is constant, but it takes consumers longer to wait in lines, the total price has really risen.

T F 6. If markets are flexible and no market restrictions exist, then surpluses and shortages won't occur, even in the short run.

T F 7. Minimum wage laws are a form of price ceiling.

T F 8. Rent controls help the poor who are looking for apartments, because rents are lower.

T F 9. Black markets, in effect, cause price to rise for certain buyers.

T F 10. Agricultural surpluses arise when governments put price ceilings on such goods.

MULTIPLE CHOICE QUESTIONS

Circle the letter that corresponds to the best answer.

1. Because resources are scarce,
   a. buyers compete with buyers for outputs.
   b. there must be some method for rationing goods.
   c. people cannot have all they want at a zero price.
   d. All of the above

2. If markets are free and prices are flexible,
   a. equilibrium price cannot be established.
   b. shortages and surpluses eventually disappear.
   c. shortages and surpluses can't arise.
   d. equilibrium quantity cannot be established.

3. If demand shifts to the right (given supply), then equilibrium
   a. quantity will rise.
   b. price is indeterminate.
   c. price and equilibrium quantity are indeterminate.
   d. price will fall.

4. If supply shifts to the right (given demand), then equilibrium
   a. quantity will rise.
   b. price will rise.
   c. price and equilibrium quantity will fall.
   d. price and equilibrium quantity rises.

5. If both supply and demand shift to the left, then equilibrium
   a. price is indeterminate and equilibrium quantity rises.
   b. price is indeterminate and equilibrium quantity falls.
   c. price falls and equilibrium quantity falls.
   d. price falls and equilibrium quantity is indeterminate.

6. If the demand for good A falls relative to its supply, then
   a. good A is now relatively more scarce.
   b. good A is now relatively less scarce.
   c. the relative price of good A will rise.
   d. the total price of good A will rise, even if A is not price flexible.

7. If the demand for good B rises relative to its supply, then
   a. good B is now relatively more scarce.
   b. the relative price of good B will rise.
   c. the total price of good B will rise, even if good B is price inflexible.
   d. All of the above

8. If the demand for good A rises relative to its supply, and markets are price flexible, then
   a. no shortage of A can exist in the long run.
   b. no shortage of A can exist in the short run.
   c. the published price of A remains constant, but its total price falls.
   d. the published price of A remains constant, but its total price rises.

9. If the demand for good A rises relative to its supply, and markets are price inflexible, then
   a. a shortage can exist in the short run.
   b. a shortage can exist in the long run.
   c. the published price of A might remain constant, but its total price rises.
   d. All of the above

10. If the demand for economists falls relative to their supply, then
    a. more college students will major in economics.
    b. some economists will change professions.
    c. a shortage of economists will result, in the long run.
    d. All of the above

11. Which of the following can influence how a society rations a specific good?
    a. Price system that rations to the highest bidder.
    b. Political power.
    c. Religion.
    d. All of the above

12. Prolonged shortages arise if
    a. demand increases relative to supply.
    b. price floors are set by governments.
    c. prices are not allowed to rise to equilibrium.
    d. buyers are allowed to compete for goods.

13. Black markets may arise if
    a. price ceilings exist.
    b. price floors exist.
    c. governments do not intervene in the market.
    d. equilibrium price is too low.

14. Rent controls
    a. are a form of price floor.
    b. help the homeless who need apartments.
    c. make tenants less mobile.
    d. reduce litigation in society.

15. If an effective minimum wage is imposed, then
    a. more workers will be unable to find jobs.
    b. the quantity of labor demanded will fall.
    c. some workers will move to sectors not covered by minimum wages.
    d. All of the above

16. Prolonged agricultural surpluses can arise if governments
    a. set price above equilibrium.
    b. institute price floors, or price supports.
    c. purchase the excess supply.
    d. All of the above

MATCHING
Choose the item in Column (2) that best matches an item in Column (1).

	(1)		(2)
a.	price floor	e.	buyer competition
b.	price ceiling	f.	rent control
c.	scarce resources	g.	minimum wage law
d.	nonprice rationing	h.	black market, long lines

CHAPTER 4: EXTENSIONS OF DEMAND AND SUPPLY ANALYSIS

WORKING WITH GRAPHS

1. Consider the graphs below, then answer the questions that follow.

a. The market clearing price is _____.
b. If the government imposes a price ceiling at P_1, what will be the quantity supplied? The quantity demanded? What exists at that price?
c. Given the quantity that will be forthcoming at the permitted price of P_1, what will the actual or black market price be?
d. Other than via a black market transaction, how can the actual price paid by buyers exceed the permitted price, P_1.
e. If price had been permitted to rise to equilibrium, what would be the quantity supplied by sellers? Is that amount greater or less than the quantity at P_1? Why?

2. Consider the following supply and demand curves for labor, and then answer the questions.

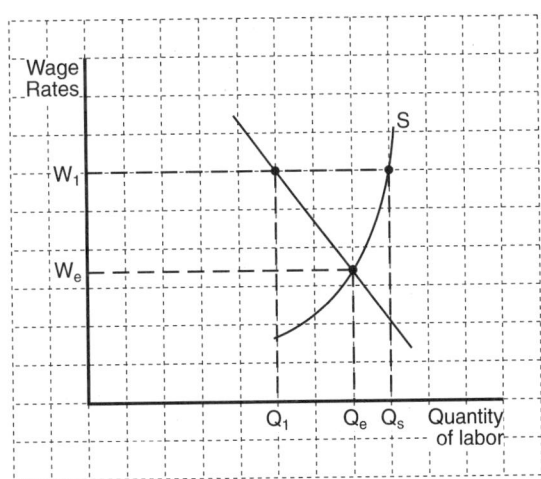

a. What is the equilibrium wage rate? The equilibrium quantity of labor?
b. If the government sets a minimum wage rate at W_1, what is the quantity of labor demanded by employers? The quantity of labor supplied by workers? What exists at the minimum wage rate?

c. Is there a shortage or surplus of *jobs*? How might such jobs be allocated (that is, how will employers go about deciding who gets the jobs)?

3. During September of 1989, the then "drug Czar" William T. Bennett, Director of the Office of National Drug Control Policy, and Nobel Prize winning economist Milton Friedman debated the case for the prohibition of drugs in various letters to the editor, in the *Wall Street Journal*. Bennett, who favors prohibition, maintained that if drugs were legalized price would fall, and, therefore, the total amount of drug usage in the U.S. would rise. Friedman, who favors legalization of drugs (to adults) maintained that, once legalized, the demand for drugs would fall because (1) the appeal to people who want the excitement of doing something "taboo" would disappear, and (2) addicts who have only a $2 a day habit have less of an incentive to get other people hooked on drugs (to support their own habit) than if they had a $200 a day habit.

   a. Is Bennett correct when he says that once legalized, price will fall? Why?
   b. If the demand for drugs shifts to the left, and the supply of drugs to the right, what happens to the price of drugs?
   c. If the demand for drugs shifts to the left (Friedman) and the supply of drugs shifts to the right (Bennett), what happens to the equilibrium quantity?
   d. How does your answer to (c) help you decide whether drug usage will rise or fall if drugs are legalized? What information is necessary to resolve this issue?

PROBLEMS

1. In a 1950's movie entitled "Under the Yum-Yum Tree," Jack Lemmon played a lecherous landlord who was extremely wealthy.
   a. How do you imagine he created a shortage of his own luxury apartments, and what criteria do you imagine he used to decide who was able to rent such apartments?
   b. Does rent control force landlords to discriminate in the selection of tenants? What criteria might they use to make such selections?

2. In 1979 the rock group The Who gave a concert in Cincinnati, and 11 people died outside Riverfront Coliseum when the gates were opened and the crowd rushed in to get choice seats. What other method of allocating the scarce resource of choice seats would have prevented this tragic event?

ANSWERS TO CHAPTER 4

COMPLETION QUESTIONS

1. zero; compete
2. fall; fall
3. fall; rise
4. is indeterminate; will rise
5. is indeterminate; will fall
6. more scarce; rise; less scarce; fall
7. risen; risen; time
8. more scarce; rise; increase
9. rationing; highest; nonprice
10. shortages; surpluses
11. ceilings
12. ceiling; reduces; reduces; causes a deterioration in; landlords and low income apartment hunters
13. left; more; rise
14. quantity
15. raise
16. surplus

CHAPTER 4: EXTENSIONS OF DEMAND AND SUPPLY ANALYSIS   **41**

TRUE-FALSE QUESTIONS

1. F The equilibrium quantity falls.
2. T
3. F Equilibrium quantity rises.
4. F Good A is now less scarce, and its relative price will fall.
5. T
6. F No, surpluses and shortages can exist—in the short run.
7. F They are a price floor.
8. F That group is hurt because they will be discriminated against and because the housing stock diminishes.
9. T
10. F Price ceilings cause shortages.

MULTIPLE CHOICE QUESTIONS

1.d; 2.b; 3.a; 4.a; 5.b; 6.b; 7.d; 8.a; 9.d; 10.b;
11.d; 12.c; 13.a; 14.c; 15.d; 16.d.

MATCHING

a and g; b and f; c and e; d and h

WORKING WITH GRAPHS

1. a. P_e
   b. Q_1; Q_2; shortage
   c. P_4
   d. quality deterioration, long lines that increase opportunity costs
   e. Q_e; greater; a higher price induces sellers to produce more.

2. a. W_e; Q_e
   b. Q_1; Q_s; surplus of labor, or unemployment
   c. shortage; family influence, political power, bribes, racial or gender preference

3. a. He is correct, because the supply curve will shift to the right as the costs and risks of drug-dealing fall.
   b. falls (Therefore Bennett is right.)
   c. It is impossible to predict the net effect on the equilibrium quantity.
   d. The real issue is an empirical one: Will supply rise by more than demand falls, or vice versa?

PROBLEMS

1. a. He set rents far below the market clearing levels, and many people wanted his apartments; he rented only to "lovely young ladies."
   b. Yes; gender, beauty, race, number of children, age, ability to pay, pets, and so on.

2. Instead of "first-come, first-served seating," ticket sellers could have raised the price of choice seats and used assigned seating. Shortly thereafter, the city of Cincinnati passed a resolution that outlawed first-come, first-served seating.

GLOSSARY TO CHAPTER 4

Black market A market in which goods are traded at prices above their legal maximum prices or in which illegal goods are sold.

Import quota A physical supply restriction on imports of a particular good, such as sugar. Foreign exporters are unable to sell in the United States more than the quantity specified in the import quota.

Minimum wage A wage floor, legislated by government, setting the lowest hourly rate that firms may legally pay workers.

Nonprice rationing devices All those methods used to ration scarce goods that are price-controlled. Whenever the price system is not allowed to work, nonprice rationing devices will evolve to ration the affected goods and services.

Price ceiling A legal maximum price that may be charged for a particular good or service.

Price controls Government mandated minimum or maximum prices that may be charged for goods and services.

Price floor A legal minimum price below which a good or service may not be sold. Legal minimum wages are an example.

Price system An economic system in which relative prices are constantly changing to reflect changes in supply and demand for different commodities. The prices of those commodities are signals to everyone within the system about what is relatively scarce and what is relatively abundant.

Rent control The placement of price ceilings on rents in particular cities.

Terms of exchange The terms under which the trading takes place. Usually, the terms of exchange are given by the price at which a good is traded.

Transaction costs All of the costs associated with exchanging, including the informational costs of finding out price and quality, service record, and durability of a product, plus the cost of contracting and enforcing that contract.

Voluntary exchange An act of trading, done on a voluntary basis, in which both parties to the trade are subjectively better off after the exchange.

CHAPTER 5
THE PUBLIC SECTOR AND PUBLIC CHOICE

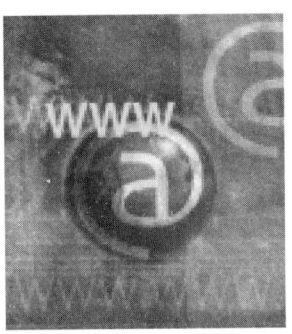

LEARNING OBJECTIVES

After you have studied this chapter, you should be able to

1. define antitrust legislation, monopoly, spillover or externality, third parties, effluent fee, market failure, property rights, private goods, public goods, principle of rival consumption, exclusion principle, free-rider problem, merit good, demerit good, transfer payment, transfers in kind, marginal and average tax rates, proportional, progressive, and regressive taxation, capital gain, capital loss, retained earnings, and tax incidence;

2. enumerate the five economic functions of government;

3. predict whether a specific good will be overproduced, underproduced, or produced in just the right amount if resources are allocated by the price system;

4. identify which graphs take into account an externality and which do not;

5. list the two ways in which a government can correct for negative externalities;

6. identify the three ways in which a government can correct for positive externalities;

7. list four characteristics of public goods that distinguish them from private goods;

8. distinguish between a marginal and an average tax rate;

9. calculate the tax burden for individuals with different incomes, given different tax structures;

10. identify similarities and differences between market and collective decision making.

CHAPTER OUTLINE

1. The government performs many economic functions that affect the way in which resources are allocated.

43

a. If a benefit or cost associated with an economic activity spills over to third parties, the price system will misallocate resources; a proper role for government is to correct such externalities.
   i. If a negative externality exists, the price system will overallocate resources to that industry; the government can correct this by taxing or regulating such activities.
   ii. If a positive externality exists, the price system will underallocate resources to that industry; the government can correct this by financing additional production, by providing special subsidies, or by regulation.
b. A legal system that defines and enforces property rights is crucial to the American capitalistic economy.
c. Because a competitive price system transmits correct signals, an important role for government is to promote competition.
d. A price system will underallocate resources to the production of public goods.
   i. Characteristics of public goods include the following:
      1. They are usually indivisible.
      2. They can be used by more people at no additional cost.
      3. Additional users of public goods do not deprive others of any of the services of the good.
      4. It is difficult to charge individual users a fee based on how much they themselves consume of the public good.
   ii. Because public goods must be consumed collectively, individuals have an incentive to take a free ride and not pay for them.
   iii. Because the price system underproduces public goods, a proper role of government may be to ensure their production.
e. In recent years the government has taken on the economic role of ensuring economy-wide stability: full employment, price stability, and economic growth.

2. The government performs political functions that also affect resource allocation.
   a. Governments subsidize the production of merit goods and tax or prohibit the production of demerit goods.
   b. By combining a progressive tax structure with transfer payments, the government attempts to redistribute income from higher to lower income groups (although many "loopholes" frustrate such a policy).

3. Governments tax in order to obtain revenues to finance expenditures.
   a. The marginal tax rate is the change in the tax payment divided by the change in income.
   b. The average tax rate equals the total tax payment divided by total income.

4. There are three main types of taxation systems.
   a. Under a proportional taxation system, as a person's income rises, the percentage of income paid (rate of taxation) in taxes remains constant.
   b. Under a progressive taxation system, as a person's income rises, the percentage of income paid in taxes rises.
   c. Under a regressive taxation system, as a person's income rises, the percentage of income paid in taxes falls.

5. The federal government imposes income taxes on individuals and corporations, and it collects Social Security taxes and other taxes.
   a. The most important tax in the U.S. economy is the personal income tax; recently some have proposed a consumption tax, which taxes people based on what they actually spend.
   b. The difference between the buying and selling price of an asset, such as a share of stock or a plot of land, is called a capital gain if a profit results, and a capital loss if it doesn't.

6. The corporate income tax is a moderately important source of revenue for the various governments in the U.S. economy.
   a. Corporate stockholders are taxed twice: once on corporate income and again when dividends are received or when the stock is sold.
   b. The incidence of corporate taxes falls on people—consumers, workers, management, and stockholders—not on such inanimate objects as "corporations."

7. An increasing percentage of federal tax receipts is accounted for each year by taxes (other than income) levied on payrolls, such as Social Security taxes and unemployment compensation.

8. Major sources of revenue for states and local governments are sales and excise taxes.

9. The theory of public choice is the study of collective decision making.
   a. Collective decision making involves the actions that voters, politicians, and other interested parties undertake to influence nonmarket choices.
   b. Market and collective decision making are similar in the sense that both involve competition for scarce resources and people motivated by self-interest.
   c. Market and collective decision making are different because the government goods are available for consumption at a price of zero, decisions about what government goods to provide are determined by majority rule, and government can use legally sanctioned force to ensure that its decisions are followed.

KEY TERMS
Antitrust legislation
Monopoly
Capital loss
Capital gain
Merit good
Collective decision making
Incentive structure

Effluent fee
Transfer payment
Retained earnings
Demerit good
Theory of public choice
Government, or political, goods

KEY CONCEPTS
Externality
Third parties
Market failure
Principle of rival consumption
Exclusion principle
Private goods
Public goods

Marginal tax rate
Average tax rate
Transfers in kind
Proportional taxation
Progressive taxation
Regressive taxation

Free-rider problem
Property rights
Public choice
Subsidy
Tax incidence
Tax bracket

COMPLETION QUESTIONS
Fill in the blank, or circle the correct term.

1. The five economic functions of federal government in our capitalistic system are _____, _____, _____, _____, and _____.

2. If there are disputes in an economic arena, the _____ often acts as a "referee" to help settle the dispute.

3. Antitrust legislation, in theory, is supposed to (decrease, promote) competition in the private sector.

4. If externalities are an important result of an economic activity, then the price system is (inefficient, efficient).

5. If Mr. Johnson buys an automobile from General Motors, those people not directly involved in the transaction are considered _____.

6. Pollution is an example of a (negative, positive) externality.

7. When there are spillover costs, a price system will (under, over) allocate resources to the production of the good in question.

8. If third parties benefit from a transaction, then (negative, positive) externalities exist, and the price system will allocate resources (inefficiently, efficiently).

9. Positive and negative externalities are examples of market _____.

10. A government can correct negative externalities by imposing taxes and by _____ the industry or firms in question.

11. A government can correct positive externalities by _____, _____, and _____.

12. If a positive externality exists for good B, a price system will produce too _____ of good B.

13. Public goods have four distinguishing characteristics. They are usually _____; they can be used by more people at _____ additional cost; additional users (do, do not) deprive others of the services of a public good; it is very (easy, difficult) to charge individuals based on how much they used the public good.

14. A free rider has an incentive to (pay, not pay) for a public good.

15. Demerit goods are goods for which society wants to (decrease, increase) production.

16. Many government, or political, goods are provided to consumers at a (zero, positive) price; but the opportunity cost to society of providing government goods is (zero, positive).

17. If the price of an asset rises after its purchase, the owner receives a(n) _____ gain; if the price falls, the owner suffers a(n) _____ loss.

18. The marginal tax rate applies only to the (first, last) tax bracket.

19. The corporate income tax is paid by one or more of the following groups: _____, _____, and _____.

20. In contrast to goods sold in private markets, government goods are not (scarce, explicitly priced).

21. In the government sector, decisions concerning what goods to produce are determined by (majority, proportional) rule.

TRUE-FALSE QUESTIONS
Circle the **T** if the statement is true, the **F** if it is false. Explain to yourself why a statement is false.

T F 1. In the U.S. economy the government plays only a minor role in resource allocation, because the country is capitalistic.

T F 2. Governments provide a legal system, but this important function is not considered an economic function.

T F 3. One aim of antitrust legislation is the promotion of competition.

T F 4. If externalities, or spillovers, exist, then a price system misallocates resources, so that inefficiency exists.

T F 5. If a negative externality exists, buyers and sellers are not faced with the true opportunity costs of their actions.

T F 6. If a positive externality exists when good A is produced, a price system will underallocate resources into the production of good A.

T F 7. One way to help correct for a negative externality is to tax the good in question, because that will cause the price of the good to fall.

T F 8. A price system will tend to overallocate resources to the production of free goods, due to the free-rider problem.

T F 9. Scarcity exists in the market sector, but not in the public sector.

T F 10. If third parties are hurt by the production of good B and they are not compensated, then too many resources have been allocated to industry B.

T F 11. Deciding what is a merit good and what is a demerit good is easily done and does not require value judgments.

T F 12. The federal individual income tax is regressive.

T F 13. The largest source of receipts for the federal government is the individual income tax.

T F 14. In a progressive tax structure, the average tax rate is greater than the marginal tax rate.

T F 15. Positive economics confirms that a progressive taxation system is more equitable than a regressive taxation system.

T F 16. In the United States the tax system that yields the most revenue to all governments combined is the corporate tax.

T F 17. When corporations are taxed, consumers and corporate employees are also affected.

T F 18. Government goods are produced solely in the public sector.

T F 19. A nation's "tax freedom day" is the date when an average resident has earned sufficient income to pay his or her total tax bill for the year.

MULTIPLE CHOICE QUESTIONS
Circle the letter that corresponds to the best answer.

1. Which of the following is **NOT** an economic function of government?
   a. income redistribution
   b. providing a legal system
   c. ensuring economy-wide stability
   d. promoting competition

2. A price system will misallocate resources if
   a. much income inequality exists.
   b. demerit goods are produced.
   c. externalities exist.
   d. All of the above

3. Which of the following does **NOT** belong with the others?
   a. positive externality
   b. negative externality
   c. demerit good
   d. public good

4. The exclusion principle
   a. does not work for public goods.
   b. does not work for private goods.
   c. causes positive externalities.
   d. makes it easy to assess user fees on true public goods.

5. Which of the following statements concerning externalities is true?
   a. If a positive externality exists for good A, A will be overproduced by a price system.
   b. If externalities exist, then resources will be allocated efficiently.
   c. Efficiency may be improved if the government taxes goods for which a positive externality exists.
   d. The output of goods for which a positive externality exists is too low, from society's point of view.

6. Which of the following is **NOT** a characteristic of public goods?
   a. indivisibility
   b. high extra cost to additional users
   c. exclusion principle does not work easily
   d. difficult to determine how each individual benefits from public goods

7. Market failure exists if
   a. Mr. Smith cannot purchase watermelons in his town.
   b. buyers and sellers must pay the true opportunity costs of their actions.
   c. third parties are injured and are not compensated.
   d. the government must provide merit goods.

8. Which of the following will properly correct a negative externality that results from producing good B?
   a. subsidizing the production of good B
   b. letting the price system determine the price and output of good B
   c. forcing buyers and sellers of good B to pay the true opportunity costs of their actions
   d. banning the production of good B

9. Merit and demerit goods
   a. are examples of public goods.
   b. are examples of externalities.
   c. indicate market failure.
   d. are not easily classified.

10. A switch from the current progressive income tax to a national sales tax
    a. would not change our tax system very much.
    b. would lead to more taxes on savings.
    c. would cause the current structure of the IRS to be greatly reduced.
    d. would cause more Internal Revenue agents to be hired.

11. If the government taxes group A and gives to group B, then economic incentives for
    a. group A may be reduced.
    b. group B may be reduced.
    c. both may change so as to reduce output.
    d. All of the above

12. If Mr. Ayres loves good A, he can convey the intensity of his wants if good A is
    a. a private good.
    b. a public good.
    c. not subject to the exclusion principle.
    d. expensive.

13. The free-rider problem exists
    a. for private goods.
    b. for goods that must be consumed collectively.
    c. only if people can be excluded from consumption.
    d. All of the above

14. In a progressive tax structure,
    a. the marginal tax rate exceeds the average tax rate.
    b. equity exists.
    c. the average tax rate rises as income falls.
    d. All of the above

15. Which of the following statements is true?
    a. Under a regressive tax structure, the average tax rate remains constant as income rises.
    b. If upper-income people pay more taxes than lower-income people, equity must exist.
    c. The U.S. federal personal income tax system is progressive.
    d. At very high income levels, the Social Security tax and employee contribution become progressive.

16. The tax incidence of the corporate income tax falls on
    a. corporate stockholders.
    b. corporate employees.
    c. consumers of goods and services produced by corporations.
    d. All of the above

17. Which of the following statements about the Social Security tax is **NOT** true?
    a. It is a progressive tax.
    b. It came into existence in 1935.
    c. It is imposed on employers and employees.
    d. It is a payroll tax.

18. If Mr. Romano faces a 90 percent marginal tax rate,
    a. the next dollar he earns nets him ninety cents.
    b. his total tax payments equal 90 percent of his total income.
    c. he has a strong incentive not to earn extra income.
    d. his average tax rate must be falling.

19. A proportional tax system
    a. is unfair.
    b. cannot be consistent with people's ability to pay such taxes.
    c. means that upper-income people pay smaller percentages of their income in taxes than do lower-income people.
    d. requires upper-income people to pay more tax dollars than lower-income people pay.

20. Which one of the following is true of both market and collective decision making? Within both contexts,
    a. resources are scarce.
    b. people face identical incentive structures.
    c. production and allocation decisions arise from majority rule.
    d. production and allocation decisions arise from proportional rule.

21. Which one of the following is true of government goods?
    a. They are always produced within the public sector.
    b. They are always produced within the private sector.
    c. They are provided free of charge.
    d. They have no opportunity cost.

MATCHING

Choose the item in Column (2) that best matches an item in Column (1).

(1)	(2)
a. antitrust legislation	g. pollution
b. spillover	h. externality
c. positive externality	i. national defense
d. negative externality	j. alcohol
e. government good	k. monopoly
f. demerit good	l. flu shots

PROBLEMS

1. Complete the following table for three taxes, and then indicate what type of tax each is.

Income	Tax 1		Tax 2		Tax 3	
	Tax paid	Average tax rate	Tax paid	Average tax rate	Tax paid	Average tax rate
$ 1,000	$ 30	___	$ 10	___	$ 100	___
3,000	90	___	60	___	270	___
6,000	180	___	180	___	480	___
10,000	300	___	400	___	700	___
15,000	450	___	750	___	900	___
20,000	600	___	1200	___	1000	___
30,000	900	___	2100	___	1200	___

2. Suppose the above table had a fourth tax as shown below. Find the average and marginal tax rates, and explain what type tax it would be.

Income	Tax paid	Average tax rate	Marginal tax rate
$ 1,000	$ 30	_____	_____
3,000	120	_____	_____
6,000	300	_____	_____
10,000	500	_____	_____
15,000	600	_____	_____
20,000	700	_____	_____
30,000	900	_____	_____

3. One important purely economic function of government is to promote competition, which presumably makes the price system more efficient. During the 1970s, the OPEC oil cartel was able to restrict output dramatically, which permitted the cartel to charge much higher prices and earn higher profits. How did consumers, businesses, and other governments react to the higher relative price of oil? Were such actions rational, from the point of view of the individuals involved? Did such decisions lead to a misallocation of resources from *society's* point of view? (Hint: the OPEC price was artificially high because the cartel reduced output and repressed competition.)

4. In the text, five economic and two political functions of the government were analyzed. Place each of the following governmental activities in one (or more) of these seven categories.

   a. Providing aid to welfare recipients _____
   b. Passing antitrust laws _____
   c. Subsidizing the arts _____
   d. Prohibiting the sale and possession of drugs _____
   e. Providing national defense _____
   f. Enforcing a progressive tax structure _____
   g. Enforcing contracts _____
   h. Providing public education to children _____
   i. Prosecuting fraud _____
   j. Providing funds for AIDS research _____
   k. Creating jobs to reduce unemployment _____

WORKING WITH GRAPHS

1. Consider the graph below, then answer the questions. Assume S represents industry supply and S' includes pollution costs to society as well as industry private costs.

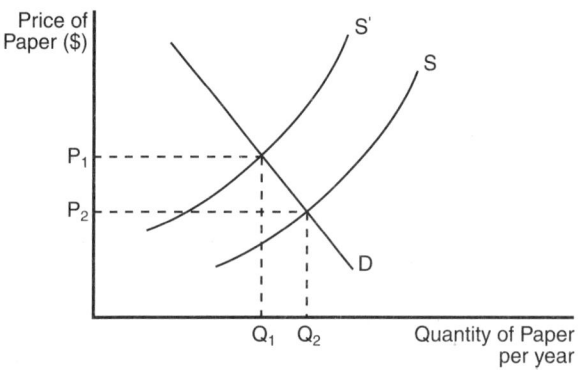

   a. If no governmental intervention takes place, what will be the market equilibrium price? The market equilibrium quantity?

   b. At the market equilibrium quantity (Q_2), which is higher: private costs or social costs?

   c. From *society's* point of view, what is the price that reflects the true opportunity costs of paper? From that same point of view, what is the optimal quantity of paper?

   d. Considering your answers in the above three questions, will a price system produce too little or too much paper?

   e. Does a negative externality or a positive externality exist?

2. Consider the graphs below, then answer the questions that follow. Assume that D represents private market demand and that D' represents benefits that accrue to third parties as well as private benefits.

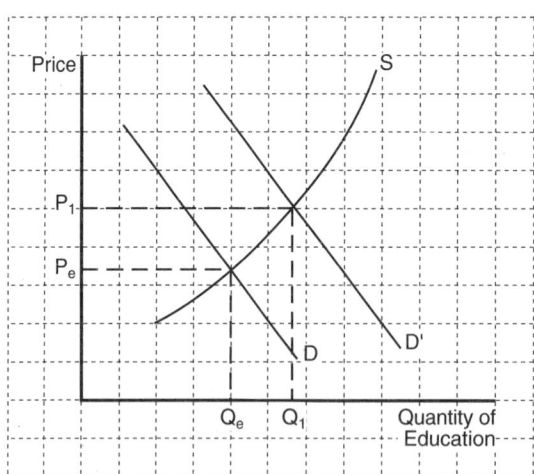

   a. If no government intervention occurs, what will be the market equilibrium price? The market equilibrium quantity?

   b. At the market equilibrium quantity, which is greater, private benefits or social benefits?

c. From *society's* point of view, what is the optimal price and the optimal quantity of education?

d. In this example, does the price system provide too much or too little education?

e. Is there a positive externality or a negative externality for this good?

3. Suppose you know the demand and supply of fertilizer locally, and you have graphed them as shown in the graph that follows. The fertilizer plant that operates in your town is also producing pollution. This pollution is a constant amount per unit of output (proportional to output) at the plant. If the government decides to try to combat the pollution problem by imposing a $20-per-ton tax on fertilizer produced, show graphically what will happen to the fertilizer market. Will the level of pollution in your town be reduced? If so, by how much? If not, can you offer a solution to the pollution problem?

4. a. Draw supply and demand curves for good A, for which no externalities exist, and indicate the optimal quantity of output, the price that reflects the opportunity cost to buyers and sellers of that good, and whether the price system has over-, or under-, or properly allocated resources into industry A.

b. Draw private supply and demand curves for good B, for which negative externalities exist. Draw another curve on that coordinate system which reflects negative externalities. Indicate the optimal output quantity and price from society's point of view, and compare them to the output quantity and price that would result from a price system.

c. Draw private supply and demand curves for good C, for which positive externalities exist. Draw another curve which reflects the positive externalities associated with good C. Indicate the optimal price and output quantity of good C from society's point of view, and compare them to the output quantity and price that result from the price system.

ANSWERS TO CHAPTER 5

COMPLETION QUESTIONS

1. providing a legal system, promoting competition, correcting externalities, providing public goods, ensuring economy-wide stability
2. government
3. promote
4. inefficient
5. third parties
6. negative
7. over
8. positive; inefficiently
9. failure
10. regulating
11. subsidizing production, financing production, regulation
12. little
13. indivisible; zero; do not; difficult
14. not pay
15. decrease
16. zero; positive
17. capital; capital
18. last
19. stockholders, consumers, employees
20. explicitly priced
21. majority

TRUE-FALSE QUESTIONS

1. F Even in capitalist countries the government plays a major role.
2. F It is an economic function because by enforcing contracts government can promote trade and commerce.
3. T
4. T
5. T
6. T
7. F A tax will cause the price of the good to *rise,* which is a movement in the correct direction.
8. F The free-rider problem deals with goods that are *scarce,* but for which the exclusion principle does not work well.
9. F Scarcity exists in the public sector too; after all, the government uses and allocates scarce goods.
10. T
11. F Whether or not a good is a merit good requires value judgments.
12. F It is progressive.
13. T
14. F For average taxes to rise with income (a progressive tax), the marginal tax rate must exceed the average tax rate.
15. F "Equitable" requires normative statements.
16. F No, the personal income tax does so.
17. T
18. F Governments can also buy privately produced goods for distribution at no charge.
19. T

MULTIPLE CHOICE QUESTIONS

1.a;   2.c;   3.c;   4.a;   5.d;   6.b;   7.c;   8.c;   9.d;   10.c;
11.d; 12.a; 13.b; 14.a; 15.c; 16.d; 17.a; 18.c; 19.d; 21.a;
22. c.

CHAPTER 5: THE PUBLIC SECTOR AND PUBLIC CHOICE

MATCHING

a and k; b and h; c and l; d and g; e and i; f and j

PROBLEMS

1. Tax 1: 3 percent; 3 percent; 3 percent; 3 percent; 3 percent; 3 percent; 3 percent; proportional

    Tax 2: 1 percent; 2 percent; 3 percent; 4 percent; 5 percent; 6 percent; 7 percent; progressive

    Tax 3: 10 percent; 9 percent; 8 percent; 7 percent; 6 percent; 5 percent; 4 percent; regressive

2. ATR: 3 percent; 4 percent; 5 percent; 5 percent; 4 percent; 3.5 percent; 3 percent

    MTR: 3 percent; 4.5 percent; 6 percent; 5 percent; 2 percent; 2 percent; 2 percent

    The average tax rate for this tax initially rises and then falls, as does the marginal tax rate. As a result, this tax is progressive up to an income of $6,000, proportional from there to $10,000, and regressive for levels of income above $10,000. Thus this tax is a combination of all three types of taxes as income varies. Can you graph the ATR and MTR for this tax? Can you think of any taxes that might behave in this manner?

3. Consumers joined car pools, drove less often, bought smaller cars, and endured less comfortable temperatures at home; businesses invested in the production of such oil substitutes as solar energy, nuclear energy, shale oil, coal, etc.; governments subsidized the production of gasohol and shale oil, etc. Such actions were rational because they were responses to a perceived increase in the relative price of oil and its distillates. From society's point of view, such actions led to a misallocation because the lack of competition caused the price system to transmit an incorrect signal. The signal was that oil had become more scarce—but the signal was induced by an artificial restriction of supply.

4. a. redistribution
    b. promoting competition
    c. providing merit goods
    d. discouraging demerit goods
    e. providing public goods
    f. redistribution
    g. providing legal systems
    h. correcting positive externality
    i. providing legal system
    j. correcting negative externality
    k. stabilizing economy

WORKING WITH GRAPHS

1. a. P_2; Q_2
    b. social costs
    c. P_1; Q_1
    d. too much
    e. negative

2. a. P_e; Q_e
    b. social benefits
    c. P_1; Q_1
    d. too little
    e. positive

3. The supply curve after the tax is imposed shifts to S_1—that is, upward by $20 at each quantity.

    The equilibrium quantity falls from 45 tons per month to below 40 tons per month as a result. Thus the quantity of fertilizer produced has declined by more than 10 percent. This means that the output of pollution has declined by more than 10 percent, because the output of pollution is a constant per unit of output of fertilizer.

    The result of the analysis should not be extended in a general fashion without regard to other possible effects that a tax of this nature might have. We might also wish to consider other factors before imposing a pollution tax. Among these factors are the effects of the increased price of the fertilizer, the likely reduction in employment as a result of the reduced quantity of fertilizer produced, and the ability of alternative methods of pollution control to achieve the same results.

4. a. The market price and the equilibrium quantity are at the socially optimal values because no externalities exist; resources are allocated properly into industry A.
    b. The *new* curve you draw, which reflects a negative externality, should be a supply curve that lies to the left of (above) the original curve, labeled S_1. The optimal price-quantity combination exists where S_1 intersects the demand curve; the socially optimal price is higher than the market price, and the socially optimal quantity is lower than the market quantity.
    c. The new curve should be a demand curve, D_1, that lies to the right of (above) the original demand curve. The socially optimal price-output combination is where D_1 intersects the supply curve; price will be higher and output will be higher than the market price-output combination.

GLOSSARY FOR CHAPTER 5

Antitrust legislation Laws that restrict the formation of monopolies and regulate certain anticompetitive business practices.

Average tax rate The total tax payment divided by total income. It is the proportion of total income paid in taxes.

Capital gain The positive difference between the purchase price and the sale price of an asset. If a share of stock is bought for $5 and then sold for $15, the capital gain is $10.

Capital loss The negative difference between the purchase price and the sale price of an asset.

Collective decision making How voters, politicians, and other interested parties act and how these actions influence nonmarket decisions.

Demerit good A good that has been deemed socially undesirable through the political process. Heroin is an example.

Effluent fee A charge to a polluter that gives the right to discharge into the air or water a certain amount of pollution; also called a *pollution tax*.

Exclusion principle The principle that no one can be excluded from the benefits of a public good even if that person has not paid for it.

Externality A consequence of an economic activity that spills over to affect third parties. Pollution is an externality.

Free-rider problem A problem that arises when individuals presume that others will pay for public goods, so that, individually, they can escape paying for their portion without a reduction in production.

Government, or political, goods Goods (and services) provided by the public sector; they can be either private or public goods.

Incentive structure The system of rewards and punishments individuals face with respect to their own actions.

Majority rule A collective decision-making system in which group decisions are made on the basis of more than 50 percent of the vote. In other words, whatever more than half of the electorate votes for, the entire electorate has to accept.

Marginal tax rate The change in the tax payment divided by the change in income, or the percentage of additional dollars that must be paid in taxes. The marginal tax rate is applied to the last tax bracket of taxable income reached.

Market failure A situation in which an unrestrained market economy leads to too few or too many resources going to a specific economic activity.

Merit good A good that has been deemed socially desirable through the political process. Museums are an example.

Monopoly A firm that has control over the price of a good. In the extreme case, a monopoly is the only seller of a good or service.

Principle of rival consumption The recognition that individuals are rivals in consuming private goods because one person's consumption reduces the amount available for others to consume.

Private goods Goods that can only be consumed by one individual at a time. Private goods are subject to the principle of rival consumption.

Progressive taxation A tax system in which as income increases, a higher percentage of the additional income is taxed. The marginal tax rate exceeds the average tax rate as income rises.

Property rights The rights of an owner to use and to exchange property.

Proportional rule A decision-making system in which actions are based on the proportion of the "votes" cast and are in proportion to them. In a market system, if 10 percent of the "dollar votes" are cast for blue cars, 10 percent of the output will be blue cars.

Proportional taxation A tax system in which regardless of an individual's income, the tax bill comprises exactly the same proportion.

Public goods Goods for which the principle of rival consumption does not apply; they can be jointly consumed by many individuals simultaneously at no additional cost and with no reduction in quality or quantity.

Regressive taxation A tax system in which as more dollars are earned, the percentage of tax paid on them falls. The marginal tax rate is less than the average tax rate as income rises.

Retained earnings Earnings that a corporation saves, or retains, for investment in other productive activities; earnings that are not distributed to stockholders.

Tax bracket A specified interval of income to which a specific and unique marginal tax is applied.

Tax incidence The distribution of tax burdens among various groups in society.

Theory of public choice The study of collective decision making.

Third parties Parties who are not directly involved in a given activity or transaction.

Transfer payments Money payments made by governments to individuals for which in return no services or goods are concurrently rendered. Examples are welfare, Social Security, and unemployment insurance benefits.

Transfers in kind Payments that are in the form of actual goods and services, such as food stamps, subsidized public housing, and medical care, and for which no goods or services are rendered concurrently.

CHAPTER 6
TAXES, TRANSFERS, AND PUBLIC SPENDING

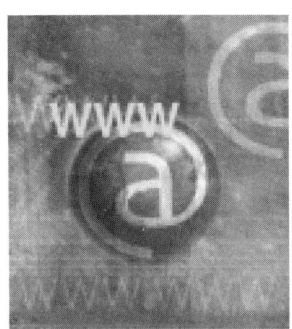

LEARNING OBJECTIVES

After you have studied this chapter, you should be able to

1. identify the main ways that governments tax sales of goods and services;

2. recognize the difference between static and dynamic tax analysis;

3. explain how levying taxes on goods and services affects market prices and equilibrium quantities;

4. assess the ways in which Medicare affects the incentives to consume medical services;

5. provide reasons why higher government spending on public education has not necessarily improved student performance;

6. discuss the key forces that caused the tremendous rise in Social Security spending;

7. explain why the Social Security Trust Fund is not a stock of savings which the nation may draw upon at a later date, and evaluate how Social Security could be reformed.

CHAPTER OUTLINE

1. The government budget constraint indicates that government spending, transfers, and repayments of borrowed funds are limited to total taxes and user charges the government collects during a given period.

2. When governments attempt to fund their operations by taxing market activities, one issue they must consider is how the tax rates they assess relate to the tax revenues they ultimately receive.
    a. Sales taxes are levied under a system of ad valorem taxation, meaning that the tax is applied to the value of final purchases of a good or service, as determined by its market price, which is the sales tax base. The total sales taxes collected by a government equal the sales tax rate multiplied by the sales tax base, so a sales tax is a proportional tax.
    b. Whereas static tax analysis indicates that a government can unambiguously increase its sales tax collections by boosting the sales tax rate, dynamic tax analysis takes into account the fact that higher tax rates give consumers an incentive to cut back on purchases of goods and services. Dynamic tax analysis indicates that at some point a further increase in the tax

rate reduces the tax base sufficiently to result in lower tax revenues for the government. Consequently, in principle there is a single tax rate at which the government can collect the maximum possible revenues.

3. When contemplating how to structure a system for taxing market transactions, governments must also consider how the taxes they impose affect market prices and equilibrium quantities
   a. Excise taxes are taxes on sales of specific commodities, and governments commonly levy certain excise taxes as a constant tax per unit sold, or a unit tax.
   b. Imposing a unit excise tax on a good or service reduces the net price that a producer receives for each unit sold by exactly the amount of the tax. Following assessment of a unit excise tax, a producer will continue to supply any given quantity only if the price received for that quantity is higher by exactly the amount of the tax. Thus levying a unit excise tax on sales of a good or service causes the market supply curve to shift upward by the amount of the tax.
   c. If the demand curve has its usual downward slope, the upward shift in the supply curve caused by imposing a unit excise tax causes the equilibrium quantity produced and consumed to decline. The market price rises by less than the amount of the tax. Producers pay part of the tax in the form of higher per-unit costs, and consumers pay the remainder of the tax when they purchase the item at the higher market price.

4. Governments use tax revenues to fund expenditures on public goods and merit goods, such as Medicare.
   a. Federal funding of health-care services implies that effective prices that consumers pay for health-care services are less than the prices that health-care providers receive to provide those services, which explains the large quantities of health-care services demanded and supplied under Medicare.
      i. Because the government pays a per-unit subsidy for consuming a health-care service covered by Medicare, the out-of-pocket expense that a Medicare recipient pays for each unit of service—the effective price to the consumer—is relatively low; thus, the quantity of health-care services demanded by Medicare patients is relatively large.
      ii. Suppliers of health-care services are willing to provide the quantity of services demanded by Medicare patients, because the per-unit price they receive is equal to the out-of-pocket expense of Medicare patients plus the government subsidy.
      iii. The Medicare program's total expense for a particular health-care service equals the per-unit subsidy times the quantity of the service demanded by Medicare patients; taxpayers must fund this expense.
   b. In the absence of Medicare subsidies, the equilibrium prices and quantities of health-care services both would be lower than they are with the subsidies provided by this federal program.
      i. This means that Medicare has encouraged increased consumption and production of health-care services.
      ii. As a result, the total expense of the program—the per-unit government subsidy times the quantity of health-care services demanded—is higher than the government estimated using equilibrium quantities as a guide.
   c. To try to contain overall federal spending on Medicare, the government often imposes reimbursement caps, or limits, on specific medical procedures; this can have the unintended effect of worsening patient care and driving the program's costs up even further.

5. Education is another merit good that receives considerable public funding, which currently amounts to more than 5 percent of total U.S. national income.
   a. The basic economics of public funding of education is similar to the economics of public subsidies of health-care programs such as Medicare: Public schools provide educational services at a price below the market price and provide the amount of services demanded at

the below-market price as long as they receive sufficiently large per-unit subsidies from state and local governments.

    b. Since 1960, the inflation-adjusted average government subsidy for U.S. primary and secondary education has increased by $5,000 per student, but measures of student performance have remained flat or even declined. A possible explanation is that a higher per-pupil subsidy increases the difference between the per-student cost of providing educational services and the lower valuation of the services by parents and students; thus schools may have allocated resources to activities that have not necessarily enhanced learning.

6. Social Security faces long-term difficulties.
    a. People older than 65 already consume more than one-third of the federal government's budget, but the U.S. population continues to age; the population's median age has risen from 28 in 1970 to over 35 today.
    b. Social Security's rate of return adjusted for price changes has fallen below rates available on stocks and other savings instruments; thus, many would be better off if they were able to drop out of Social Security and save for retirement on their own.
    c. There are several possible reforms that could preserve Social Security as a "social compact" that spans generations of U.S. residents.
        i   One of these is to increase Social Security contributions by raising the payroll tax and/or increasing the wage base to which the payroll tax is applied.
        ii. Another reform would entail reducing total benefits, perhaps by means-testing benefit eligibility, reducing benefits to spouses of covered retirees, and/or raising the benefit retirement age.
        iii. Reducing restrictions on immigration by well-trained workers could expand the payroll tax base, thereby increasing current Social Security contributions.
        iv. Using Social Security funds to purchase shares of stock could raise the program's inflation-adjusted rate of return, provided that the returns on stocks remain relatively high; problems with this idea are that returns on stocks are not guaranteed to remain high and that deciding which stocks to buy could pose political difficulties.

KEY TERMS
Ad valorem taxation
Dynamic tax analysis
Excise tax
Government budget constraint

Inflation-adjusted return
Rate of return
Sales taxes
Social Security contributions

Static tax analysis
Tax base
Unit tax

KEY CONCEPTS
Education vouchers
Medicare subsidies

Payroll tax rate
Payroll tax wage base

User charges

COMPLETION QUESTIONS
Fill in the blank, or circle the correct term.

1. Ultimately, all government spending, transfers, and borrowing are primarily financed by (taxes, user charges).

2. The _____ is the limitation that taxes and user charges place on the total amount of government expenditures and transfer payments.

3. Under an *ad valorem* sales tax system, the government applies a (tax rate, constant tax) to the price of an item to determine the tax owed on purchase of the item.

4. _____ tax analysis emphasizes the potential for ever-higher tax rates to induce a reduction in the tax base.

5. (A sales, An excise) tax is levied on purchases of a particular good or service.

6. If the demand and supply curves for an item have their typical shapes, then imposing a unit excise tax on the item results in (a decrease, an increase) in the market price of the item and (a decrease, an increase) in the equilibrium quantity purchased and sold.

7. Because the Medicare program pays a per-unit subsidy for health-care expenses of people covered by the program, the price that they pay for health-care services is (greater than, equal to, less than) the market price, and the quantity of health-care services that they desire to consume is (greater than, equal to, less than) the equilibrium quantity.

8. Because the Medicare program pays a per-unit subsidy for health-care expenses of people covered by the program, the price that providers receive for health-care services is (greater than, equal to, less than) the market price, and the quantity of health-care services they are willing to supply is (greater than, equal to, less than) the equilibrium quantity.

9. An increase in the number of people covered by Medicare will tend to cause the demand for covered health-care services to _____, thereby causing a(n) _____ in both the equilibrium and actual quantities of the service demanded and supplied.

10. When governments provide subsidies to providers of educational services, the result is that the cost of the last unit of services provided is (lower, higher) than the marginal value of the services to parents and students.

11. A government-operated system of educational vouchers provides funds directly to (consumers, producers) of educational services.

12. A rate of return adjusted for the effects of price changes is called the _____ return.

13. The maximum wage earnings subject to the Social Security payroll tax _____ assessed against the earnings is called the wage _____ of the payroll tax system.

14. By increasing the number of workers who make payroll tax contributions, increased (immigration, emigration) could help the long-term prospects of Social Security.

15. Using Social Security contributions to purchase shares of _____ in companies might yield a higher rate of return for Social Security, but there is no guarantee of this.

TRUE-FALSE QUESTIONS
Circle the **T** if the statement is true, the **F** if it is false. Explain to yourself why a statement is false.

T F 1. A sales tax is typically a constant amount charged on the sale of a particular item.

T F 2. Static tax analysis indicates that raising the tax rate by 1 percentage point will always increase tax revenues by an amount equal to 1 percent of the tax base.

T F 3. Every U.S. state government relies on sales taxes to fund at least a portion of its spending and transfer programs.

T F 4. According to dynamic tax analysis, there is likely to be a single tax rate that maximizes government tax collections.

T F 5. Consumers always pay the full amount of a unit excise tax.

CHAPTER 6: TAXES, TRANSFERS, AND PUBLIC SPENDING

T F 6. The price that Medicare patients pay for covered care that they receive is lower than the market price of that care.

T F 7. Not including any administration costs, the direct expense that taxpayers incur in paying the government's share of the total costs of a particular type of care equals the per-unit subsidy that the government pays times the quantity of care demanded under the subsidy.

T F 8. The price that the supplier of a service covered by Medicare receives is higher than the market price of providing that service.

T F 9. If market demand and supply curves have their normal shapes, then the difference between the market price of a health-care service covered by Medicare and the price that Medicare recipients actually pay is equal to the per-unit Medicare subsidy.

T F 10. Since 1960, more than tripling the inflation-adjusted expenditures on U.S. public education has more than doubled the measured performance of U.S. public school students.

T F 11. A key problem for the Social Security system is that the generation following the Baby Boom generation is larger.

T F 12. One possible way to help fund Social Security in future years would be to raise the payroll tax rate for Social Security contributions.

T F 13. One possible way to reduce the future obligations of the Social Security program would be to reduce the initial age that a person is eligible for retirement benefits.

T F 14. Emigration of large numbers of working age people from the United States could do much to reduce the long-term financial problems of Social Security.

T F 15. Loosening restrictions on immigration by poorly trained people who would have trouble finding jobs would do more to aid the long-term financial health of the Social Security program, as compared with allowing immigration by highly qualified workers.

T F 16. There is no guarantee that purchasing stocks with Social Security funds would yield a higher future rate of return for the program.

MULTIPLE CHOICE QUESTIONS
Circle the letter that corresponds to the best answer.

1. If the government establishes a sales tax on a broad set of goods and services by levying a tax rate equal to the market price of each unit purchased, then it uses a system of
   a. unit taxes.
   b. excise taxes.
   c. *ad valorem* taxes.
   d. constant per-unit taxes.

2. The value of goods, services, or incomes subject to taxation is known as the
   a. tax base.
   b. unit base.
   c. *ad valorem* constraint.
   d. government budget constraint.

3. A key assumption of static tax analysis is that
   a. the tax base declines as the government raises the tax rate.
   b. there is a single tax rate that maximizes government tax revenues.
   c. the government's tax revenues always rise with increases in the tax rate.
   d. the government's tax revenues eventually decline when it levies ever-higher tax rates.

4. Imposing a unit excise tax results in
   a. an upward shift in the market supply curve equal to the amount of the tax.
   b. a downward shift in the market supply curve equal to the amount of the tax.
   c. an upward shift in the market demand curve equal to the resulting price increase.
   d. a downward shift in the market demand curve equal to the resulting price decline.

5. If market demand and supply curves have their normal shapes, then when a government levies a unit excise tax on an item equal to $5 per unit, the market price of the item will
   a. decline by an amount less than $5 per unit.
   b. increase by an amount less than $5 per unit.
   c. decline by an amount more than $5 per unit.
   d. increase by an amount more than $5 per unit.

6. If market demand and supply curves have their normal shapes, then a $1 increase in a unit excise tax on a good causes
   a. the price consumers pay for each unit to rise by $1.
   b. the costs suppliers incur to supply each unit to rise by $1.
   c. the price consumers pay for each unit to rise by more than $1.
   d. the costs suppliers incur to supply each unit to rise by less than $1.

7. Suppose that the government has been paying a fixed per-unit subsidy for a health-care service covered by Medicare. Then officials who administer the program tell patients and doctors and other health-care providers that they plan to cut the per-unit subsidy. Other things being equal, the result will be
   a. a rise in the market price and a decline in the equilibrium quantity in the market for the service.
   b. a rise in the price paid by each Medicare recipient, and a reduction in the quantity of the service demanded and supplied.
   c. a rise in the price received by each health-care supplier, and an increase in the quantity of the service demanded and supplied.
   d. a fall in the price received by each health-care supplier, and an increase in the quantity of the service demanded and supplied.

8. Suppose that, until this year, a health-care service was not covered by Medicare. Recently, however, the government has extended Medicare coverage to this service and has started paying a fixed per-unit subsidy to providers of the service. Other things being equal, the result will be
   a. a fall in the market price and an increase in the equilibrium quantity in the market for the service.
   b. a rise in the price paid by each Medicare recipient, and a reduction in the quantity of the service demanded and supplied.
   c. a rise in the price received by each health-care supplier, and an increase in the quantity of the service demanded and supplied.
   d. a fall in the price received by each health-care supplier, and an increase in the quantity of the service demanded and supplied.

CHAPTER 6: TAXES, TRANSFERS, AND PUBLIC SPENDING   **65**

9. In future years, the number of people covered by Medicare will increase, so the demand for each covered health-care service will rise. Suppose that the per-unit subsidy that the government pays for each covered service remains unchanged. Other things being equal, which one of the following will **NOT** occur as a result?
    a. The market price of the service will increase, and the equilibrium quantity in the market for the service will rise.
    b. There will be a rise in the price paid by each Medicare recipient, and there will be an increase in the quantity of the service demanded.
    c. There will be a rise in the price received by each health-care supplier, and there will be an increase in the quantity of the service supplied.
    d. Because the per-unit subsidy paid by the government remains unchanged, the total expense incurred by taxpayers will remain unaffected.

10. Today, the Social Security payroll tax rate is closest to
    a. 2 percent.
    b. 4 percent.
    c. 10 percent.
    d. 14 percent.

11. In 1935, only the first $3,000 of a person's wage earnings was subject to a Social Security payroll tax. Today, the wage base to which this payroll tax is applied is closest to the first _____ of a person's wage earnings.
    a. $5,000
    b. $25,000
    c. $80,000
    d. $100,000

12. Which one of the following would **NOT** help resolve current financial problems faced by Social Security, as it is currently structured?
    a. eliminating the Social Security payroll tax
    b. raising the Social Security payroll tax rate
    c. eliminating the cap on wage earnings subject to the payroll tax rate
    d. raising the wage base to which the Social Security payroll tax rate is applied

13. Which one of the following would **NOT** help resolve current financial problems faced by Social Security, as it is currently structured?
    a. raising the Social Security retirement age
    b. raising benefits paid to spouses of retirees who are eligible for benefits
    c. eliminating benefits for retirees who already earn relatively high incomes from other sources
    d. reducing benefits for all retirees irrespective of the incomes they receive from other sources

14. Increased immigration could help the long-term financial prospects of Social Security as long as immigrants are
    a. U.S. residents who already are beneficiaries of Social Security benefits.
    b. eligible for Social Security benefits within a short time after entering the United States.
    c. capable of finding jobs and earning wages that are subject to Social Security payroll taxes.
    d. unemployable spouses, children and other relatives of people who immigrated to the United States in prior years.

15. Which one of the following is a common rationale for purchasing shares of stock with Social Security contributions?
    a. In recent years, the inflation-adjusted rate of return has been much higher for stocks than for the Social Security system.
    b. Purchasing shares of stock will permit the federal government to exercise more influence over U.S. companies.
    c. Unlike the rate of return on the current Social Security system, the rate of return on shares of stock is guaranteed.
    d. Buying shares of stock in large quantities will cause the market rate of return on stocks to decline in the future.

MATCHING
Choose an item in Column (2) that best matches an item in Column (1).

(1)	(2)
a. Medicare subsidy	f. assumes that ever-higher tax rates eventually reduce the tax base
b. sales tax	g. assumes that ever-higher tax rates leave the tax base unaffected
c. *ad valorem* tax	h. tax levied as percentage of market price
d. dynamic tax analysis	i. difference between the price a consumer pays and the price received by a seller
e. static tax analysis	j. tax on market prices of many items

PROBLEMS

1. Consider the situation below in a market for health-care services covered by Medicare, where the program pays a per-unit subsidy equal to $20 to suppliers. Suppose that the government expands Medicare and increases the per-unit subsidy by $20. What happens to the market price and equilibrium quantity of health-care services? What happens to the prices paid by Medicare patients and received by health-care providers and to the actual quantity of services consumed and provided under Medicare?

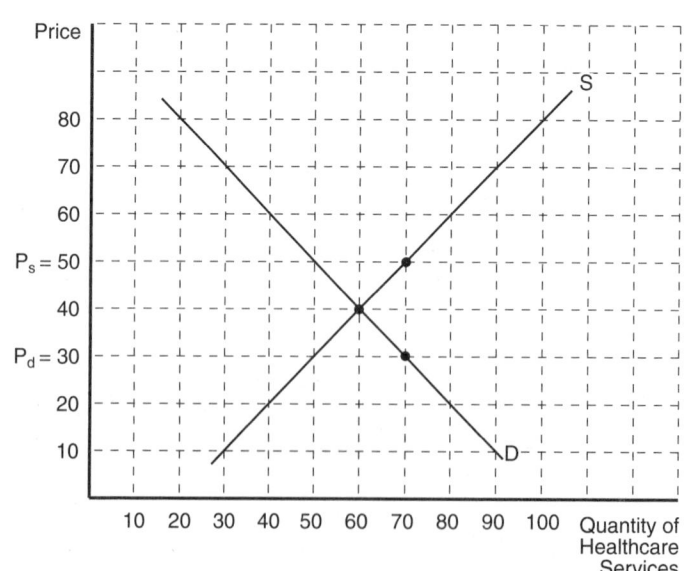

2. In the past, some economists have accused the American Medical Association of restricting the entry of doctors into markets for health-care services. Suppose that these critics are correct and that the AMA successfully reduces the number of doctors offering their services at any given price of health-care services they provide. As a result, the quantity of services provided at each price falls by 20 units. As shown below, the Medicare program pays a per-unit subsidy of $20 to the doctors whom the AMA permits to provide services in this market. Use the diagram below to illustrate the effects of the AMA's action on (1) the market price and equilibrium quantity of health-care services, (2) the price paid by patients covered by Medicare, and (3) the price received by doctors.

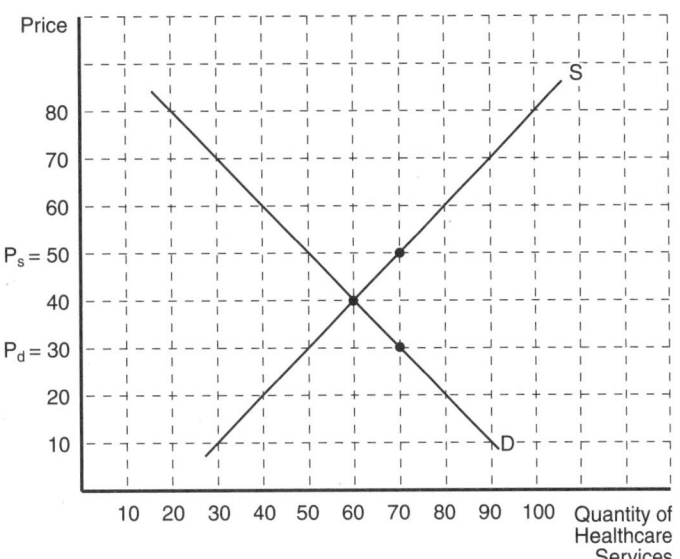

ANSWERS TO CHAPTER 6

COMPLETION QUESTIONS

1. taxes
2. government budget constraint
3. tax rate
4. dynamic
5. An excise
6. an increase; a decrease
7. less than; greater than
8. greater than; greater than
9. increase; increase
10. higher
11. consumers
12. inflation-adjusted
13. rate; base
14. immigration
15. stock

TRUE-FALSE QUESTIONS

1. F A sales tax covers a large set of items and typically is levied as a fraction of the price.
2. T
3. F There are no sales taxes in Delaware, Montana, New Hampshire, and Oregon.
4. T
5. F Consumers pay the full tax only if demand is completely unresponsive to price.
6. T
7. T
8. T
9. F The Medicare subsidy equals the difference between the price that suppliers receive and the price the recipients pay.
10. T Measures of student performance have either shown little change or declined.
11. F The problem is a smaller working age population that must fund benefits for a larger number of older people, including retiring members of the Baby Boom generation.
12.
13. F Reducing the retirement age would increase total benefit payments, thereby adding to payouts.
14. F Emigration of working age residents would reduce the tax base, thereby reducing Social Security contributions.
15. F This would add to total payouts from the program, which would worsen its problems.
16. T

MULTIPLE CHOICE QUESTIONS

1. c;   2. a;   3. c;   4. a;   5. b;   6. d;   7. b;   8. c;
9. d;   10. d;   11. c;   12. a;   13. b;   14. c;   15. a.

MATCHING

a and i; b and j; c and h; d and f; e and g

PROBLEMS

1. When the subsidy increases, the price paid by Medicare patients declines from $30 per unit to $20 per unit, and the price received by health-care providers increases from $50 per unit to $60 per unit. The quantity of services provided under Medicare increases from 70 units to 80 units. The market price remains equal to $40 per unit, and the equilibrium quantity remains equal to 60 units.

CHAPTER 6: TAXES, TRANSFERS, AND PUBLIC SPENDING   69

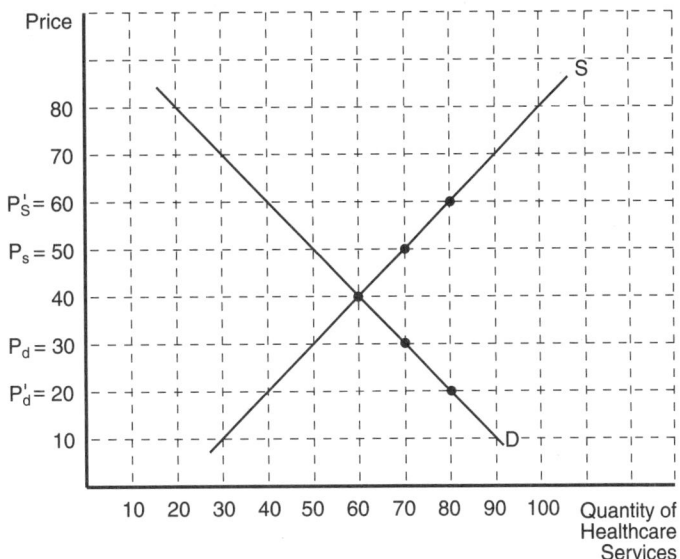

2. The supply curve shifts leftward, so the market price rises from $40 per unit to $50 per unit, and the equilibrium quantity falls from 60 units to 50 units. The subsidy remains equal to $20 per unit, however, so the price paid by Medicare patients increases from $30 per unit to $40 per unit, as does the price received by doctors, from $50 per unit to $60 per unit.

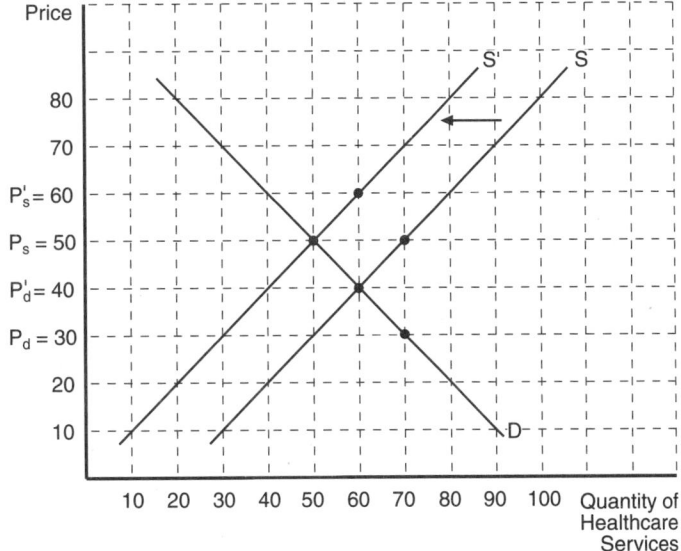

GLOSSARY TO CHAPTER 6

Ad valorem **taxation:** Assessing taxes by charging a tax rate equal to a fraction of the market price of each unit purchased.

Dynamic tax analysis: Economic evaluation of tax rate changes that recognizes that the tax base eventually declines with ever-higher tax rates, so that tax revenues may eventually decline if the tax rate is raised sufficiently.

Excise tax: A tax levied on purchases of a particular good or service.

Government budget constraint: The limit on government spending and transfers imposed by the fact that every dollar the government spends, transfers, or uses to repay borrowed funds must ultimately be provided by the taxes it collects.

Inflation-adjusted return: A rate of return that is measured in terms of real goods and services; that is, after the effects of inflation have been factored out.

Rate of return: The future financial benefit to making a current investment.

Sales taxes: Taxes assessed on the prices paid on a large set of goods and services.

Social Security contributions: The mandatory taxes paid out of workers' wages and salaries. Although half are supposedly paid by employers, in fact the net wages of employees are lower by the full amount.

Static tax analysis: Economic evaluation of the effects of tax rate changes under the assumption that there is no effect on the tax base, so that there is an unambiguous positive relationship between tax rates and tax revenues.

Tax base: The value of goods, services, incomes, or wealth subject to taxation.

Unit tax: A constant tax assessed on each unit of a good that consumers purchase.

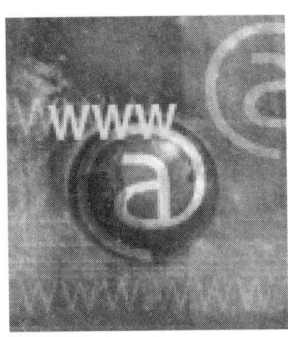

CHAPTER 19
CONSUMER CHOICE

LEARNING OBJECTIVES

After you have studied this chapter, you should be able to

1. define utility, util, marginal utility, marginal analysis, diminishing marginal utility, consumer optimum, substitution effect, principle of substitution, purchasing power, and real income effect;

2. distinguish between total utility and marginal utility, and answer questions that require an understanding of how they are related;

3. define marginal utility, and answer questions that require an understanding of this concept;

4. apply the concept of diminishing marginal utility to the law of demand;

5. predict what happens to the marginal utility per dollar's worth of a good when (a) its price changes, other things being constant and (b) more or less is consumed, other things being constant;

6. predict what a consumer will do if the marginal utility per dollar's worth of good A is greater (less) than the marginal utility per dollar's worth of good B;

7. predict how a change in price generates a real income effect and a substitution effect;

8. answer questions that require an understanding of how economists can explain the diamond-water paradox.

CHAPTER OUTLINE

1. Utility analysis is the study of consumer decision making based on utility maximization.
   a. A util is an artificial unit by which utility is measured.
   b. Total utility is the sum of all the utils derived from consumption; marginal utility is the change in total utility due to a one-unit change in the quantity of a good consumed.
   c. Economists maintain that economic decisions are made by comparing the marginal benefit of an activity with its marginal cost.
   d. As long as marginal utility is positive, total utility will rise.
   e. If marginal utility becomes negative—the good becomes a nuisance—total utility will fall.

2. The principle of diminishing marginal utility states that as more of any good or service is consumed, eventually its extra benefit declines.

72 CHAPTER 19: CONSUMER CHOICE

3. Consumers are assumed to optimize their consumption choices; the consumer attempts to maximize total utility subject to such constraints as income and relative prices.

4. When relative price changes, the consumer optimum is affected and the consumer reacts consistently and predictably.
    a. A consumer is optimizing when she allocates all of her money income in such a way that the marginal utility per dollar's worth of each good and service purchased is equal.
    b. If the relative price of a good falls, consumers will substitute it for the now relatively more expensive substitutes; this is the substitution effect.
    c. If the price of a good falls, given money income and given the prices of all other goods, a consumer's real income rises and she normally will purchase more of that good whose price has fallen; this is the real income effect.
    d. The substitution effect and the income effect help to explain the law of demand.

5. The "law" of diminishing marginal utility can account for the law of demand; because the marginal benefit falls to consumers as they consume more per unit of time, price must fall to induce them to purchase more.

6. The diamond-water paradox is that diamonds are unessential to life and have a high relative price, while water is essential to life yet has a low relative price.
    a. The total utility of water to humans far exceeds the total utility of diamonds to humans, but the marginal utility of water is relatively low while the marginal utility of diamonds is high.
    b. The price of a good, therefore, reflects its value on the margin—not its total or average value.

KEY TERMS
Utility
Util
Marginal utility

KEY CONCEPTS
Utility analysis
Purchasing power
Diminishing marginal utility
Substitution effect
Real income effect
Consumer optimum
Principle of substitution

COMPLETION QUESTIONS
Fill in the blank, or circle the correct term.

1. The want-satisfying power that a good or service possesses is referred to as _____.

2. The _____ is an artificial unit by which utility is measured.

3. The change in total utility due to a one-unit change in quantity consumed is called _____.

4. _____ analysis is the study of what happens when small changes take place relative to the status quo.

5. If marginal utility is positive, total utility must (fall, rise); if marginal utility is negative, total utility must _____; if marginal utility falls (but is positive) then total utility must (fall, rise) at a decreasing rate.

6. Economists maintain that as more of a good or service is consumed, per unit of time, its marginal benefit (falls, rises); therefore before buyers will purchase more and more of a good, its price must (fall, rise).

7. The consumer optimum exists when consumers _____ their total utility, subject to such constraints as _____ and relative price; in order to optimize, a consumer should allocate his income so that the marginal utility per dollar's worth of each good or service he purchases is _____.

8. Assume a consumer is in consumer optimum and then the price of good A rises, other things being constant. It is now true that the marginal utility per dollar's worth of good A is (less, greater) than the marginal utility per dollar's worth of other goods; the consumer will now feel (richer, poorer) and probably spend (more, less) on good A; furthermore, the consumer will tend to substitute (A for other goods, other goods for A).

9. Although the (marginal, total) utility of water is greater than that of diamonds, the (marginal, total) utility of diamonds is higher; the price of a good reflects its (marginal, total) utility.

10. The explicit price of time spent surfing the Internet is (zero, infinite), but the law of diminishing marginal utility implies that a person who places a relatively high value on her time will tend to spend (more, less) time "Net-surfing."

TRUE-FALSE QUESTIONS
Circle the **T** if the statement is true, the **F** if it is false. Explain to yourself why a statement is false.

T F 1. Economists today maintain that utility can be measured cardinally.

T F 2. It is possible for a person marginal utility to be negative if consuming more of an item causes a the individual's total utility to decline.

T F 3. Positive economics permits economists to say that person 1 gets more utility from ice cream than does person 2.

T F 4. If total utility rises at a decreasing rate, then marginal utility must be falling.

T F 5. If marginal utility is positive, then consuming the last unit of output reduced total utility.

T F 6. Economists typically assume that as a person consumes more of any good, that good's total utility must fall.

T F 7. If the MU of good X/price of good X exceeds the MU of good Y/price of good Y, the consumer can increase her total utility by substituting good X for good Y.

T F 8. The law of diminishing marginal utility implies the law of demand, assuming consumers wish to optimize.

T F 9. When the price of hamburgers falls, other things constant, everyone's real income will rise.

T F 10. When the price of butter falls, other things constant, people will tend to substitute butter for margarine.

T F 11. Because price reflects total utility rather than marginal utility, diamonds are more expensive than water.

CHAPTER 19: CONSUMER CHOICE

MULTIPLE CHOICE QUESTIONS
Circle the letter that corresponds to the best answer.

1. If marginal utility is positive, but falling, then total utility
   a. falls.
   b. falls at a decreasing rate.
   c. rises.
   d. rises at a decreasing rate.

2. Which of the following words is most **UNLIKE** the others?
   a. marginal
   b. average
   c. incremental
   d. extra

3. When an individual's total utility increases with consumption of one more unit of an item, it must be true that the person's
   a. marginal utility from consuming this unit is negative.
   b. marginal utility from consuming this unit is positive.
   c. marginal utility is increasing at the current level of consumption.
   d. marginal utility is decreasing at the current level of consumption.

4. As more of good A is consumed per week, over broad ranges
   a. the marginal utility of good A falls.
   b. the total utility of good A rises.
   c. the total utility of good A rises at a decreasing rate.
   d. All of the above

5. If marginal utility is negative, then
   a. total utility falls.
   b. total utility rises at a decreasing rate.
   c. total utility must be negative.
   d. None of the above

6. Which of the following helps to explain the law of demand?
   a. the law of diminishing marginal utility
   b. the substitution effect
   c. the income effect
   d. All of the above

7. Consumer optimizing requires that the consumer
   a. maximize income.
   b. maximize total utility, subject to an income constraint.
   c. maximize income, subject to a marginal utility constraint.
   d. maximize marginal utility, subject to an income constraint.

8. If the marginal utility per dollar's worth of good A exceeds that of good B for Mr. Capra, then he
   a. is optimizing.
   b. will substitute good A for good B.
   c. will substitute good B for good A.
   d. is minimizing, not maximizing.

9. If the price of good A rises, other things being constant, then
   a. the marginal utility of good A falls.
   b. the marginal utility of good A rises.
   c. the marginal utility per dollar's worth of good A falls.
   d. the relative price of good A falls.

10. If the price of steak rises, other things constant,
    a. everyone's real income will rise.
    b. everyone's money income will rise.
    c. the real income of steak buyers will rise.
    d. the real income of steak buyers will fall.

11. If the price of steak rises, other things constant,
    a. a real income effect will induce people to purchase less steak.
    b. people will substitute hamburgers for steak.
    c. the quantity demanded for steak will fall.
    d. All of the above

12. Diamonds have a higher price than water because
    a. people are shallow and shortsighted.
    b. price reflects total, not marginal, utility.
    c. price reflects marginal, not total, utility.
    d. the total utility of diamonds is greater, but the marginal utility of water is greater.

WORKING WITH GRAPHS

1. Use the information given below to complete the table.

Hamburgers consumed per month	Total utility (in utils)	Marginal utility (in utils)
0	0	
1	5	
2	14	
3	22	
4	28	
5	33	
6	36	
7	35	
8	32	

   a. Graph the total and marginal utility curves on the graph provided below. (Plot the marginal utilities at the midpoint between quantities.)

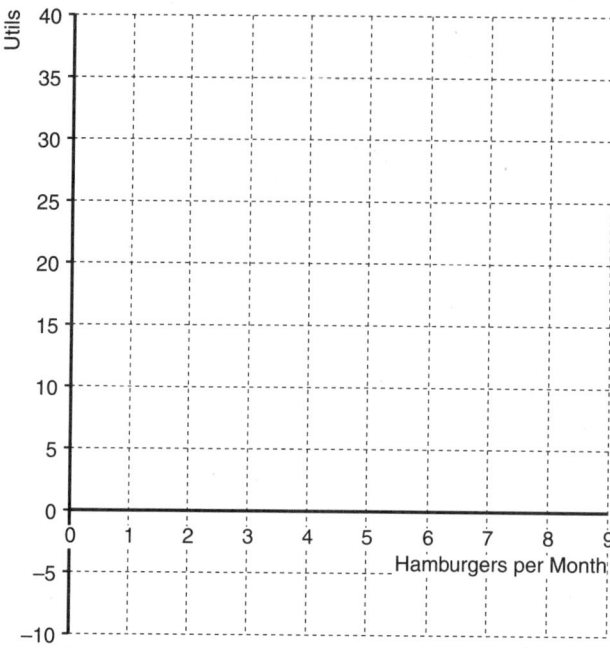

b. At what quantity does diminishing marginal utility set in?

2. Consider the graphs below, then answer the questions that follow.

a. Which panel indicates constant marginal utility?
b. Which panel indicates increasing marginal utility?
c. Which panel indicates decreasing marginal utility?

PROBLEMS

1. Consider the following information.

Quantity Consumed per week	Candy Bars Total utility	Candy Bars Marginal utility	Apples Total utility	Apples Marginal utility
0	0		0	
1	10	_____	15	_____
2	18	_____	24	_____
3	25	_____	30	_____
4	29	_____	32	_____
5	31	_____	31	_____
6	30	_____	29	_____

   a. Complete the columns containing the marginal utilities of each good.
   b. With unlimited income, a consumer described by the above information would consume _____ candy bars and _____ apples.
   c. If candy bars cost 25 cents each and apples are two for a quarter (12.5 cents each) and the consumer has $1.50 to spend on candy and apples, what quantity of candy bars and apples will allow the above individual to reach consumer optimum?
   d. Now suppose the consumer suffers a loss of income and has 20 cents to spend. In addition, the price of candy bars is now 10 cents and the price of apples is 2 cents. What quantities of each will allow the individual to reach consumer optimum?

2. Mr. Smith does not believe that economists are correct when they say that diminishing marginal utility is the rule for most goods. He claims that *increasing* marginal utility is the rule: as he consumes more and more of any good, his marginal utility rises.

   Assume that Mr. Smith spends his income one dollar at a time, and that he can purchase one dollar's worth of any good. Assume further that he wishes to maximize his total utility.

   On what good does Mr. Smith spend his first dollar? The second? The third? What predictions can you make about his behavior? Do most people behave that way? Does anyone?

3. Conduct the same analysis that you did in question (2) above for Mrs. Smith, who claims that, for her, *constant* marginal utility is the rule.
   a. How do your answers differ from those in question (2)?
   b. Can you think of *anything* for which diminishing marginal utility does not occur eventually, *per unit of time*?

ANSWERS TO CHAPTER 19

COMPLETION QUESTIONS

1. utility
2. util
3. marginal utility
4. marginal
5. rise; fall; rise
6. falls; fall
7. maximize; income; equal
8. less; poorer; less; other goods for A
9. total; marginal; marginal
10. zero; less

TRUE-FALSE QUESTIONS

1. F They need only to assume that it can be measured ordinally.
2. T
3. F Interpersonal utility comparisons require normative judgments.
4. T
5. F Marginal utility is positive only if total utility increased with the last unit consumed.
6. F They assume that its *marginal utility* falls.
7. T
8. T
9. F Only hamburger buyers will experience an increase in real income.
10. T
11. F Price reflects marginal utility.

MULTIPLE CHOICE QUESTIONS

1. d; 2. b; 3. b; 4. d; 5. a; 6. d; 7. b; 8. b; 9. c; 10. d;
11. d; 12. c.

WORKING WITH GRAPHS

1. a. 5; 9; 8; 6; 5; 3; -1; -3

   b. with the third hamburger consumed each month

2. a. 3
   b. 1
   c. 2

PROBLEMS

1. a. marginal utility of candy bars: 10, 8, 7, 4, 2, -1; marginal utility of apples: 15, 9, 6, 2, -1, -2
   b. 5, 4
   c. 4 candy bars and 4 apples
   d. 1 candy bar and 4 apples. Note that the consumer has 2 cents left over, cannot purchase another candy bar, and will not purchase another apple, since the additional apple has a negative marginal utility (total utility declines).

2. Mr. Smith will spend every dollar of his income on the same good—that which gives him the highest marginal utility per dollar's worth of his first dollar spent. Only drug addicts, perhaps, behave that way.

3. a. The answers are the same as in (2) above.
   b. Given the qualifications in the question, it is difficult to think of any good for which that is not the case.

GLOSSARY TO CHAPTER 19

Consumer optimum A choice of a set of goods and services that maximizes the level of satisfaction for each consumer, subject to limited income.

Diminishing marginal utility The principle that as more of any good or service is consumed, its extra benefit declines. Otherwise stated, increases in total utility from the consumption of a good or service become smaller and smaller as more is consumed during a given time period.

Marginal utility The change in total utility due to a one-unit change in the quantity of a good or service consumed.

Principle of substitution The principle that consumers and producers shift away from goods and resources that become priced relatively higher in favor of goods and resources that are now priced relatively lower.

Purchasing power The value of money for buying goods and services. If your money income stays the same but the price of one good that you are buying goes up, your effective purchasing power falls, and vice versa.

Real-income effect The change in people's purchasing power that occurs when, other things being constant, the price of one good they purchase changes. When that price goes up, real income, or purchasing power, falls, and when that price goes down, real income increases.

Substitution effect The tendency of people to substitute cheaper commodities for more expensive commodities.

Util A representative unit by which utility is measured.

Utility The want-satisfying power of a good or service.

Utility analysis The analysis of consumer decision making based on utility maximization.

APPENDIX E
MORE ADVANCED CONSUMER CHOICE THEORY

LEARNING OBJECTIVES

After you have studied Appendix E, you should be able to

1. define indifference curve, budget constraint, income-consumption curve, and price-consumption curve;

2. draw an indifference curve based on data presented in a table;

3. answer questions that require a proper interpretation of an indifference curve and of an indifference map;

4. recognize properties of indifference curves;

5. explain the meaning of the slope of an indifference curve and the slope of a budget line;

6. recognize the consumer optimum combination of goods, given an indifference map and a budget line;

7. interpret and sketch an income-consumption curve and a price-consumption curve;

8. predict what happens to a budget line when each price changes and when income changes.

APPENDIX OUTLINE

1. This appendix presents a more rigorous and more formal analysis of consumer behavior.
    a. An indifference curve is the set of consumption alternatives which yield the same total amount of satisfaction.
    b. Indifference curves have important properties.
        i. Indifference curves are negatively sloped.
        ii. Indifference curves are never linear; they are convex with respect to the origin.
    c. The slope of an indifference curve is referred to as the marginal rate of substitution, which is the change in the quantity of one good that just offsets a one-unit change in the consumption of another good, so that total satisfaction remains constant.

80

2. An indifference map is a set of indifference curves; higher indifference curves represent higher levels of satisfaction (because they permit more consumption of *both goods*), and lower indifference curves represent less satisfying combinations of goods.

3. A budget constraint represents the set of opportunities facing a decision maker.
   a. The budget line is derived assuming a fixed money income and a given set of relative prices.
   b. The slope of a budget line is (the negative of) the ratio of the prices of the relevant goods.
   c. The position of a budget line depends on the level of nominal income; if nominal income changes, a parallel shift in the budget line results.

4. Consumer optimum exists at that point (combination of goods and services) where the slope of the indifference curve equals the slope of the budget line; at that point the consumer is maximizing utility.

5. If nominal and relative prices are held constant and income is increased, an income-consumption curve can be derived.

6. A price-consumption curve is the set of consumer optimum combinations of two goods that results when the price of one good changes, holding money income and the price of the other good constant.

7. A demand curve can be derived from the indifference map-budget line model; as the price of one good changes, other things being constant (the price of the other good and money income), consumer optimum changes so as to indicate an inverse relationship between price and quantity demanded.

KEY TERMS
Income–consumption curve   Price–consumption curve

KEY CONCEPTS
Indifference curve   Budget constraint

COMPLETION QUESTIONS
Fill in the blank, or circle the correct term.

1. A curve that indicates combinations of goods and services that yield an equal level of satisfaction is called a(n) _____ curve; such a curve is (positively, negatively) sloped.

2. Ignoring its sign, the slope of an indifference curve (falls, rises) as we move down the curve; a set of indifference curves is called an indifference _____.

3. If indifference curve B lies below indifference curve A, it (is, is not) preferred; if indifference curve C lies above indifference curve A, indifference curve C permits a consumer to consume (less, more) of both goods.

4. A budget constraint line is derived holding relative _____ constant and holding nominal _____ constant; the slope of a budget constraint line is determined by _____, and the position of such a line depends on _____.

5. Consumer optimum exists where the budget constraint line is _____ to a(n) _____ curve; at such a point the (lowest, highest) indifference curve is achieved.

6. If income falls, other things being constant, the budget line _____; generally a reduction in income will lead to (a decrease, an increase) in the quantity demanded.

7. If the price of one good changes, the slope of an indifference curve (remains constant, changes); if the price of one good changes, the slope of a budget constraint line (remains constant, changes); if nominal income changes, the slope of a budget constraint line (remains constant, changes).

8. Along a price-consumption curve, which relates the combinations of good A and good B that a consumer will purchase, the price of good A falls while the price of good B (rises, falls, remains constant) and nominal income (rises, falls, remains constant).

TRUE-FALSE QUESTIONS
Circle the **T** if the statement is true, the **F** if it is false. Explain to yourself why a statement is false.

T F 1. Along an indifference curve, a consumer has the same level of marginal utility.

T F 2. Indifference curves are negatively sloped.

T F 3. Indifference curves are usually linear.

T F 4. The slope of the budget constraint line is referred to as the marginal rate of substitution.

T F 5. Points below a budget constraint line are not attainable goods combinations for a consumer.

T F 6. If indifference curve 3 lies above indifference curve 2, curve 3 is not preferable to the consumer.

T F 7. Indifference curves that lie entirely above a budget constraint line are unattainable for the consumer.

T F 8. If nominal income changes, then the slope of an indifference curve changes.

T F 9. If nominal income changes, then the slope of a budget constraint line changes.

T F 10. If relative prices change, then the slope of a budget constraint line changes, but the slope of an indifference curve is unaltered.

T F 11. Consumer optimum is attained where the budget constraint line is tangent to the highest possible indifference curve.

T F 12. Along an income-consumption curve, prices remain constant.

T F 13. Along a price-consumption curve, relative prices change, but money income is constant.

MULTIPLE CHOICE QUESTIONS
Circle the letter that corresponds to the best answer.

1. Along an indifference curve,
    a. total utility stays the same.
    b. marginal utility stays the same.
    c. marginal utility increases as consumption rises.
    d. All of the above

2. In indifference curve analysis, if combination A is preferred to combination B and combination B is preferred to combination C, then
    a. A is on a higher indifference curve than B or C.
    b. C is on a lower indifference curve than A or B.
    c. A, B, and C are on different indifference curves.
    d. All of the above

3. Indifference curves
    a. are upward sloping.
    b. are linear.
    c. are convex with respect to the origin.
    d. indicate objective, not subjective, valuations of a consumer.

4. As we move down an indifference curve, the marginal rate of substitution
    a. remains constant.
    b. remains constant, but total utility rises.
    c. changes.
    d. changes, but total utility rises.

5. The negative of the slope of a(n) _____ is the marginal rate of substitution.
    a. production possibilities curve
    b. budget constraint line
    c. income-consumption curve
    d. indifference curve

6. Where consumer optimum is reached,
    a. the slope of the budget constraint line equals the slope of an indifference curve.
    b. the ratio of relative prices equals the marginal rate of substitution.
    c. the consumer attains the highest indifference curve, given the budget constraint line.
    d. All of the above

7. The slope of the budget constraint line
    a. reflects the relative prices of the two goods in question.
    b. reflects the consumer's income.
    c. varies as nominal income varies.
    d. always equals the slope of the indifference curve.

8. If income rises, other things being constant, then
    a. an indifference curve shifts outward.
    b. a parallel, rightward shift in the budget constraint line occurs.
    c. the slope of the budget constraint line falls.
    d. the slope of the budget constraint line rises.

9. When a price-consumption curve is derived,
    a. the relative price of both goods changes.
    b. the relative price of only one good changes.
    c. money income changes.
    d. consumer optimum is not attained.

84 APPENDIX E: MORE ADVANCED CONSUMER CHOICE THEORY

10. When an income-consumption curve is derived,
    a. relative prices remain constant.
    b. income changes.
    c. consumer optimum exists at each point along such a curve.
    d. All of the above

11. When the price of good A rises, other things being constant,
    a. the indifference map does not change.
    b. the slope of the budget constraint line changes.
    c. a new consumer optimum is reached, where less of good A is purchased.
    d. All of the above

WORKING WITH GRAPHS

1. Suppose that a consumer is faced with the choice of only two goods: food and entertainment. After some consideration, the consumer provides the following information about various combinations of food and entertainment per month to which she is indifferent, given some particular level of satisfaction.

Units of entertainment per month	Units of food per month
35	7
20	11
10	15
5	20
3	30
2	45

    a. Use this information and the following grid to plot this consumer's indifference curve for entertainment and food for a given level of satisfaction. Label the curve I.

    Suppose the consumer is asked to provide the same type of information for some higher level of satisfaction. In this case the consumer supplies the information given below.

Units of entertainment per month	Units of food per month
40	11
30	15
25	18
15	25
10	35
7	45

    b. Use this new information and the grid above to plot this additional indifference curve. Label this curve II.

2. Suppose that the consumer in problem 1 has a monthly income of $400 and that the price of entertainment is $10 per unit and the price of food is $20 per unit.
    a. Plot the consumer's budget line on the above grid and label it BL1.
    b. Given the consumer's indifference map and the above prices and income, what combination of entertainment and food will put the consumer at an optimum point?
    c. Suppose that the price of food drops to $10 per unit but the price of entertainment and the consumer's income remain unchanged. Draw the new budget line in the above grid and label it BL2.
    d. After the change in part (c), which combination of entertainment and food will put the consumer at an optimum point?

3. Draw a price-consumption curve for each of the following combinations of goods.
    a. Hot dogs and hot dog buns, with the price of buns changing
    b. Coke and Pepsi, with the price of Pepsi changing
    c. Potatoes and guitar strings, with the price of guitar strings changing

ANSWERS TO APPENDIX E

COMPLETION QUESTIONS

1. indifference; negatively
2. falls; map
3. is not; more
4. prices; income; relative prices; income
5. tangent; indifference; highest
6. shifts inward (parallel); decrease
7. remains constant; changes; remains constant
8. remains constant; remains constant

TRUE-FALSE QUESTIONS

1. F Total utility stays the same, not marginal.
2. T
3. F A linear indifference curve implies a constant marginal rate of substitution.
4. F The slope of the budget line reflects relative prices.
5. F They are attainable, but not optimal.
6. F It is preferable if it lies above 2.
7. T
8. F Indifference curves are independent of income.
9. F Slope stays the same, but the budget line shifts.
10. T
11. T
12. T
13. T

MULTIPLE CHOICE QUESTIONS

1.a; 2.d; 3.c; 4.c; 5.d; 6.d; 7.a; 8.b; 9.a; 10.d; 11.d.

WORKING WITH GRAPHS

1. a. see graph below; b. see graph below

2. a. see graph above; b. 10 units of entertainment per month and 15 units of food per month; c. see graph above; d. 15 units of entertainment per month and 25 units of food per month.

3.

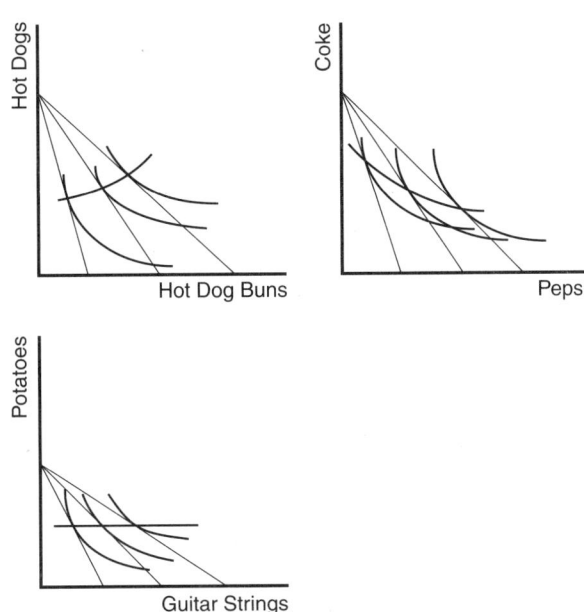

GLOSSARY TO APPENDIX E

Budget constraint All of the possible combinations of goods that can be purchased (at fixed prices) with a specific budget.

Income-consumption curve The set of optimal consumption points that would occur if income were increased, relative prices remaining constant.

Indifference curve A curve composed of the set of consumption alternatives, each of which yields the same total amount of satisfaction.

Price-consumption curve The set of consumer-optimum combinations of two goods that the consumer would choose as the price of one good changes, while money income and the price of the other good remain constant.

CHAPTER 20
DEMAND AND SUPPLY ELASTICITY

LEARNING OBJECTIVES

After you have studied this chapter, you should be able to

1. define price elasticity of demand, elastic demand, unit elastic demand, inelastic demand, perfectly inelastic demand, perfectly elastic demand, cross price elasticity of demand, income elasticity of demand, price elasticity of supply, perfectly elastic supply, and perfectly inelastic supply;

2. calculate price elasticity of demand in two ways, given the relevant information;

3. predict what will happen to a firm's total revenues if the firm changes price, given price elasticity of demand;

4. classify an elasticity coefficient as indicating whether demand is elastic, unit elastic, or inelastic, in the relevant price range;

5. recognize from a graph whether the demand for a good is perfectly elastic or perfectly inelastic in the specified price range;

6. identify the determinants of price elasticity of demand;

7. calculate the cross price elasticity of demand coefficient, and determine from the sign of that coefficient whether or not the goods in question are substitutes or complements;

8. calculate income elasticity of demand from relevant information and distinguish price elasticity of demand from income elasticity of demand;

9. calculate price elasticity of supply, identify the determinants of price elasticity of supply, and recognize a graph of a perfectly elastic supply curve and a perfectly inelastic supply curve.

CHAPTER OUTLINE

1. Elasticity measures quantity responsiveness to price changes.
   a. Price elasticity of demand is defined as the percentage change in quantity demanded divided by the percentage change in price.

CHAPTER 20: DEMAND AND SUPPLY ELASTICITY

       i. Because of the law of demand, the price elasticity of demand is always negative; by convention the sign is ignored.

       ii. Price elasticity of demand relates percentage changes, not absolute changes.

  b. There are two ways to calculate the price elasticity of demand.

       i. Price elasticity of demand may be calculated by dividing the change in quantity demanded over the original quantity demanded by the change in price over the original price; this method yields a different elasticity over the same range of the demand curve, depending on whether price rises or falls.

       ii. In order to get consistent results over the same range of a demand curve, it is possible to calculate price elasticity by using average values for base price and base quantity.

2. If the calculated price elasticity of demand for a good is greater than one, the demand is called elastic; if it is equal to one, the demand is called unit elastic; if it is less than one, the demand is called inelastic.

3. Elasticity is related to a firm's total revenues.
   a. In the range of elastic demand, if a firm lowers price its total revenues will rise; if it raises price its total revenues will fall.
   b. In the range of unit elastic demand, small changes in price leave the firm's total revenues unaltered.
   c. In the range of inelastic demand, if a firm lowers price its total revenues will fall; if it raises price its total revenues will rise.
   d. Along a linear demand curve (which has a constant slope, by definition), a good has an elastic, a unit elastic, and an inelastic range.
   e. There are two extreme price elasticities of demand.
      i. Perfectly inelastic demand indicates no change in quantity demanded as price changes; such a demand curve is vertical at the given quantity.
      ii. Perfectly elastic demand indicates that even a slight increase in price will lead to a zero quantity demanded; such a demand curve is horizontal at the given price.

4. As long as the market supply curve has its typical upward slope, the price elasticity of demand is an important factor affecting who actually pays most of a per-unit tax on a good or service after imposition of the tax shifts the supply curve upward by the amount of the tax.
   a. If demand is perfectly inelastic, then the market price will rise by the full amount of the tax; as a result, consumers pay the entire tax.
   b. If demand is perfectly elastic, then the market price does not change when the tax is imposed, so producers pay all of the tax.
   c. When demand is neither perfectly inelastic nor perfectly elastic, both consumers and producers pay portions of the tax.

5. There are three major determinants of the price elasticity of demand.
   a. The closer the substitutes for a particular good, and the more available they are, the greater will be its price elasticity of demand.
   b. The higher the proportion of total expenditures that people allocate to a good, the higher will be that good's price elasticity of demand.
   c. The longer any price change persists, the greater the price elasticity of demand; the distinction between the short-run and long-run consumer adjustment period varies with the good in question.

6. Cross price elasticity of demand is defined as the percentage change in the demand for one good (holding its price constant) divided by the percentage change in the price of a related good.
   a. If the sign of the cross price elasticity of demand is positive, the two goods are substitutes.

b. If the sign of the cross price elasticity of demand is negative, the two goods are complements.

7. Income elasticity of demand is defined as the percentage change in the demand for a good (holding its price constant) divided by the percentage change in money income.

8. Price elasticity of supply is defined as the percentage change in quantity supplied divided by the percentage change in price.
   a. One extreme is perfectly elastic supply, where a slight decrease in price leads to a zero quantity supplied; such a supply curve is horizontal at the given price.
   b. Another extreme is perfectly inelastic supply, where quantity supplied is constant, regardless of what happens to price; such a supply curve is vertical at the given quantity.
   c. The longer the time for adjustment, the more price elastic is the supply curve.
   d. Empirical evidence indicates that short-run elasticities for goods are often considerably smaller than long-run elasticities.

KEY TERMS
Elastic demand
Unit elasticity of demand
Inelastic demand

KEY CONCEPTS
Price elasticity of demand
Perfectly inelastic demand
Perfectly elastic demand
Perfectly elastic supply
Cross price elasticity of demand
Price elasticity of supply
Income elasticity of demand
Perfectly inelastic supply

COMPLETION QUESTIONS
Fill in the blank, or circle the correct term.

1. Price elasticity of demand is a measure of buyer _____ to price changes.

2. Price elasticity of demand is defined as the percentage change in _____ divided by the percentage change in _____; the problem with this measure is that we get (the same, a different) numerical value when we move up, as opposed to down, the same range of the demand curve.

3. In order to correct for the problem in question 2 above, the _____ value method of calculating the price elasticity of demand can be used.

4. Assume a 1 percent change in price. If quantity demanded changes by less than 1 percent, then we say that in that range the demand for the good is _____; if quantity demanded changes by 1 percent, then in that range demand is _____; if quantity demanded changes by more than 1 percent, then in that range demand is _____.

5. If price falls and total revenues rise, then in that range demand was price _____ if price falls and total revenues remain constant, then in that range demand was price _____; if price falls and total revenues fall, then in that range demand was price _____.

6. If price rises and total revenues fall, then demand was price _____; if total revenues rise, then demand was price _____; if total revenues remain constant, then demand was _____.

7. A demand curve that exhibits zero responsiveness to price changes is _____; such a demand curve is (horizontal, vertical) at the given quantity; a demand curve in which even the

slightest increase in price will lead to a zero quantity demanded is _____; such a demand curve is (horizontal, vertical) at the given price.

8. The determinants of price elasticity of demand are _____, _____, and _____.

9. Cross price elasticity of demand is defined as the percentage change in the _____ for one good, holding its _____ constant, divided by the percentage change in the _____ of another good.

10. If the cross price elasticity of demand is positive, then the two goods are _____; if it is negative, the two goods are _____.

11. The income elasticity of demand is defined as the percentage change in _____ for a good, holding its _____ constant, divided by the percentage change in _____.

12. The price elasticity of supply measures the responsiveness of the _____ of a good to a change in its price; a supply curve in which a slight decrease in price leads to a zero quantity supplied is _____; if quantity supplied remains constant no matter what happens to price, the supply curve is _____.

TRUE-FALSE QUESTIONS
Circle the **T** if the statement is true, the **F** if it is false. Explain to yourself why a statement is false.

T F 1. Price elasticity of demand measures the responsiveness of price to changes in quantity demanded.

T F 2. Because of the law of demand, price elasticity of demand will always (implicitly) be a negative number.

T F 3. Price elasticity of demand deals with absolute, not relative, values.

T F 4. When price elasticity of demand is used by the average value approach, price elasticity is the same whether price rises or falls over a given demand curve range.

T F 5. If the price elasticity of demand is 3, then over the relevant price range demand is inelastic.

T F 6. When the demand for an item is perfectly elastic, the slightest increase in the price of that item causes the quantity demanded to drop to zero. As a result, the demand curve for the item is horizontal.

T F 7. When the demand for an item is perfectly elastic and the supply of the item has its normal upward slope, consumers will pay all of a per-unit tax that the government has imposed on sales of the item.

T F 8. If price falls and total revenues rise, then over that price range demand is inelastic.

T F 9. If a firm discovers that at current prices the price elasticity of demand is 0.5, the firm may want to raise prices to increase profits.

T F 10. The price elasticity of demand for McDonald's hamburgers is less than the price elasticity of demand for hamburgers.

T F 11. If the demand for good A is perfectly elastic, its demand curve is vertical at that price.

T F 12. If the demand for good A is perfectly inelastic over *all* prices, good A violates the law of demand.

T F 13. The less time people have to respond to a price change, the higher is the price elasticity.

T F 14. If the cross price elasticity of demand for goods A and B is negative, A and B are complements.

T F 15. Income elasticity of demand is calculated for a horizontal shift in the demand curve, given price.

T F 16. If supply is perfectly inelastic, the curve will be horizontal at the given quantity.

MULTIPLE CHOICE QUESTIONS
Circle the letter that corresponds to the best answer.

1. Price elasticity of demand measures responsiveness of
    a. quantity demanded to changes in price.
    b. quantity demanded to changes in income.
    c. price to changes in quantity demanded.
    d. price to changes in demand.

2. If the price elasticity of demand is 0.33, then
    a. demand is inelastic.
    b. demand is inelastic over that price range.
    c. demand is elastic.
    d. demand is elastic over that price range.

3. Which of the following is **NOT** true concerning the price elasticity of demand?
    a. Its sign is always negative, due to the law of demand.
    b. It is a unitless, dimensionless number.
    c. It equals the percentage change in price divided by the percentage change in quantity demanded.
    d. It measures the responsiveness of quantity demanded to changes in price.

4. If price elasticity of demand is calculated using the original price and quantity, then over a given range in the demand curve price elasticity of demand
    a. differs, depending on whether price rises or falls.
    b. is the same, regardless of whether price rises or falls.
    c. is equal to 1.
    d. rises as price falls.

5. If price falls by 1 percent and quantity demanded rises by 2 percent, then the price elasticity of demand
    a. is inelastic over that range.
    b. is 0.5.
    c. is elastic over that range.
    d. cannot be calculated from this information.

6. If price rises and total revenue rises, then the price elasticity of demand over that range is
   a. elastic.
   b. inelastic.
   c. unit elastic.
   d. equal to 1.

7. If price falls and over that price range demand is inelastic, total revenues will
   a. remain constant.
   b. fall.
   c. rise.
   d. fall, then rise.

8. If the demand for good A is perfectly inelastic at all prices,
   a. quantity demanded does not change as price changes.
   b. the law of demand is violated.
   c. the demand curve is vertical at the given quantity.
   d. All of the above

9. If the demand for good A is perfectly elastic,
   a. quantity demanded does not vary with price.
   b. the demand curve is horizontal.
   c. the demand curve is vertical.
   d. the demand curve is positively sloped.

10. If the government imposes a per-unit tax of $1 on sales of an item for which demand is perfectly inelastic at all prices and for which the supply curve slopes upward,
    a. quantity supplied falls to zero at all post-tax prices of the item.
    b. quantity demanded falls to zero at all post-tax prices of the item.
    c. the market price does not change, so producers pay the entire tax.
    d. the tax is fully reflected in the market price, so consumers pay the entire tax.

11. If the government imposes a per-unit tax of $1 on sales of an item for which demand is perfectly elastic at all prices and for which the supply curve slopes upward,
    a. quantity supplied falls to zero at all post-tax prices of the item.
    b. quantity demanded falls to zero at all post-tax prices of the item.
    c. the market price does not change, so producers pay the entire tax.
    d. the tax is fully reflected in the market price, so consumers pay the entire tax.

12. Which of the following is **NOT** a determinant of the price elasticity of demand?
    a. existence and closeness of substitutes
    b. proportion of the good to the consumer's budget
    c. price elasticity of supply
    d. length of time allowed for adjustment to a price change

13. If the cross price elasticity of demand between good A and good B is positive, the goods are
    a. substitutes.
    b. complements.
    c. unrelated.
    d. necessities.

14. If the cross price elasticity between good A and good B is -10, then A and B are
    a. close substitutes.
    b. near substitutes.
    c. strongly complementary.
    d. mildly complementary.

15. Baseballs and baseball bats are
    a. substitutes.
    b. complements.
    c. not related goods.
    d. necessities.

16. When the income elasticity of demand for good A is calculated,
    a. the price of good A varies.
    b. income changes, which lead to horizontal shifts in the demand curve for good A, are measured.
    c. a movement along the demand curve for good A is measured.
    d. All of the above

17. *Analogy*: A movement along a demand curve is to price elasticity of demand as a shift in the demand curve is to
    a. an increase in demand.
    b. changes in taxes or subsidies.
    c. income elasticity of demand.
    d. substitutes and complements.

18. At current prices for salt, salt is highly price
    a. elastic.
    b. inelastic.
    c. cross elastic.
    d. unit elastic.

19. Which of the following goods is probably the most highly income elastic?
    a. salt
    b. food
    c. alcoholic beverages
    d. private education

20. A perfectly inelastic supply curve
    a. shows great quantity supplied responsiveness to price changes.
    b. is horizontal at the given price.
    c. indicates zero quantity supplied responsiveness to price changes.
    d. is a normal situation.

21. If the supply of good B is perfectly elastic and price falls, quantity supplied will
    a. remain unchanged.
    b. rise.
    c. fall.
    d. fall to zero.

22. If price rises, the quantity supplied will be greater the
    a. longer the time that elapses.
    b. more income elastic is the good.
    c. higher the price elasticity of demand for the good.
    d. All of the above

CHAPTER 20: DEMAND AND SUPPLY ELASTICITY   95

MATCHING

Choose the item in column (2) that best matches an item in column (1).

(1)
a. perfectly inelastic demand
b. perfectly elastic demand
c. perfectly inelastic supply
d. perfectly elastic supply
e. determinant of price elasticity
f. cross-price elasticity of demand
g. inelastic

(2)
h. elasticity coefficient less than 1
i. horizontal supply curve
j. complementary or substitute goods
k. quality of substitutes
l. horizontal demand curve
m. vertical demand curve
n. vertical supply curve

PROBLEMS

1. Suppose you are given the following data on the market demand and supply for used CDs in a small record store. (Use the average elasticity measure.)

Price	Quantity demanded (per week)	Quantity supplied (per week)
$4.00	50	10
4.50	45	15
5.00	40	25
5.50	35	35
6.00	30	45

   a. What is the equilibrium price for CDs?
   b. What is the price elasticity of demand over the price range $4.50 to $5? Over the range $5.50 to $6?
   c. What is the price elasticity of supply over the same two ranges of price?
   d. Now suppose that most students in the area are working for the minimum wage and that the minimum wage has gone up. As a result, at each price, two more CDs per week are demanded. Calculate the price elasticity of demand over the same ranges as in part (b).
   e. After comparing your answers from parts (b) and (d), what can you conclude about the price elasticity of demand as the demand curve shifts to the right?

2. Suppose we have the following information for a low-income family:

	Income per month	Quantity of hamburger demanded per month	Quantity of steak demanded per month
Period 1	$750	8 lbs.	2 lbs.
Period 2	$950	5 lbs.	4 lbs.

   a. What is the income elasticity of demand for hamburger?
   b. What is the income elasticity of demand for steak?
   c. From our study of demand in an earlier chapter, we know _____ is a normal good, whereas _____ is an inferior good.

3. Suppose the price of color print film has recently risen by 10 percent due to an increase in the cost of the silver that is used to make film. As a result, less film is being sold in the camera store where you work. You do some checking and find that camera sales are down by 4 percent. What is the cross-price elasticity of cameras and film? Are these two goods complements or substitutes?

ANSWERS TO CHAPTER 20

COMPLETION QUESTIONS

1. responsiveness
2. quantity demanded; price; a different
3. average
4. inelastic; unit elastic; elastic
5. elastic; unit elastic; inelastic
6. elastic; inelastic; unit elastic
7. perfectly inelastic; vertical; perfectly elastic; horizontal
8. closeness of available substitutes; proportion of the good in consumer budgets; length of time to respond
9. demand; price; price
10. substitutes; complements
11. demand; price; money income
12. quantity supplied; perfectly elastic; perfectly inelastic

TRUE-FALSE QUESTIONS

1. F   It measures quantity demanded responsiveness to price changes.
2. T
3. F   It deals with relative values.
4. T
5. F   It is price elastic because the coefficient exceeds 1.
6. T
7. F   The supply curve shifts upward by the amount of the per-unit tax, and because demand is perfectly elastic the market price does not change, so consumers pay none of the tax.
8. F   It must have been elastic.
9. T
10. F   It is greater, because there are more substitutes for *McDonald's* hamburgers than for hamburgers.
11. F   It is horizontal at that price.
12. T
13. F   Elasticity increases over time because substitutes become more readily available over time.
14. T
15. T
16. F   It will be vertical, at the given quantity.

MULTIPLE CHOICE QUESTIONS

1.a; 2.b; 3.c; 4.a; 5.c; 6.b; 7.b; 8.d; 9.b; 10.d;
11.c; 12.c; 13.a; 14.c; 15.b; 16.b; 17.c; 18.b; 19.d; 20.c;
21.d 22.a.

MATCHING

a and m;   b and l;   c and n;   d and i;   e and k;   f and j;   g and h

PROBLEMS

1. a. $5.50
   b. 1.12; 1.77
   c. 4.75; 2.88
   d. 1.07; 1.67
   e. As the demand curve shifts to the right, for any price range, demand becomes less elastic—or, alternatively stated, more inelastic.

2. a. -1.96
   b. 2.83
   c. steak; hamburger

3. -0.4; complements

GLOSSARY TO CHAPTER 20

Cross price elasticity of demand (E_{xy}) The percentage change in the demand for one good (holding its price constant) divided by the percentage change in the price of a related good.

Elastic demand (E_i) A demand relationship in which a given percentage change in price will result in a larger percentage change in quantity demanded. Total expenditures and price are inversely related in the elastic portion of the demand curve.

Income elasticity of demand The percentage change in demand for any good, holding its price constant, divided by the percentage change in income; the responsiveness of the demand to changes in income, holding the good's relative price constant.

Inelastic demand A demand relationship in which a given percentage change in price will result in a less than proportionate percentage change in the quantity demanded. Total expenditures and price are directly related in the inelastic region of the demand curve.

Perfectly elastic demand A demand that has the characteristic that even the slightest increase in price will lead to a zero quantity demanded.

Perfectly elastic supply A supply characterized by a reduction in quantity supplied to zero when there is the slightest decrease in price.

Perfectly inelastic demand A demand that exhibits zero responsiveness to price changes; that is, no matter what the price is, the quantity demanded remains the same.

Perfectly inelastic supply A supply for which quantity supplied remains constant, no matter what happens to price.

Price elasticity of demand (E_p) The responsiveness of the quantity demanded of a commodity to changes in its price; defined as the percentage change in quantity demanded divided by the percentage change in price.

Price elasticity of supply (E_s) The responsiveness of the quantity supplied of a commodity to a change in its price; the percentage change in quantity supplied divided by the percentage change in price.

Unit elasticity of demand A demand relationship in which the quantity demanded changes exactly in proportion to the change in price. Total expenditures are invariant to price changes in the unit elastic portion of the demand curve.

CHAPTER 21
RENTS, PROFITS, AND THE FINANCIAL ENVIRONMENT OF BUSINESS

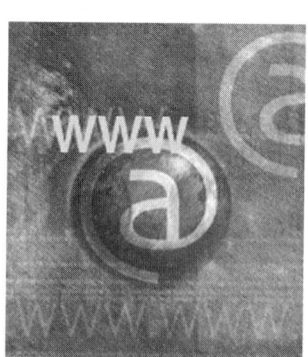

LEARNING OBJECTIVES

After you have studied this chapter you should be able to

1. define economic rent, firm, proprietorship, partnership, corporation, unlimited liability, limited liability, explicit costs, implicit costs, accounting profit, economic profit, normal rate of return, opportunity cost of capital, interest, nominal rate of interest, real rate of interest, present value, rate of discount, discounting financial capital, dividends, share of stock, bond, reinvestment, random walk theory, and inside information;

2. understand the allocative function of economic rents;

3. distinguish among proprietorships, partnerships, and corporations;

4. identify the advantages and disadvantages of proprietorships, partnerships, and corporations;

5. distinguish between accounting profits and economic profits and between explicit costs and implicit costs;

6. explain the importance of earning a normal rate of return and taking into account the opportunity cost of capital;

7. explain the distinction between the nominal interest rate and the real interest rate and calculate the (approximate) nominal interest rate, given the real interest rate and the anticipated rate of inflation;

8. list three factors that account for variations in interest rates;

9. calculate the present value of an amount of money to be received at a future date;

CHAPTER 21: RENTS, PROFITS, AND THE FINANCIAL ENVIRONMENT OF BUSINESS

10. describe the differences between stocks and bonds and the basic features of securities markets.

CHAPTER OUTLINE

1. *Economic rent* is a payment for the use of any resource that is in fixed supply.
    a. Land is often believed to be in fixed supply.
    b. Even if land is absolutely in fixed supply, rent payments help society to decide how land is to be used.
    c. Economic rents also accrue to factors of production other than land.
    d. Rents help society decide how to allocate a factor fixed in supply.

2. A firm is an organization that brings together different factors of production, such as labor, land, capital, and entrepreneurial skill, to produce a product or service which it is hoped can be sold for a profit.

3. A proprietorship is owned by a single individual who makes the business decisions, receives all the profits, and is legally responsible for all the debts of the firm.
    a. Advantages: a proprietorship is easy to form and dissolve; all decision-making powers reside with the sole proprietor; a proprietorship is taxed only once.
    b. Disadvantages: the proprietorship faces unlimited liability for debts of the firm and has limited ability to raise funds; the business normally ceases to exist with the death of the proprietor.

4. A partnership is owned by two or more who share profits or losses.
    a. Advantages: partnerships are easy to form, experience relatively low costs of monitoring job performance, permit more specialization than sole proprietorships, and are only taxed once.
    b. Disadvantages: partnerships face unlimited liability and more difficulty in decision-making (relative to proprietorship); dissolution of the partnership is usually necessary when a partner dies or leaves the partnership.

5. A corporation is a legal entity that may conduct business in its own name, just as an individual does. The owners of the corporation are its shareholders.
    a. Advantages: shareholders enjoy limited liability; a corporation continues to exist even if some owners cease to remain owners; a corporation has the ability to raise large sums of money for investments.
    b. Disadvantages: owners are subject to double taxation because corporations pay taxes on profits and shareholders pay taxes on dividends received; ownership and control are separated in a corporation.
        i. Professional managers, who may have little or no ownership in the firm, may pursue their own, not shareholder-owner, interests.
        ii. Shareholders may experience high costs to monitor the behavior of professional managers.

6. It is widely assumed by economists that the goal of the firm is to maximize total profits.
    a. Accounting profits equal total revenues minus explicit costs.
    b. The opportunity cost of capital, or the normal rate of return to invested capital, is the rate of return that must be paid to an investor to induce him or her to invest in a business.
    c. There is also an opportunity cost to labor; single-owner proprietors, after all, could earn wages elsewhere.
        i. There is an opportunity cost to all inputs.

ii. Economic profits equal total revenues minus the opportunity cost of all inputs; stated differently, total profits equal total revenues minus the sum of explicit and implicit costs.

7. The term *interest* is used to mean two things: (1) the price paid by debtors to creditors for the use of loanable funds, and (2) the market return earned by (nonfinancial) capital as a factor of production.
   a. Interest is the payment for obtaining credit.
   b. Interest rates vary with the length of loan, risk, and handling charges.
   c. The *nominal interest* rate is (approximately) equal to the sum of the real interest rate and the expected rate of inflation.
   d. The interest rate, ultimately, allocates physical capital to various firms for investment projects.

8. Interest rates link the present with the future.
   a. A money value in the future can be expressed in today's value by a process referred to as *discounting* to present worth.
   b. Discounting is the method by which the present value of a future sum, or a stream of future sums, is obtained.
   c. The *rate of discount* is the interest rate used in the discounting to present worth equation.

9. Stocks, bonds, and reinvestment of retained earnings are the most important sources of corporate financing.
   a. From the investor's point of view, stocks offer the highest risk (and, therefore, the highest potential rate of return), and the greatest control over the firm's decisions.
   b. Bonds are relatively safer (and yield a correspondingly lower rate of return) and provide little control over decision-making.

10. Some people believe that the stock market is an efficient market, in the sense that it follows a random walk.
    a. The random walk theory predicts that the best forecast of tomorrow's stock price is today's price, because today's price incorporates all the information important to stock price determination.
    b. Only inside information will permit people to beat the stock market.

KEY TERMS

Proprietorship
Partnership
Corporation
Explicit costs
Implicit costs
Accounting profit

Economic profit
Normal rate of return
Interest
Nominal rate of interest
Real rate of interest

Rate of discount
Financial capital
Share of stock
Dividends
Bond

KEY CONCEPTS

Economic rent
Unlimited liability
Limited liability

Opportunity cost of capital
Reinvestment
Discounting

Present value
Random walk theory
Inside information

CHAPTER 21: RENTS, PROFITS, AND THE FINANCIAL ENVIRONMENT OF BUSINESS

COMPLETION QUESTIONS
Fill in the blank or circle the correct term.

1. A payment for the use of any resource that is _____ in supply is an economic rent.

2. The three major forms of U.S. business organizations are _____, _____, and _____.

3. While the highest percentage of U.S. firms are (proprietorships, partnerships, corporations), the highest percentage of total business revenue is attributed to _____.

4. A _____ is a legal entity that may conduct business in its own name, just as an individual does; its owners are called (shareholders, bondholders), and such owners enjoy (unlimited, limited, partially limited) liability.

5. (Explicit, Implicit) costs are usually considered by accountants, but _____ costs typically are not.

6. Economists consider implicit costs because such costs (do, do not) include the opportunity costs of the resources used.

7. Accounting profits equal _____ minus _____; economic profits equal _____ minus _____; economic profits are less than accounting profits because economic profits subtract _____ costs from total revenues.

8. Economists usually assume that the firm's goal is _____.

9. Interest is the cost of obtaining _____. Interest is used to mean two different things: (1) _____, and (2) _____.

10. Interest rates vary due to _____, _____, and _____.

11. The nominal interest rate equals the real interest rate plus the _____; ultimately the interest rate allocates _____ to various firms for investment projects.

12. The process of finding the value today of a sum of money in the future is called _____; the interest rate used in that process is called the _____ rate.

13. According to the efficient markets theory, the stock market is a _____ walk; the best prediction of tomorrow's price is _____.

TRUE-FALSE QUESTIONS
Circle the **T** if the statement is true, the **F** if it is false. Explain to yourself why a statement is false.

T F 1. Economic rent accrues only to the factor land.

T F 2. Economic rent is the price paid to a factor that is perfectly elastic in supply.

T F 3. If economic rent was totally taxed away, society would have to decide who gets to use the resource in question.

T F 4. For a factor fixed in supply, economic rent has no economic function.

T F 5. Economic rent occurs because specific resources have perfect substitutes.

T F 6. If a rock star prices tickets at a price way below equilibrium, that is an efficient way to help poor people.

T F 7. Corporations are the most common form of business organization in the United States.

T F 8. Proprietorships account for the highest percentage of total business revenues in the United States.

T F 9. Proprietorships and partnerships face unlimited liability for the debts of their firms.

T F 10. The main advantage of corporations is that they offer limited liability to shareholders.

T F 11. Accountants typically do not consider implicit costs.

T F 12. Explicit costs include the opportunity cost of a resource.

T F 13. Accounting profits equal total revenues minus explicit costs.

T F 14. Accounting profits always exceed economic profits.

T F 15. Economists usually assume that the firm's goal is to maximize profits.

T F 16. Other things being constant, the greater the risk of nonrepayment, the higher the interest rate.

T F 17. The nominal interest rate (approximately) equals the real rate of interest plus the expected interest rate.

T F 18. Ultimately, the interest rate allocates physical capital to *specific firms* and households.

T F 19. Discounting is the process of converting future money values to present worth.

T F 20. Stocks offer a higher risk and return, relative to bonds, but bonds offer investors greater control over the firm's decisions.

T F 21. Reinvestment of retained earnings is the most important source of corporate finance.

T F 22. According to the efficient market theory, the best prediction of tomorrow's stock price is today's price.

T F 23. According to the efficient market theory, the only way to earn abnormal profits (in the long run) is to have inside information.

CHAPTER 21: RENTS, PROFITS, AND THE FINANCIAL ENVIRONMENT OF BUSINESS

MULTIPLE CHOICE QUESTIONS
Circle the letter that corresponds to the best answer.

1. For a factor that earns economic rent,
    a. its quantity varies only in the long run.
    b. its supply is perfectly elastic.
    c. its supply curve is perfectly inelastic.
    d. no taxation is possible because no surplus exists.

2. In David Ricardo's economic model,
    a. land was fixed in supply.
    b. wages and salaries were set by government.
    c. land rent falls as industrialization occurs.
    d. All of the above

3. Economic rents
    a. have no allocative function.
    b. have no economic function.
    c. do not bring forth a greater quantity of the resource.
    d. exist only for land.

4. Economic rents
    a. accrue only to land.
    b. accrue only to labor.
    c. accrue only to entrepreneurs.
    d. can accrue to any factor, in principle.

5. Which of the following is **NOT** true, concerning a proprietorship?
    a. Most U.S. firms are proprietorships.
    b. They are easy to form and to dissolve.
    c. They offer limited liability.
    d. The owner is taxed only once on business income.

6. Which of the following is a disadvantage of a proprietorship?
    a. Unlimited liability for the firm's debts.
    b. Limited ability to raise funds.
    c. The firm ends with the death of the proprietor.
    d. All of the above

7. Which of the following is **NOT** true, concerning partnerships?
    a. There are fewer partnerships than proprietorships in the United States.
    b. They permit more effective specialization than proprietorships.
    c. Business income is taxed only once.
    d. Partners have limited liability for the firm's debts.

8. Which of the following is an advantage of partnerships?
    a. Partners have unlimited liability.
    b. They enjoy reduced cost in monitoring job performance.
    c. They must be dissolved if one partner dies.
    d. All of the above

9. A corporation
   a. is a legal entity that conducts business in its own name.
   b. permits unlimited liability to shareholders.
   c. must be dissolved if a majority stockholder dies.
   d. has severely limited abilities to attract financial resources.

10. Explicit costs
    a. are considered by accountants.
    b. are greater than implicit costs.
    c. are considered irrelevant by economists.
    d. are considered by accountants, but not by economists.

11. Implicit costs
    a. are considered important to accountants, but not to economists.
    b. are usually less than explicit costs.
    c. include the opportunity costs of resources.
    d. are considered irrelevant by businesses.

12. Accounting profits
    a. equal total revenues minus explicit costs.
    b. exceed economic profits.
    c. do not take implicit costs into account.
    d. All of the above

13. The opportunity cost of capital is
    a. an explicit cost of doing business.
    b. not an important cost of doing business.
    c. the normal rate of return on capital invested in a business.
    d. purely a technological concept.

14. Which of the following is **NOT** explicit?
    a. wages
    b. opportunity cost of capital
    c. taxes
    d. rent

15. *Analogy*: Rent is to explicit costs as _____ are to implicit costs.
    a. labor services of a proprietor
    b. taxes
    c. wages
    d. accounting profits

16. Which of the following goals of the firm is most widely assumed by economists?
    a. staff maximization
    b. sales maximization
    c. growth maximization
    d. profit maximization

17. Other things being constant, the interest rate varies with the
    a. length of a loan.
    b. risk of nonrepayment.
    c. handling charges.
    d. All of the above

CHAPTER 21: RENTS, PROFITS, AND THE FINANCIAL ENVIRONMENT OF BUSINESS   105

18. The nominal interest rate approximately equals the real interest rate
    a. minus the expected interest rate.
    b. plus the expected interest rate.
    c. plus the expected rate of inflation.
    d. minus the expected inflation rate.

19. Interest rates
    a. have no economic function.
    b. allocate financial capital to less efficient firms.
    c. allocate physical capital to firms in a random manner.
    d. allocate physical capital to specific firms for investment projects.

20. Discounting
    a. converts future dollar values into present values.
    b. connects the future with the present.
    c. uses the interest rate.
    d. All of the above

21. If the interest rate is 5 per cent, the present value of $100 that is to be received one year from now is about
    a. $90
    b. $950
    c. $95
    d. $105

22. When Miller won the $1,000,000 lottery in Florida, he found out that the money would be paid to him at the rate of $50,000 per year for the next twenty years. Which of the following is probably true?
    a. Miller will refuse the money, after he finds out what the lottery is really worth.
    b. The lottery winnings are worth considerably less than $1 million.
    c. Miller would *prefer* to receive his lottery winnings over twenty years, instead of all at once.
    d. Miller would have preferred to receive $25,000 per year for 40 years.

23. Shareholders
    a. are the owners of corporations.
    b. are less at risk than are bondholders.
    c. are subject to unlimited risk.
    d. have less control over firm decisions than do bondholders.

24. According to the efficient market theory, in an efficient market
    a. only lucky people can earn abnormal profits in the long run.
    b. tomorrow's price is easily determined.
    c. only inside information permits abnormal profits.
    d. a pattern of price changes will emerge.

CHAPTER 21 RENTS, PROFITS, AND THE FINANCIAL ENVIRONMENT OF BUSINESS

MATCHING
Choose the item in column (2) that best matches an item in column (1).

(1)

a. economic rent
b. share of stock
c. bond
d. present value calculation
e. total profits
f. corporation
g. real rate of interest

(2)

h. corporate debt
i. payment to resource fixed in supply
j. limited liability
k. total revenues minus total costs
l. corporate ownership
m. discount rate
n. inflation expectation

WORKING WITH GRAPHS
Use the following diagram to answer the questions that follow.

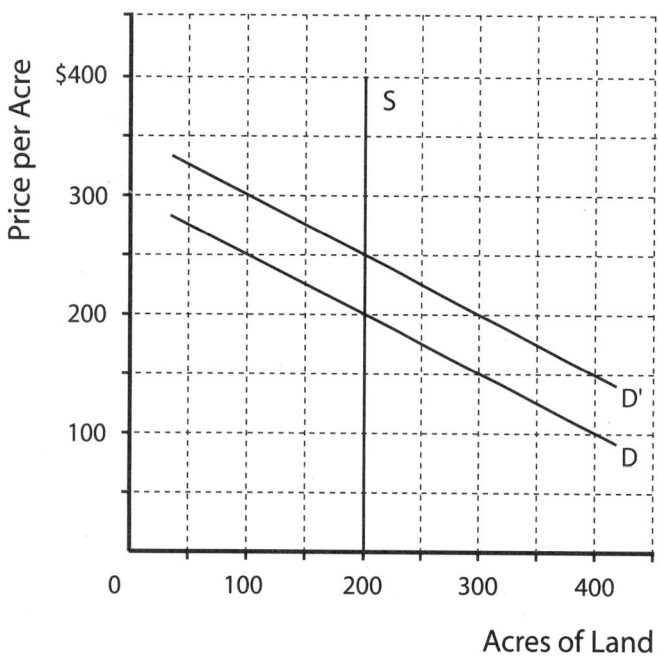

1. If the demand for land is represented by D, what is the total rent received by the owner of the 200 acres of land?

2. If the demand for land increases to D', what is the rent received by the landowner?

PROBLEMS

1. Suppose you win a lottery that offers the following payoff. At the end of each year for the next 3 years you are to receive $1000. At the end of each of the following 3 years you will receive $500, for a total of $4500 over the six-year period. If the current going rate of interest is 8%, what is the present value of your winnings? If someone offered you $3700 today for your lottery ticket, should you take it?

2. Gladstone Gander just learned that a long-lost aunt has set up a trust for him, whereby he will receive $1 million exactly ten years from now. Assume that the relevant interest rate is 10 percent.

   a. Can Gladstone sell his inheritance, right now, for $1 million? Why or why not?

   b. What is the present value of Gladstone's inheritance?

3. Suppose that you had used a discount rate of 20 percent in question (2) above. How would you answer (a) and (b) now?

   c. How are present value and the interest rate related?

ANSWERS TO CHAPTER 21

COMPLETION QUESTIONS

1. fixed
2. proprietorships; partnerships; corporations
3. proprietorships; corporations
4. corporation; shareholders; limited
5. Explicit; implicit
6. do
7. total revenues; explicit costs; total revenues; implicit plus explicit costs; implicit
8. profit maximization
9. credit; price paid by creditors to debtors, return to capital
10. length of loan, risk of nonrepayment, handling charges
11. expected inflation rate; physical capital
12. discounting; discount
13. random; today's price

TRUE-FALSE QUESTIONS

1. F It accrues to any factor fixed in supply.
2. F It is the price paid to a perfectly *in*elastic resource supply.
3. T
4. F It allocates the fixed factor to its highest-valued use.
5. F Rent is earned by resources that cannot be replicated exactly.
6. F Giving them money income directly would be more efficient.
7. F Proprietorships account for about 70 percent of total business organizations.
8. F Corporations do.
9. T
10. T
11. T
12. F Implicit costs do.
13. T
14. T
15. T
16. T
17. F Plus the expected *inflation (not expected interest)* rate.
18. T
19. T
20. F Stocks also give investors greater control than bonds.

21. T
22. T
23. T

MULTIPLE CHOICE

1.c; 2.a; 3.c; 4.d; 5.c; 6.d; 7.d; 8.b; 9.a; 10.a;
11.c; 12.d; 13.c; 14.b; 15.a; 16.d; 17.d; 18.c; 19.d; 20.d;
21.c; 22.b; 23.a; 24.c

MATCHING

a and i; b and l; c and h; d and m; e and k; f and j; g and n

WORKING WITH GRAPHS

1. $40,000
2. $50,000

PROBLEMS

1. From Table 21-3 on page 517 of your text we can see:

Year	Present Value	(Found by)
1	$ 926.00	(.926 x 1000)
2	857.00	(.857 x 1000)
3	794.00	(.794 x 1000)
4	367.50	(.735 x 500)
5	340.50	(.681 x 500)
6	315.00	(.630 x 500)
Total	$3600.00	

    Yes, you would be $100 better off, as is seen by the present value calculation.

2. a. No, no one would give him $1 million right now because such a sum could be invested and earn interest for ten years, and at the end of that period it would be worth $1 million plus the accumulated interest.

    b. $\frac{\$1,000,000}{(1.1)^{10}} = \frac{\$1,000,000}{2.5937425} = \$385,543$ • Or from Table 21-3, use the discount factor of 0.385, or an answer of $385,000.

3. a. See (2) above
    b. $161,506 (or rounded to $162,000 if the discount factor of 0.162 from Table 21-3 is used)
    c. They are inversely related.

GLOSSARY TO CHAPTER 21

Accounting profit Total revenues minus total explicit costs.

Bond A legal claim against a firm, usually entitling the owner of the bond to receive a fixed annual coupon payment, plus a lump sum payment at the bond's maturity date. Bonds are issued in return for funds lent to the firm.

Corporation A legal entity that may conduct business in its own name just as an individual does; the owners of a corporation, called shareholders, own shares of the firm's profits and enjoy the protection of limited liability.

Discounting The method by which the present value of a future sum or a future stream of sums is obtained.

Dividends Portion of a corporation's profits paid to the its owners (shareholders).

Economic profits Total revenues minus total opportunity costs of all inputs used, or the total of all implicit and explicit costs.

Economic rent A payment for the use of any resource over and above its opportunity cost.

Explicit costs Costs that business managers must take account of because they must be paid; for example, wages, taxes, and rent.

Financial capital Funds used to purchase physical capital goods such as plant and equipment.

Firm A business organization that employs resources to produce goods or services for profit. A firm normally owns and operates at least one plant in order to produce.

Implicit costs Expenses that managers do not have to pay out of pocket and hence do not normally calculate, such as the opportunity cost of factors of production that are owned; examples are owner-provided capital and owner-provided labor.

Inside information Information that is not available to the general public about what is happening in a corporation.

Interest The payment for current rather than future command over resources; the cost of obtaining credit. Also, the return paid to owners of capital.

Limited liability A legal concept whereby the responsibility, or liability of the owners of a corporation is limited to the value of the shares in the firm that they own.

Nominal rate of interest The market rate of interest expressed in today's dollars.

Normal rate of return The amount that must be paid to an investor to induce investment in a business; also known as the *opportunity cost of capital*.

Opportunity cost of capital The normal rate of return, or the available return on the next-best alternative investment. Economists consider this a cost of production, and it is included in our cost examples.

Partnership A business owned by two or more joint owners, or partners, who share the responsibilities and profits of the firm, and who are individually liable for all the debts of the partnership.

Present value The value of a future amount expressed in today's dollars; the most that someone would pay today to receive a certain sum at some point in the future.

Proprietorship A business owned by one individual who makes the business decisions, receives all the profits, and is legally responsible for the debts of the firm.

Random walk theory The theory that there are no predictable trends in securities prices that can be used to "get rich quick."

Rate of discount That rate of interest used to discount future sums back to present value.

Real rate of interest The nominal rate of interest minus the anticipated rate of inflation.

Reinvestment Profits (or depreciation reserves) used to purchase new capital equipment.

Securities Stocks and bonds.

Share of stock A legal claim to a share of a corporation's future profits; if it is *common stock*, it incorporates certain voting rights regarding major policy decisions of the corporation; if it is *preferred stock*, its owners are accorded preferential treatment in the payment of dividends.

Unlimited liability A legal concept whereby the personal assets of the owner of a firm may be seized to pay off the firm's debts.

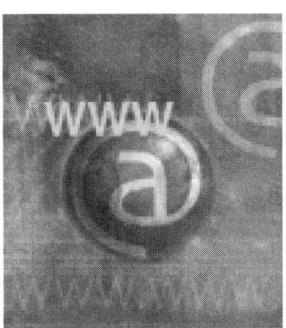

CHAPTER 22
THE FIRM: COST AND OUTPUT DETERMINATION

LEARNING OBJECTIVES

After you have studied this chapter, you should be able to

1. define short run, long run, production, production function, law of diminishing (marginal) returns, average physical product, marginal physical product, total costs, fixed costs, variable costs, average fixed costs, average variable cost, average total costs, marginal costs, planning horizon, long-run average cost curve, planning curve, economies of scale, constant returns to scale, diseconomies of scale, and minimum efficient scale;

2. distinguish between the firm's short run and its long run;

3. apply the law of diminishing (marginal) returns to account for the shape of the firm's short-run marginal cost curve, average total cost curve, and average variable cost curve;

4. classify firm costs as fixed or variable costs;

5. calculate average total cost, average fixed cost, average variable cost, and marginal cost, given sufficient information;

6. apply the concepts of economies of scale, diseconomies of scale, and constant returns to scale to predict the shape of a firm's long-run average cost curve;

7. list reasons for economies of scale and for diseconomies of scale;

8. understand the concept of minimum efficient scale (MES).

CHAPTER OUTLINE

1. The short run is defined as that time period in which a firm cannot alter its current size of plant; the long run is that time period in which all factors of production can be varied.

2. Total costs are identical to total fixed costs plus total variable costs.
   a. Total fixed costs do not vary with output.
   b. Total variable costs are the sum of all those costs that vary with output.
   c. There are several short-run average cost curves.
      i. Average total costs equal total costs divided by output.

ii. Average variable costs equal total variable costs divided by output.
iii. Average fixed costs equal total fixed costs divided by output.
d. Marginal cost equals the change in total costs divided by the change in output.
e. When marginal cost is above average cost, average cost rises; when marginal cost is below average cost, average cost falls; when marginal cost equals average cost, average cost remains constant.
f. The marginal cost curve intersects the average total cost curve and the average variable cost curve at their respective minimum points.

3. The production function is a relationship between inputs and outputs; it is a technological, not an economic, relationship.
   a. The law of diminishing (marginal) returns comes into play when the firm increases output in the short run.
   b. The marginal physical product is the change in total product that occurs when a variable input is increased and all other inputs are held constant.
   c. The law of diminishing (marginal) returns implies that the marginal physical product of labor eventually falls.

4. Diminishing marginal product causes the marginal cost curve, the average total cost curve, and the average variable cost curve to rise.

5. In the long run, all inputs are variable, and long-run cost curves must take this into account.
   a. The long-run average cost curve is the locus of points representing the minimum unit cost of producing any given rate of output, given current technology and resource prices.
   b. Another name for the long-run average cost curve is the planning horizon.

6. The long-run average cost curve is also U-shaped.
   a. Initially a firm experiences economies of scale due to specialization, a dimensional factor, or improved productive equipment.
   b. Eventually a firm might experience diseconomies of scale because a disproportionate increase in management and staff may be needed, and because the costs of information and communication also grow more than proportionally with output.

7. The minimum efficient scale is the lowest rate of output per unit time period at which average costs reach a minimum for a particular firm.

8. At the output rate when economies of scale end and constant economies of scales start, the minimum efficient scale for the firm occurs. It is the lowest rate of output at which long-run average costs are minimized.

KEY TERMS
Average physical product
Marginal physical product
Total costs
Fixed costs
Variable costs
Average fixed costs
Average variable costs
Average total costs
Marginal costs
Long-run average cost curve
Planning curve
Economies of scale
Constant returns to scale
Production

CHAPTER 22: THE FIRM: COST AND OUTPUT DETERMINATION   **113**

KEY CONCEPTS
Short run
Production function
Long run
Diseconomies of scale

Law of diminishing returns
Planning horizon
Minimum efficient scale

COMPLETION QUESTIONS
Fill in the blank, or circle the correct term.

1. Our definition of the short run is the time during which _____ is fixed, but _____ is variable;

2. In the long run (no, all) factors are variable.

3. Fixed costs (do, do not) vary with output; variable costs (do, do not) vary with output.

4. (Rent, wages) and (mortgage interest payments, raw materials costs) are examples of fixed costs; (rent, wages) and (mortgage interest payments, raw materials costs) are examples of variable costs.

5. Short-run average cost curves eventually are upward sloping due to _____.

6. If marginal cost exceeds average total cost, then average total cost will (fall, rise, remain constant).

7. At the minimum of the average total cost curve, marginal cost is (less than, greater than, equal to) average total cost.

8. If marginal cost is less than average total cost, then average total cost will (fall, rise, remain constant).

9. Because of diminishing (marginal) returns, in the (short, long) run the marginal product of labor will eventually (fall, rise, remain constant).

10. The long-run cost curve may also be U-shaped because initially as a firm expands its scale of operations, it realizes _____ of scale; then it may realize _____ returns to scale; eventually it realizes _____ of scale.

11. Reasons for economies of scale include _____, _____, and _____.

12. A firm might experience diseconomies of scale due to _____ and _____.

TRUE-FALSE QUESTIONS
Circle the **T** if the statement is true, the **F** if it is false. Explain to yourself why a statement is false.

T F   1. Short-run cost curves that include variable costs eventually reflect the influence of the law of diminishing marginal returns.

T F   2. Fixed costs vary with output.

T F   3. Eventually, as output expands, the short-run marginal cost curve must rise.

T F   4. When average total cost exceeds marginal cost, marginal cost must be rising.

T F   5. When average variable cost is less than marginal cost, marginal cost must be falling.

T F 6. At the minimum average total cost output level, marginal cost equals average total cost.

T F 7. In the short run, the supply of labor to the firm is usually fixed.

T F 8. Because of the law of diminishing marginal returns, the marginal product of labor will rise.

T F 9. Long-run cost curves are U-shaped due to the law of diminishing returns.

T F 10. The minimum efficient scale is the lowest scale of output at which long-run average total cost is as low as possible.

MULTIPLE CHOICE QUESTIONS
Circle the letter that corresponds to the best answer.

1. In the short run, for our purposes,
   a. all factors are variable.
   b. labor is variable.
   c. capital is variable
   d. both capital and labor are variable.

2. The long run
   a. permits the variation of all factors of production.
   b. is different for different firms.
   c. permits a firm to avoid the consequences of the law of diminishing returns.
   d. All of the above

3. Fixed costs
   a. vary with output.
   b. do not vary with output.
   c. reflect the effect of diminishing returns.
   d. include labor and raw material costs.

4. In the short run, which cost is **NOT** fixed?
   a. rent
   b. wages
   c. opportunity cost of capital
   d. interest payments on borrowed money

5. If marginal cost is above average total cost, then average total cost
   a. will rise.
   b. will fall.
   c. will remain constant.
   d. cannot be calculated.

6. At that output where average total cost is at a minimum,
   a. marginal cost equals average total cost.
   b. marginal cost equals average variable cost.
   c. average total cost is rising.
   d. total cost is constant.

7. Which short-run curve is **NOT** U-shaped?
   a. average total cost
   b. marginal cost
   c. average variable cost
   d. average fixed cost

8. The production function
   a. is a technological relationship.
   b. is not an economic relationship.
   c. relates output to inputs.
   d. All of the above

9. Because of the law of diminishing marginal returns,
   a. long-run average cost eventually rises.
   b. marginal cost falls.
   c. the marginal product of labor eventually falls.
   d. the average total cost curve falls.

10. Which is **NOT** due to the law of diminishing marginal returns?
    a. rising short-run marginal cost
    b. rising long-run average total cost
    c. rising short-run average variable cost
    d. rising short-run average total cost

11. *Analogy*: Diminishing returns is to rising short-run average total costs as _____ is to rising long-run average total costs.
    a. economies of scale
    b. diseconomies of scale
    c. law of diminishing returns
    d. constant returns to scale

12. Which of the following helps to account for a U-shaped short-run average total cost curve?
    a. economies of scale
    b. diseconomies of scale
    c. law of diminishing (marginal) returns
    d. constant returns to scale

13. A firm might experience diseconomies of scale due to
    a. disproportionate rises in specialization.
    b. dimensional factors.
    c. information and communication costs that rise disproportionately.
    d. the ability to use larger-volume machinery that is efficient only at large outputs.

14. If the minimum efficient scale is relatively low, then
    a. there will likely be a relatively large number of firms in the industry.
    b. there will likely be a relatively small number of firms in the industry.
    c. economies of scale are very great.
    d. long-run average costs decline over broad ranges of output.

116 CHAPTER 22: THE FIRM: COST AND OUTPUT DETERMINATION

MATCHING
Choose the item in column (2) that best matches an item in column (1).

(1)	(2)
a. long run	i. falling long-run average cost
b. short run	j. rising long-run average cost
c. fixed cost	k. fixed plant size
d. variable cost	l. diminishing marginal product
e. marginal cost	m. overhead
f. economies of scale	n. wages of laborers
g. diseconomies of scale	o. additional cost of producing next unit
h. law of diminishing returns	p. all factors variable

WORKING WITH GRAPHS

1. Assume that the High Rise Bakery produces a single product: loaves of bread. Further assume that the bread is produced using a fixed plant size, with ten ovens and varying quantities of labor. John Doe, the owner and manager of the High Rise Bakery, notices that as he hires additional workers, the total output of bread goes up for a while. Then he finds that after hiring several additional workers, the workers begin to get in one another's way and extra output begins to decline. John knows the principles of economics and something about diminishing marginal physical product. Given the information below, calculate the marginal physical product of John's bakers. Graph total and marginal products on the next page and tell John how many bakers he can employ before diminishing marginal returns set in. (Plot the marginal product at the midpoint between the number of bakers employed.)

Bakers	Output (loaves per day)	Marginal product
0	0	
1	8	_____
2	19	_____
3	32	_____
5	60	_____
6	71	_____
7	75	_____
8	77	_____
9	77	_____
10	75	_____
11	65	_____

2. Complete the following table of cost figures and then graph the information on the graphs provided below. Assume total fixed costs are $3.

Output	Total variable costs	Total costs	Average variable cost	Average total cost	Marginal cost
0	0.00	3.00	___	___	___
1	3.00	___	___	___	___
2	___	___	___	4.00	___
3	___	9.20	___	___	___
4	___	___	___	___	2.30
5	___	___	2.38	___	___
6	___	___	___	___	5.00
7	23.90	___	___	___	___
8	___	36.90	___	___	___

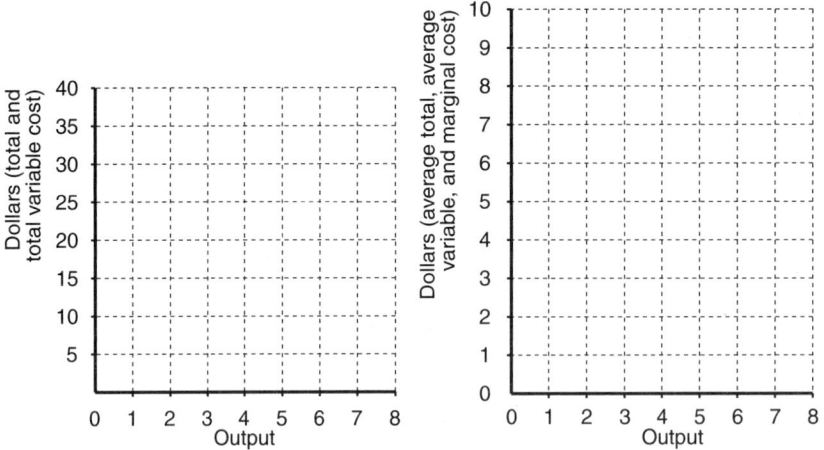

3. Use the graphs below to answer the questions that follow.

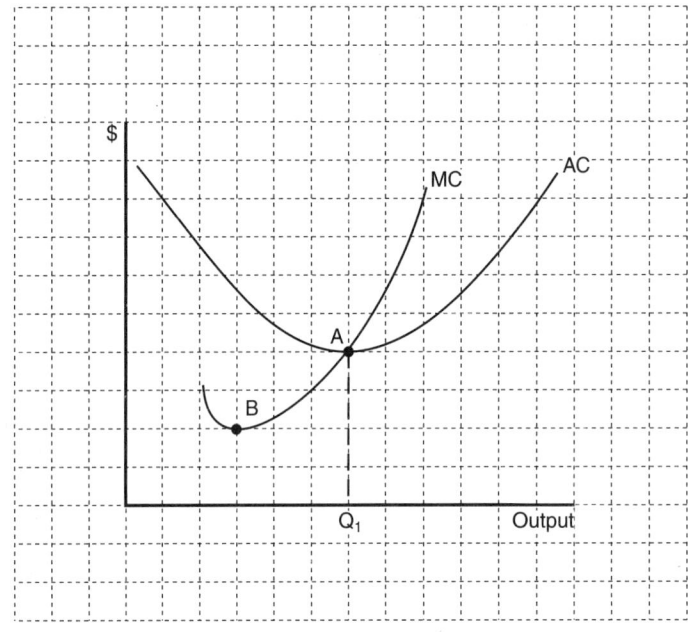

a. At what point do diminishing marginal returns begin?
b. At any output less than Q_1, why is AC falling?
c. At any output greater than Q_1, why is AC rising?
d. What is AC doing at the exact output Q_1?

4. Use the graphs below to answer the questions that follow. Assume that A and B are minimum points.

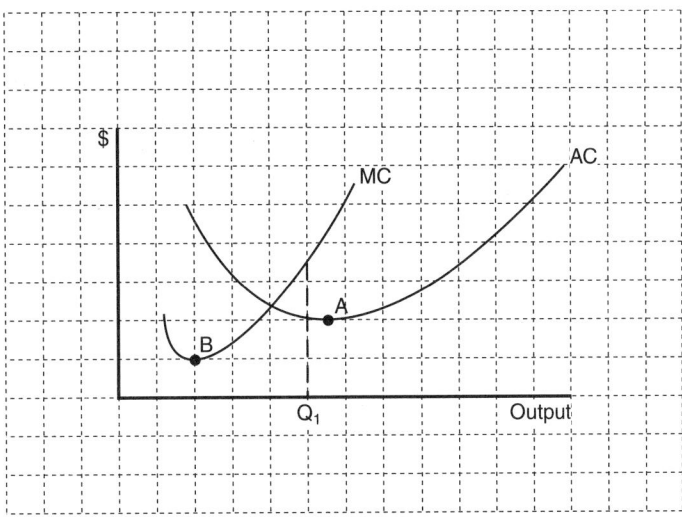

a. Something is wrong with the graphs above. What is it?
b. According to the graphs above, what is happening at output Q_1, with respect to MC and AC? Is this possible?

PROBLEM

1. Fill in the information in each blank below so that the equation is correct. (Note: Q is quantity of output.)

   a. TC = TFC + _____
   b. AFC = _____ - AVC
   c. ATC = (TVC/Q) + _____
   d. TFC = Q x _____
   e. AVC = (TC/Q) - _____/Q
   f. TVC = (Q x ATC) - Q x _____

ANSWERS TO CHAPTER 22

COMPLETION QUESTIONS

1. capital; labor
2. all
3. do not; do
4. rent; mortgage interest payments; wages; raw material costs
5. diminishing (marginal) returns
6. rise
7. equal to
8. fall
9. short; fall
10. economies; constant; diseconomies
11. specialization; dimensional factors; improved productive equipment
12. disproportionate requirements for managers and staff; disproportionate costs of information and communication

TRUE-FALSE QUESTIONS

1. T
2. F By definition they do not.
3. T
4. F Not necessarily.
5. F When AVC is less than MC, the MC curve has already crossed through the minimum point of AVC, so MC must be rising.
6. T
7. F Capital is fixed in the short run.
8. F It falls due to the law of diminishing returns.
9. F Diminishing marginal returns occur in the short run.
10. T

MULTIPLE CHOICE QUESTIONS

1.b; 2.d; 3.b; 4.b; 5.a; 6.a; 7.d; 8.d; 9.c; 10.b;
11.b; 12.c; 13.c; 14.a.

MATCHING

a and p; b and k; c and m; d and n; e and o; f and i; g and j; h and l

WORKING WITH GRAPHS

1. Marginal product: 8; 11; 13; 13; 15; 11; 4; 2; 0; -2; -10
   Diminishing returns set in when John hires the sixth baker.

CHAPTER 22: THE FIRM: COST AND OUTPUT DETERMINATION

2.

Output	Total variable costs	Total costs	Average variable cost	Average total cost	Marginal cost
0	0.00	3.00	--	--	--
1	3.00	6.00	3.00	6.00	3.00
2	5.00	8.00	2.50	4.00	2.00
3	6.20	9.20	2.07	3.07	1.20
4	8.50	11.50	2.13	2.88	2.30
5	11.90	14.90	2.38	2.98	3.40
6	16.90	19.90	2.82	3.32	5.00
7	23.90	26.90	3.41	3.84	7.00
8	33.90	36.90	4.24	4.61	10.00

122 CHAPTER 22: THE FIRM: COST AND OUTPUT DETERMINATION

3.   a. B
    b. MC is below AC, due to specialization
    c. MC is above AC
    d. AC is constant, because MC = AC.

4.   a. MC cuts the AC curve to the left of AC's minimum point.
    b. MC > AC, yet AC is falling. No.

PROBLEM

1.   a. TVC   b. ATC   c. AFC   d. AFC   e. TFC   f. AFC

GLOSSARY TO CHAPTER 22

Average fixed costs   Total fixed costs divided by the number of units produced.

Average physical product   Total product divided by the variable input.

Average total costs   Total costs divided by the number of units produced; sometimes called *average per unit total costs*.

Average variable costs   Total variable costs divided by the number of units produced.

Constant returns to scale   No change in long-run average costs when output increases.

Diseconomies of scale   Increases in long-run average costs that occur as output increases.

Economies of scale   Decreases in long-run average costs resulting from increases in output.

Fixed costs   Those costs that do not vary with output. Fixed costs include such things as rent on a building. These costs are fixed for a certain period of time; in the long run they are variable.

Law of diminishing (marginal) returns   The observation that fter some point, successive increases in a variable factor of production, such as labor, added to fixed factors of production, will result in smaller increases in output.

Long run   That time period during which all factors of production can be varied.

Long-run average cost curve (LAC)   The locus of points representing the minimum unit cost of producing any given rate of output, given current technology and resource prices.

Marginal costs The change in total costs due to a one-unit change in production rate.

Marginal physical product The physical output that is due to the addition of one more unit of a variable factor of production; the change in total product occurring when a variable input is increased and all other inputs are held constant; also called *marginal product* or *marginal return*.

Minimum efficient scale The lowest rate of output per unit time at which long-run average costs for a particular firm are at a minimum.

Planning curve The long-run average cost curve.

Planning horizon The long run, during which all inputs are variable.

Plant size The physical size of factories that a firm owns and operates to produce its output. Plant size can be defined by square footage, maximum physical capacity, and other physical measures.

Production Any activity that results in the conversion of resources into product that can be used in consumption.

Production function The relationship between inputs and maximum physical output. A production function is a technological, not an economic, relationship.

Short run The time period during which at least one input, such as plant size, cannot be changed.

Total costs The sum of total fixed costs and total variable costs.

Variable costs Those costs that vary with the rate of production. They include wages paid to workers and the purchases of materials.

CHAPTER 23
PERFECT COMPETITION

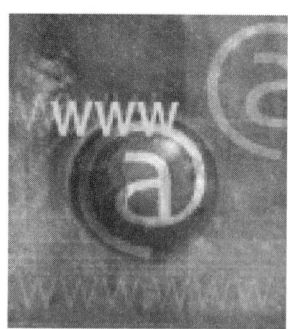

LEARNING OBJECTIVES
After you have studied this chapter, you should be able to

1. define price taker, total revenues, marginal revenue, short-run shutdown price, short-run break-even price, industry supply curve, long-run industry supply curve, constant-cost industry, increasing-cost industry, decreasing-cost industry, and marginal-cost pricing;

2. list four characteristics of the perfect competition market structure;

3. recognize the shape of a competitive firm's demand curve and recognize reasons for its shape;

4. determine a perfect competitor's optimal output rate, given sufficient information;

5. calculate the value of a perfect competitor's short-run profits, given sufficient information;

6. recognize and determine the perfectly competitive firm's short-run shutdown price and its short-run break-even price;

7. recognize a perfectly competitive firm's short-run supply curve and recognize how an *industry* short-run supply curve is derived;

8. distinguish among constant-cost, increasing-cost, and decreasing-cost industries;

9. recognize the long-run equilibrium position for a firm in a perfectly competitive industry;

10. indicate why a perfectly competitive market structure is socially efficient;

11. recognize how the asymmetry of information problem affects the perfect competition model.

CHAPTER OUTLINE

1. There are four major characteristics of the perfect competition market structure: a large number of buyers and sellers, homogeneous product, unimpeded industry exit and entry, and equally good information for both buyers and sellers.

2. Because in the perfect competition model many firms produce a homogeneous product, a single firm's demand curve is perfectly elastic at the "going" market price.

3. In order to predict how much the perfect competitor will produce, we assume that it wants to maximize total profits.
   a. Total revenues equal quantity sold times price per unit.
   b. In the short run, total costs are the sum of total fixed costs and total variable costs.
   c. Total revenues minus total costs equal total profits.
   d. Marginal revenue equals the change in total revenue divided by the change in output.
   e. Total profits are maximized at that rate of output where marginal revenue equals marginal cost.

4. Because a normal rate of return to investment is included in the average total cost curve, the "profits" we calculate are economic profits.

5. The firm's short-run shutdown price occurs at its minimum average variable cost value: At a higher price, the firm should produce and contribute to payment of fixed costs; it should not produce at a lower price.

6. The firm's short-run break-even price is found at the minimum point on its average total cost curve: At a higher price the firm will earn abnormal profits, at a lower price it suffers economic losses, and at the minimum point, economic profits equal zero.

7. The firm's short-run supply curve is its marginal cost curve above the short-run shutdown point.

8. The short-run industry supply curve is derived by summing horizontally all the firm supply curves; the industry supply curve shifts when nonprice determinants of supply change.

9. In a competitive market, the "going" price is set where the market demand curve intersects the industry supply curve.

10. In the long run, because abnormal industry profits induce entry and because negative industry profits induce exit, firms in a competitive industry will earn zero economic profits.
    a. Long-run supply curves relate price and quantity supplied after firms have time to enter or exit from an industry.
    b. A constant-cost industry is one whose long-run supply curve is horizontal because input prices are unaffected by output.
    c. An increasing-cost industry is one whose long-run supply curve is positively sloped because the price of specialized (or essential) inputs rises as industry output increases.
    d. A decreasing-cost industry is one whose long-run supply curve is negatively sloped because specialized input prices fall as industry output expands.

11. In a perfectly competitive industry, a firm operates where price equals marginal revenue equals marginal cost equals short-run minimum average cost equals long-run minimum average cost—in the long run.
    a. Perfectly competitive industries are efficient from society's point of view because for such industries price equals marginal cost in long-run equilibrium.
    b. They are also efficient because in long-run equilibrium the output rate is produced at minimum average cost.
    c. The perfectly competitive model is not a realistic description of any real-world industry; nevertheless it helps economists explain and predict economic events.

CHAPTER 23: PERFECT COMPETITION

KEY TERMS
Total revenues
Marginal revenue
Short-run shutdown price
Short-run break-even price
Market failure

Long-run industry supply curve
Perfectly competitive firm
Total costs
Industry supply curve

KEY CONCEPTS
Profit-maximizing rate of production
Perfect competition
Price taker
Signals

Marginal-cost pricing
Increasing-cost industry
Decreasing-cost industry
Constant-cost industry

COMPLETION QUESTIONS
Fill in the blank, or circle the correct term.

1. The four major characteristics of a perfect competition market structure are _____, _____, _____, and _____.

2. The demand curve facing a perfect competitor is _____ elastic.

3. We assume that the goal of the firm is to _____; if so, the perfect competitor should produce up to the point where MR equals _____. Total profits are defined as _____ minus _____.

4. Marginal revenue equals _____ divided by _____.

5. Because we include the opportunity cost of capital as a cost of production, the profits we define are (accounting, economic) profits.

6. If the firm's selling price cannot cover its short-run variable costs, then it should _____; if the selling price equals minimum average total cost, the firm is just _____, and its economic profits are (negative, positive, zero).

7. If the firm is earning zero economic profits, it (will, will not) continue to operate.

8. The competitive firm's short-run supply curve is the portion of its _____ curve lying above minimum AVC; the industry short-run supply curve is derived by _____ all the firm supply curves.

9. In the long run, a firm in a perfectly competitive industry will earn exactly zero economic profits. This is true because if economic profits are positive, some firms will _____ the industry and price will fall; if economic profits are negative, some firms will _____ the industry and price will rise.

10. If an industry expands and input prices do not change, such an industry is a(n) _____-cost industry and the long-run supply curve is horizontal. If input prices rise, the industry is a(n) _____-cost industry and the long-run industry supply curve is _____ sloping. If input prices fall, the industry is a(n) _____-cost industry and the industry's long-run supply curve is _____ sloping.

11. In the long run a perfectly competitive firm will earn (negative, positive, zero) economic profits. Its price will be (greater than, less than, equal to) marginal cost, and output (will, will not) be produced at minimum average total cost. From society's point of view, all of this is (efficient, inefficient).

TRUE-FALSE QUESTIONS
Circle the **T** if the statement is true, the **F** if it is false. Explain to yourself why a statement is false.

T F 1. A firm in a perfectly competitive industry is a price taker.

T F 2. Because firms in a perfectly competitive industry are all price takers, price cannot change in that industry.

T F 3. The demand curve facing a perfect competitor is perfectly elastic.

T F 4. The perfectly competitive firm attempts to maximize marginal profits.

T F 5. The total profit maximization output occurs at the point where the firm's marginal cost equals its marginal revenue.

T F 6. Average revenue minus average cost equals total profits.

T F 7. If price is below minimum average variable costs in the short run, the firm will shut down, assuming output is where MR = MC.

T F 8. If price is below minimum average total cost, economic profits will be negative, assuming that output is where MR = MC.

T F 9. The firm's short-run supply curve is its average variable cost curve.

T F 10. The industry supply curve is derived by summing horizontally all the firm supply curves.

T F 11. Because of the law of diminishing returns, the firm's short-run supply curve will be upward sloping.

T F 12. Because of free exit and entry, long-run accounting profits for a perfect competitor must be zero.

T F 13. A constant-cost industry has an upward-sloping long-run industry supply curve.

T F 14. If demand falls in a decreasing-cost industry, in the long run both output and price will fall.

T F 15. In the long-run equilibrium situation, the perfectly competitive firm will earn zero economic profits and produce at minimum average cost.

T F 16. Because of excessive competition, the perfectly competitive industry is believed to be inefficient from society's point of view.

MULTIPLE CHOICE QUESTIONS
Circle the letter that corresponds to the best answer.

1. Which of the following is **NOT** a characteristic of the perfect competition market structure?
   a. equally good information for both buyers and sellers
   b. homogeneous product
   c. large number of buyers and sellers
   d. restricted entry and exit

2. The demand curve facing the perfect competitor is
   a. perfectly elastic.
   b. vertical at the going price.
   c. perfectly inelastic.
   d. negatively sloped.

3. In the perfect competition model
   a. each seller is a price taker.
   b. all firms together can affect price.
   c. all firms produce a homogeneous product.
   d. All of the above

4. We assume the firm wants to maximize _____ profits.
   a. marginal
   b. average
   c. total
   d. fixed

5. The firm maximizes total profits at that output at which
   a. MC = MR.
   b. MC > MR.
   c. P = AC.
   d. AR = AC.

6. In which of these cases are economic profits negative?
   a. Total revenues exceed total costs.
   b. Average revenues exceed average costs.
   c. Price is below minimum average total cost.
   d. Average revenue is equal to price.

7. The perfect competitor
   a. can sell all it wants to sell at the going price.
   b. can sell nothing at a price higher than the going price.
   c. faces a perfectly elastic demand curve.
   d. All of the above

8. The competitive firm's short-run total profits equal
   a. average revenue minus average cost times quantity sold.
   b. average revenue minus average cost.
   c. price minus marginal cost.
   d. price minus average variable cost.

9. If selling price equals the firm's minimum average variable cost, then
   a. that is the firm's shutdown point.
   b. economic profits are negative.
   c. the firm is indifferent between producing and shutting down.
   d. All of the above

10. At the short-run break-even price,
    a. accounting profits equal economic profits.
    b. economic profits are negative.
    c. economic profits are zero.
    d. economic profits are positive.

11. The firm's short-run supply curve is its
    a. marginal cost curve above the shutdown point.
    b. average cost curve above its minimum point.
    c. average variable cost curve above the shutdown point.
    d. marginal revenue curve.

12. The industry supply curve is derived by summing horizontally all the firms'
    a. marginal cost curves above their shutdown points.
    b. average revenue curves.
    c. total revenue curves.
    d. marginal revenue curves.

13. Which of the following will **NOT** shift the industry supply curve?
    a. change in price
    b. change in the cost of raw materials
    c. change in number of firms in the industry
    d. change in wage rates

14. If economic profits are negative in an industry, then
    a. firms will enter that industry.
    b. some firms will exit from that industry.
    c. price is above minimum average total costs.
    d. accounting profits must also be negative.

15. In long-run equilibrium, a competitive firm
    a. earns zero economic profits.
    b. produces at minimum average cost.
    c. produces where price equals marginal cost.
    d. All of the above

16. If demand falls in an increasing-cost industry, then in the long run
    a. price will fall.
    b. price will return to its previous level.
    c. output will rise.
    d. output will return to its previous level.

17. In a decreasing-cost industry, the long-run industry supply curve is
    a. downward sloping.
    b. upward sloping.
    c. horizontal.
    d. perpendicular.

18. The marginal cost of producing good A
    a. includes fixed costs.
    b. represents the opportunity cost to society of producing one more unit of good A.
    c. is found by reading the average variable cost curve.
    d. includes only labor costs.

130 CHAPTER 23: PERFECT COMPETITION

MATCHING
Choose the item in column (2) that best matches an item in column (1).

(1)
a. long-run equilibrium
b. constant returns to scale
c. price taker
d. decreasing-cost industry
e. short-run shutdown price
f. short-run supply curve
g. profit maximizing output

(2)
h. horizontal long-run industry supply curve (given input prices)
i. perfectly competitive firm
j. zero economic profits
k. marginal cost curve above shutdown point
l. falling long-run industry supply curve
m. P = minimum AVC
n. MR = MC

WORKING WITH GRAPHS

1. Use the graph below to answer the following questions. Assume that the firm is a profit maximizer operating in a competitive market.

   a. How many units of output will the firm produce and sell?
   b. What is TR at this level of output?
   c. What is the ATC at this level of output?
   d. What is the TFC at this level of output?
   e. What is the AVC at this level of output?
   f. What is TC at this level of output?
   g. What is the total profit or loss at this level of output?

2. Use the graphs below to answer the questions that follow.

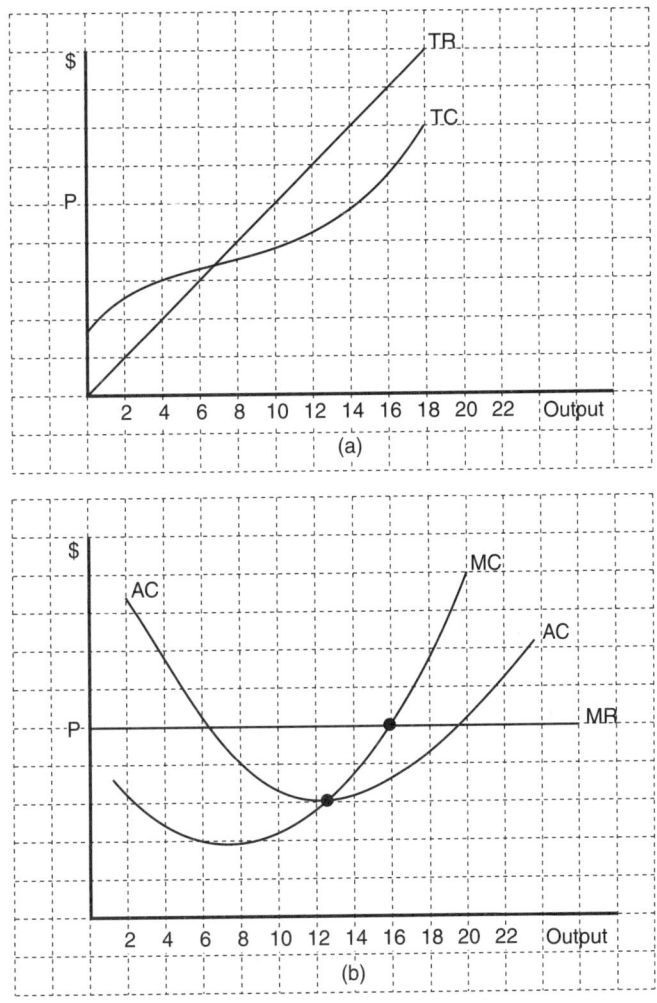

a. The total revenue curve is linear; therefore its slope is a _____; its slope equals what economic concept?

b. The slope of a tangent to a point on the TC curve is defined as what?

c. The firm tries to (minimize, maximize) _____ the positive difference between TR and TC. At what output level does that occur?

d. In panel (b), what is the firm's profit-maximizing output? Why?

e. How are your answers to parts c and d related?

PROBLEMS

1. Suppose you are hired as an economic consultant for Profmax Consulting Company. Your job is to advise the company's clients on the appropriate action to take in the short run in order to maximize the profits (or minimize the losses) of each firm. The firms you are to analyze produce indistinguishable products, and each operates independently in a different perfectly competitive market. You may assume that each is currently operating at an output level where marginal cost is increasing. Fill in the missing information, and make your suggestions about the appropriate action for each firm by placing one of the following symbols in the last row of the table of information that follows.

CHAPTER 23: PERFECT COMPETITION

C = currently operating at the correct level of output
I = increase the level of output
D = decrease the level of output
SD = shut down the plant

Firm	A	B	C	D	E	F	G
Price	$0.50	___	$3.50	___	$3.00	$5.00	___
Output	___	300	750	700	___	___	1000
TR	$500	$300	___	$2800	$1800	$4000	$5000
TC	___	$525	$2625	$2975	___	___	___
TFC	___	___	___	___	$180	$1200	___
TVC	$300	___	___	$2450	___	___	$3000
ATC	$0.40	___	Minimum	___	___	$5.50	$5.50
AVC	___	$1.20	$3.00	___	$2.00	Minimum	___
MC	$0.40	$1.00	___	$4.00	$3.50	___	$5.75
Suggestion		___	___	___	___	___	___

ANSWERS TO CHAPTER 23

COMPLETION QUESTIONS

1. large number of buyers and sellers; homogeneous product; equally good information for both buyers and sellers; unimpeded entry or exit
2. perfectly
3. maximize total profits; MC; total revenues; total costs
4. change in total revenue; change in output
5. economic
6. shut down; breaking even; zero
7. will
8. MC; summing horizontally
9. enter; exit
10. constant; increasing; upward; decreasing; downward
11. zero; equal to; will; efficient

TRUE-FALSE

1. T
2. F Price is a constant to an *individual* firm, but not to the group of firms.
3. T
4. F Firms attempt to maximize *total* profits.
5. T
6. F It equals average profits.
7. T
8. T
9. F The firm's marginal cost curve above minimum AVC is its short-run supply curve.
10. T
11. T
12. F Long-run *economic* profits must be zero.
13. F It is horizontal.
14. F Price will rise.
15. T
16. F It is efficient because P = MC and economic profits = 0 in the long run.

MULTIPLE CHOICE QUESTIONS

1.d; 2.a; 3.d; 4.c; 5.a; 6.c; 7.d; 8.a; 9.d; 10.c;
11.a; 12.a; 13.a; 14.b; 15.d; 16.a; 17.a; 18.b.

MATCHING

a and j; b and h; c and i; d and l; e and m; f and k; g and n

WORKING WITH GRAPHS

1. a. 100
   b. $260
   c. $2
   d. $65
   e. $1.35
   f. $200
   g. $60 profit

2. a. constant; MR (or P)
   b. MC
   c. maximize; 16 units of output
   d. 16 units of output; because MC = MR at that output level

e. MC = MR at 16 units of output

PROBLEMS

Firm	A	B	C	D	E	F	G
Price	$0.50	$1.00	$3.50	$4.00	$3.00	$5.00	$5.00
Output	1000	300	750	700	600	800	1000
TR	$500	$300	$2625	$2800	$1800	$4000	$5000
TC	$400	$525	$2625	$2975	$1380	$4400	$5500
TFC	$100	$165	$375	$525	$180	$1200	$2500
TVC	$300	$360	$2250	$2450	$1200	$3200	$3000
ATC	$0.40	$1.75	Minimum	$4.25	$2.30	$5.50	$5.50
AVC	$0.30	$1.20	$3.00	$3.50	$2.00	Minimum	$3.00
MC	$0.40	$1.00	$3.50	$4.00	$3.50	$4.00	$5.75
Suggestion	I	SD	C	C	D	I	D

GLOSSARY TO CHAPTER 23

Constant-cost industry An industry whose total output can be increased without an increase in long-run per-unit costs; its long-run supply curve is horizontal.

Decreasing-cost industry An industry in which an increase in output leads to a reduction in long-run per-unit costs, such that the long-run industry supply curve slopes downward.

Increasing-cost industry An industry in which an increase in industry output is accompanied by an increase in long-run per-unit costs, such that the long-run industry supply curve slopes upward.

Industry supply curve The locus of points showing the minimum prices at which given quantities will be forthcoming; also called the *market supply curve.*

Long-run industry supply curve A market supply curve showing the relationship between prices and quantities forthcoming after firms have been allowed the time to enter into or exit from an industry, depending on whether there have been positive or negative economic profits.

Marginal-cost pricing A system of pricing in which the price charged is equal to the opportunity cost to society of producing one more unit of the good or service in question. The opportunity cost is the marginal cost to society.

Marginal revenue The change in total revenues resulting from a change in output (and sale) of one unit of the product in question.

Market failure A situation in which an unrestrained market operation leads to either too few or too many resources going to a specific economic activity.

Perfect competition A market structure in which the decisions of *individual* buyers and sellers have no effect on market price.

Perfectly competitive firm A firm that is such a small part of the total industry that it cannot affect the price of the product it sells.

Price taker A competitive firm that must take the price of its product as given because the firm cannot influence its price.

Profit-maximizing rate of production The rate of production that maximizes total profits, or the difference between total revenues and total costs; also, the rate of production at which marginal revenue equals marginal cost.

Short-run break-even price The price at which a firm's total revenues equal its total costs. At the break-even price, the firm is just making a normal rate of return on its capital investment. (It is covering its explicit and implicit costs.)

Short-run shutdown price The price that covers average variable costs. It occurs just below the intersection of the marginal cost curve and the average variable cost curve.

Signals Compact ways of indicating to economic decision makers information needed to make decisions. A true signal not only conveys information but also provides the incentive to react appropriately. Economic profits and economic losses are such signals.

Total revenues The price per unit times the total quantity sold.

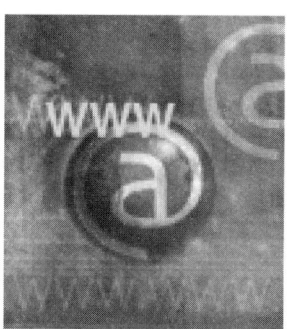

CHAPTER 24
MONOPOLY

LEARNING OBJECTIVES

After you have studied this chapter, you should be able to

1. define monopolist, natural monopoly, price discrimination, price differentiation, price searcher, tariffs, and cartel;

2. list the characteristics of a monopoly and distinguish them from the characteristics of the perfectly competitive firm;

3. distinguish between the monopolist's demand curve and the perfect competitor's demand curve;

4. determine the profit-maximizing output for the monopolist, given sufficient information, and determine the price that a monopolist would charge, given the profit-maximizing output;

5. list possible barriers to entry into an industry;

6. calculate a monopolist's total profits, given sufficient information;

7. recognize some misconceptions concerning monopoly;

8. distinguish between price discrimination and price differentiation, and list the conditions necessary for price discrimination;

9. list and recognize two costs to society of monopolies.

CHAPTER OUTLINE

1. A monopolist is a single supplier that constitutes an entire industry; the monopolist produces a good for which there are no close substitutes.

2. Barriers to entry are impediments that prevent new firms from entering an industry; there are numerous potential barriers to entry.
   a. Some monopolists gain power through the exclusive ownership of a raw material that is essential to produce a good.

CHAPTER 24: MONOPOLY

b. If an enormous capital investment is required to enter an industry, such a sum could be a barrier to entry.
c. Licenses, franchises, and certificates of convenience also constitute potential barriers to entry.
d. Patents issued to inventors constitute, for a time, effective barriers to entry.
e. If economies of scale are great relative to market demand, new entrants into an industry will be discouraged; persistent economies of scale could lead to a natural monopoly.
f. Governmental safety and quality regulations may raise fixed costs to firms in an industry significantly enough so as to deter new entrants.
g. If tariffs on imports are sufficiently high, then producers can gain some measure of monopoly power.

3. The monopolist faces the industry demand curve because the monopolist is the entire industry; examples of monopolies include local electric power companies and the post office.

4. It is instructive to compare the monopolist with the perfect competitor.
    a. The perfect competitor's demand curve is perfectly elastic at the "going" price; price is the same as average revenue, and average revenue equals marginal revenue in this model.
    b. The monopolist's demand curve is negatively sloped; price (or average revenue) falls, and therefore marginal revenue is less than price because the monopolist must lower its price on all the units it sells, and not just on the marginal unit.

5. Where marginal revenue equals zero, total revenue is maximized; at the point on the demand curve corresponding to zero marginal revenue, the price elasticity of demand equals 1; at higher prices (lower outputs) demand is elastic, and at lower prices (higher outputs) demand is inelastic.

6. By assuming that the monopolist wants to maximize total profits and that the short-run cost curves are similar in shape to those of the perfect competitor, we can determine the monopolist's optimal output-price combination.
    a. The monopolist's total revenue curve is nonlinear (unlike the perfect competitor's); optimal output exists where the positive difference between total costs and total revenues is maximized.
    b. Stated differently, optimal output exists where MR = MC.
    c. If MR > MC, the firm can increase total profits by increasing output; if MC > MR, then the firm can increase total profits by reducing output.
    d. Once the profit-maximizing output is determined, the monopolist's price is already determined; it is read on the demand curve at that quantity.

7. Graphically, total profits are calculated by subtracting average costs from average revenues and multiplying that value by the quantity produced.

8. If its average cost curve lies entirely above its demand curve, the monopolist will experience economic losses.

9. If the monopolist can prevent the resale of its homogeneous output and if it can separate its customers into different markets with different price elasticities, then it can price discriminate—and earn higher profits.

10. Monopolies are inefficient because they charge a price that is too high (P > MC) and because they produce an output that is too low.

KEY TERMS
Monopolist
Price discrimination
Price differentiation

Tariffs
Cartel

KEY CONCEPTS
Price searcher

Natural monopoly

COMPLETION QUESTIONS
Fill in the blank, or circle the correct term.

1. A monopolist is a(n) _____ supplier that constitutes the entire industry; its demand curve is _____ sloped.

2. Before a monopolist can earn long-run monopoly profits, there must be _____ to entry.

3. Examples of barriers to entry include _____, _____, _____, _____, _____, and _____.

4. Because the perfect competitor's demand curve is perfectly elastic, its selling price is constant; therefore its average revenue (falls, rises, remains constant) and its marginal revenue (falls, rises, remains constant).

5. Because the monopolist's demand curve is negatively sloped, its selling price falls with output; therefore its average revenue (falls, rises, remains constant) and its marginal revenue (falls, rises, remains constant).

6. If a monopolist must charge the same price to everyone, when it produces more, its marginal revenue will be (less than, greater than, equal to) its price.

7. When marginal revenue equals zero, total revenue is (minimized, maximized); at that point on the demand curve, the price elasticity of demand equals the number _____; at a higher price total revenues would fall, and therefore demand would be (elastic, inelastic); at a lower price total revenues would fall, and therefore demand would be _____.

8. One misconception about monopoly is that the monopolist can sell any quantity that it chooses to at any _____; instead the monopolist can sell any specific quantity at only one price. Another misconception is that a monopolist must earn economic profits; it won't, if the _____ curve is above the monopolist's demand curve.

9. The monopolist maximizes total profits at that output for which _____ equals _____; given its profit-maximizing output, the monopolist (need not, must) charge a price consistent with that quantity.

10. If a monopolist need not charge the same price to everyone, then it can _____, and its profits will rise; a monopolist can charge different prices to different groups if it can prevent the _____ of its product.

11. A monopolist charges a price that is too _____, and it produces an output that is too _____; therefore monopoly is (less, more) socially efficient than perfect competition.

CHAPTER 24: MONOPOLY

TRUE-FALSE QUESTIONS
Circle the T if the statement is true, the F if it is false. Explain to yourself why a statement is false.

T F 1. The more broadly we define an industry, the less likely it is to be a monopoly.

T F 2. Because of barriers to entry, a monopolist must earn long-run profits.

T F 3. The monopolist's marginal revenue curve lies below its demand, or average revenue, curve.

T F 4. A monopolist must charge the same price to all buyers.

T F 5. The monopolist's total revenue curve is linear.

T F 6. At that output for which total revenue is maximized, price elasticity of demand equals 1.

T F 7. The profit-maximizing monopolist will never produce on the inelastic portion of its demand curve.

T F 8. Total profits are maximized where total revenue equals total costs.

T F 9. If MR > MC, the firm can increase profits if it produces less.

T F 10. A monopolist can select only one profit-maximizing price, given the output it chooses to produce, assuming no price discrimination.

T F 11. If possible, a monopolist will charge a higher price to a price inelastic group than to a price elastic group.

T F 12. A monopolist tends to produce too little and to sell at a price that is too high.

T F 13. A monopolist is a price taker.

T F 14. Because there are no close substitutes for a monopolist's output, its demand curve is inelastic throughout.

MULTIPLE CHOICE QUESTIONS
Circle the letter that corresponds to the best answer.

1. Which of the following is **NOT** a characteristic of the monopoly market structure?
    a. one seller
    b. homogeneous product
    c. restricted entry
    d. price taker

2. Which of the following is a potential barrier to entry?
    a. government license requirement
    b. sole ownership of a key resource
    c. great economies of scale, relative to demand
    d. All of the above

3. Which is **NOT** true about monopolies?
    a. linear total revenue curve
    b. may earn long-run economic profits
    c. negatively sloped demand curve
    d. marginal revenue below price

4. The firm maximizes total profits at that output where
   a. total revenue equals total cost.
   b. marginal revenue equals marginal cost.
   c. the elasticity of demand equals 1.
   d. All of the above

5. Once a monopolist produces a profit-maximizing output,
   a. the price is determined for it, given its demand curve.
   b. it can select any price it wants.
   c. its competitors select price.
   d. price cannot be determined.

6. If MR < MC, then the firm
   a. is maximizing total profits.
   b. can increase total profits by producing more.
   c. can increase total profits by producing less.
   d. is maximizing total revenues.

7. Monopoly profit
   a. equals (average revenue - average cost) times quantity sold.
   b. equals price times quantity sold.
   c. exists only in the short run.
   d. exists because no entry barriers exist.

8. A monopolist will price discriminate if
   a. price differentiation exists.
   b. it can separate markets by different price elasticities of demand and prevent resales.
   c. it chooses to maximize average revenues.
   d. all buyers have the same price elasticity of demand.

9. Which of the following is price differentiation?
   a. Students pay a higher rental price for apartments than do nonstudents because they cause more damage.
   b. Women pay higher prices for haircuts because it takes longer to cut their hair.
   c. People in ghetto areas pay higher prices for individual items because costs are greater in such areas.
   d. All of the above

10. Assume that at a given output a monopolist's marginal revenue is $10 per unit and its marginal cost is $5. If the monopolist increases output, then
    a. price, marginal cost, and total profit will fall.
    b. price will fall, marginal cost will rise, and total profit will rise.
    c. price will rise, marginal cost will fall, and total profit will rise.
    d. price, marginal cost, and total profit will rise.

MATCHING
Choose the item in column (2) that best matches an item in column (1).

(1)	(2)
a. perfect competitor	g. nonlinear total revenue curve
b. monopolist	h. firm with a downward-sloping demand curve
c. price differentiation	i. great economies of scale
d. price discrimination	j. price taker
e. barrier to entry	k. students pay higher rents for apartments than do nonstudents
f. price searcher	l. students pay different tuition costs depending on need

CHAPTER 24: MONOPOLY

WORKING WITH GRAPHS

1. Suppose you are given the demand schedule for a monopolist and the total cost figures below. Plot the monopolist's demand curve, marginal revenue curve, and marginal cost curve on the graph provided. Determine the optimal level of output for the monopolist. What do total profits equal? (Plot MC and MR on the mid-points.)

Output per unit of time	Price	Total Cost
0	$32	$12
1	28	20
2	24	25
3	20	31
4	16	41
5	12	56
6	8	79
7	4	117

2. Suppose you are given the graphical summary of a monopolist below. Answer the following questions using this information.

a. The optimal short-term output level for the monopolist is _____.

b. At the optimal level of output, marginal cost is _____.

c. At the optimal level of output, total cost is _____.

d. At the optimal level of output, price is _____ and total revenue is _____.

e. The monopolist is earning a (profit, loss) of _____ in the given situation.

f. Suppose that the above graph represented a competitive industry and the demand curve given was the market demand curve for the entire industry. The competitive level of output would be _____, sold at a price of _____.

g. The average total cost per unit of output in the competitive case would fall by _____, as compared with the average total cost under a monopoly.

PROBLEMS

1. Indicate whether the following may characterize the perfect competitor (PC), the monopolist (M), or both (B).

_____ a. perfectly elastic demand curve

_____ b. increasing marginal cost curve

_____ c. downward-sloping demand curve

_____ d. linear total revenue curve

_____ e. total profit maximizer

_____ f. possibility of earning long-run economic profits

_____ g. P>MR

_____ h. homogeneous output

_____ i. price discriminator

_____ j. barriers to entry

_____ k. free exit and entry

_____ l. price searcher

_____ m. price taker

_____ n. produces where MR = MC

_____ o. P = MC in equilibrium

_____ p. long-run equilibrium at minimum AC

_____ q. P = MR

_____ r. P = AR

ANSWERS TO CHAPTER 24

COMPLETION QUESTIONS

1. single; negatively
2. barriers
3. ownership of resources without close substitutes; large capital requirements to enter industry; legally required licenses, franchises, or certificates of convenience; patents; economies of scale; safety and quality regulations; high tariffs
4. remains constant; remains constant
5. falls; falls
6. less than
7. maximized; 1; elastic; inelastic
8. price; average total cost
9. MR; MC; must
10. price discriminate; resale
11. high; low; less

TRUE-FALSE QUESTIONS

1. T
2. F   An inefficient monopolist need not earn economic profits.
3. T
4. F   A monopolist can price discriminate under certain conditions.
5. F   It is not linear because price falls as the monopolist produces more.
6. T
7. T
8. F   Profit maximization occurs where MR = MC; if TR = TC, then economic profits are zero.
9. F   If MR > MC, profits will rise if the firm produces more.
10. T
11. T
12. T
13. F   A monopolist is a price searcher.
14. F   A monopolist's demand curve has various ranges of elasticity.

MULTIPLE CHOICE QUESTIONS

1.d;   2.d;   3.a;   4.b;   5.a;   6.c;   7.a;   8.b;   9.d;   10.b.

MATCHING

a and j;   b and g;   c and k;   d and l;   e and i;   f and h

WORKING WITH GRAPHS

1.

The profit-maximizing level of output is 3 units sold at a price of $20 each. This can be seen graphically. Total profits equal $29 at that output.

2.   a. 300;   b. $2;   c. $1890;   d. $5, $1500;   e. loss, $390;   f. 400, $4;   g. $0.30

PROBLEMS

1. a. PC   b. B   c. M   d. PC   e. B   f. M   g. M   h. B   i. M
    j. M   k. PC   l. M   m. PC   n. B   o. PC   p. PC   q. PC   r. B

GLOSSARY TO CHAPTER 24

Cartel An association of producers in an industry that agree to set common prices and output quotas to prevent competition.

Monopolist The single supplier of a good or service for which there is no close substitute. The monopolist therefore constitutes its entire industry.

Natural monopoly A monopoly that arises from the peculiar production characteristics in an industry. It usually arises when there are large economies of scale relative to the industry's demand such that one firm can produce at a lower average cost than can be achieved by multiple firms.

Price differentiation Establishing different prices for similar products to reflect only differences in marginal cost in providing those commodities to different groups of buyers.

Price discrimination Selling a given product at more than one price, with the price difference being unrelated to cost difference.

Price searcher A firm that must determine the price-output combination that maximizes profit because it faces a downward-sloping demand curve.

Tariffs Taxes on imported goods.

CHAPTER 25
MONOPOLISTIC COMPETITION

LEARNING OBJECTIVES

After you have studied this chapter you should be able to

1. list the characteristics of the monopolistic competition market structure;

2. distinguish between the monopolistic competitor's demand curve and the perfect competitor's demand curve;

3. explain the profit-maximizing behavior of a monopolistically competitive firm;

4. discuss why brand names and trademarks are important to monopolistically competitive firms and describe different methods of and forms of advertising;

5. identify the key characteristics of information products;

6. describe the shapes of the short-run cost curves of a firm that sells information products and explain the concept of short-run economies of operation for producers of information products;

7. explain why firms that sell information products charge prices above marginal cost.

CHAPTER OUTLINE

1. There are four characteristics of the theory of *monopolistic competition*, which was developed simultaneously by Edward Chamberlin and Joan Robinson in 1933.
    a. A significant number of sellers in a highly competitive market
    b. Differentiated products
    c. Sales promotion and advertising
    d. Easy entry of new firms in the long run

2. Although there are many sellers in a monopolistically competitive industry, there are not as many as there are in the perfect competition model; each monopolistic competitor has a little control over its price, but collusion is difficult and each firm acts independently of the others.

146

3. Perhaps the most important feature of a monopolistically competitive industry is *product differentiation*.
   a. Differentiation refers to differences in physical characteristics.
   b. Each separate differentiated product has close substitutes.

4. It is possible to predict the optimal price-output combination of the monopolistic competitor.
   a. The monopolistic competitor's demand curve is downward sloping; thus its marginal revenue curve lies below its demand curve.
   b. Short-run equilibrium exists where MR = MC; economic profits or losses are possible in the short run.
   c. In the long run, because of free entry, the monopolistic competitor must earn exactly zero economic profits. Nevertheless, social inefficiency exists in the long run because the price of its product exceeds marginal cost, and its rate of output lies to the left of the minimum point on the ATC curve.

5. Because product differentiation is such an important aspect of monopolistically competitive industries, firms in these industries promote brand names via advertising.
   a. Firms can register trademarks—words, symbols, and logos—with the U.S. Patent and Trademark Office, and they can seek legal damages if anyone makes false use of trademarks and thereby damages the image of the firm's brand names.
   b. To promote their product brands, firms use three basic advertising methods: direct marketing, mass marketing, and interactive marketing.
   c. Search goods, which are items with qualities that can be assessed in advance of their purchase, are best marketed via informational advertising that acquaints consumers with their features; experience goods, which are items with qualities that can only be assessed following their purchase, are best marketed via persuasive advertising that induces consumers to discover previously unknown tastes for those items.

6. Information products are goods produced using information-intensive inputs at a relatively high fixed cost but distributed for sale at a relatively low marginal cost.
   a. Because fixed costs are relatively high, the average fixed cost of producing the first copy of an information product is significant; average fixed cost declines as the firm increases its sale of additional units.
   b. The per-unit cost of distributing additional copies of an information product is the same, relatively low amount no matter how many units are sold; thus, marginal cost and average variable cost are equal to the same constant per-unit cost.
   c. The average total cost curve for a firm that makes and sells an information product is the sum of the downward-sloping average fixed cost curve and the constant per-unit average variable cost, so the average total cost curve for the firm that produces an information product slopes downward; thus the firm experiences short-run economies of operation.
   d. If the price of an information product were equal to marginal cost, and hence average variable cost, the firm would only earn sufficient revenues to cover its variable costs but not its fixed costs.
   e. In a long-run monopolistically competitive equilibrium a firm that produces an information product just earns sufficient revenues to cover its total costs, thereby earning zero economic profits, when its price equals average total costs.

KEY TERMS
Monopolistic competition
Experience good
Information product

Short-run economies of operation
Search good

CHAPTER 25: MONOPOLISTIC COMPETITION

KEY CONCEPTS
Product differentiation   Informational advertising   Mass marketing
Direct marketing   Interactive marketing   Persuasive advertising

COMPLETION QUESTIONS
Fill in the blank or circle the correct term.

1. The four characteristics of monopolistic competition are _____, _____, _____, and _____.

2. Under monopolistic competition, collusion is (easy, difficult); each firm (must, need not) take into account the reactions of rivals, and each firm has (a little, much, no) control over its selling price.

3. The demand curve for the monopolistic competitor is _____ sloped; therefore its marginal revenue curve is (below, above) its demand, or AR curve.

4. In the short run, a profit-maximizing monopolistically competitive firm produces to the point at which (price, marginal revenue) equals (marginal cost, average total cost).

5. In a long-run monopolistically competitive equilibrium, the price of a firm's product must be (less than, greater than, equal to) marginal cost; therefore social (inefficiency, efficiency) exists in the monopolistic competition market structure.

6. In a long-run monopolistically competitive equilibrium, the price of a firm's product is (less than, equal to, greater than) the average total cost of producing its actual output level, but the price is (less then, equal to, greater than) the minimum feasible average total cost of producing the product.

7. Brand names and trademarks have value for firms in monopolistically competitive industries because these are important factors affecting the (demand for, supply of) products that are (homogeneous, differentiated) among the firms in this industry.

8. The main methods of advertising are _____ marketing, _____ marketing, and _____ marketing.

9. An item possessing qualities that are relatively easy for consumers to evaluate in advance of purchasing the item is _____ good; an item with qualities that are relatively difficult for consumers to evaluate in advance of purchasing the item is _____ good.

10. Advertising that focuses on explaining the features of a product is _____ advertising that is more likely to be used by a firm seeking to market (a search, an experience) good.

11. Advertising that is intended to induce a consumer to discover previously unknown tastes for an item is _____ advertising that is more likely to be used by a firm seeking to market (a search, an experience) good.

12. For the producer of an information product, in the short run a relatively low average _____ cost of producing the item is equal to marginal cost at any given amount of output, and the average _____ cost curve slopes downward over its entire range.

13. If the producer of an information product were required to set the price of the item equal to marginal cost, then price would equal average (fixed; variable) cost at any given amount of output, so that total revenues would exactly equal (total fixed; total variable) costs; this means that the firm would not earn sufficient total revenues to cover any of its (total fixed; total variable) costs, so it would earn (zero; negative) economic profits.

14. If the producer of an information product sets the price of the item equal to average total cost, then total revenues would exactly equal _____ costs, and the firm would earn _____ economic profits.

TRUE-FALSE QUESTIONS
Circle the **T** if the statement is true, the **F** if it is false. Explain to yourself why a statement is false.

T F 1. The monopolistic competitor has a negatively sloped demand curve.

T F 2. The monopolistic competitor must take into account the reactions of its competitors.

T F 3. The most important feature of the monopolistically competitive market is product differentiation.

T F 4. Product differentiation exists in the wheat industry.

T F 5. One important goal of advertising is to convey quality information.

T F 6. The monopolistic competition model leads to social efficiency because in the long run P = MC.

T F 7. A firm that produces a search good is likely to market the item using exclusively persuasive advertising.

T F 8. Based on the advertising expenses of U.S. firms, the most used advertising method is direct marketing.

T F 9. Informational advertising focuses on enlightening consumers about the features of a product.

T F 10. A problem with heavy spending on advertising is that it can signal that a firm is mismanaged and consequently may be exiting the market in the near future.

T F 11. The production of information products entails incurring relatively low fixed costs and relatively high marginal costs.

T F 12. The reason why a firm that sells an information product experiences short-run economies of operation is that the average total cost curves slopes downward over its entire range.

T F 13. If the price of an information product is equal to marginal cost, then the firm producing this item fails to earn sufficient revenues to cover fixed costs.

T F 14. The price of an information product exceeds average total cost in a long-run monopolistically competitive equilibrium.

CHAPTER 25: MONOPOLISTIC COMPETITION

MULTIPLE CHOICE QUESTIONS
Circle the letter that corresponds to the best answer.

1. Which is *not* a characteristic of monopolistic competition?
    a. Each firm must take into account its rivals' reactions to price changes.
    b. There are a significant number of sellers.
    c. There are differentiated products.
    d. Advertising is prevalent.

2. Which of the following *is* an important characteristic of monopolistic competition?
    a. It is difficult to enter the industry.
    b. It is easy for firms to establish collusive agreements.
    c. Each firm has very small shares of total market production and sales.
    d. Firms are all interdependent, so decisions made by each firm affect choices of others.

3. Because each separate differentiated product sold by a monopolistically competitive firm has numerous similar substitutes, we can say for certain that the demand for each individual firm's product is relatively
    a. low, so that no one firm can sell more than a few units of its output.
    b. high, so that in principle any given firm can sell the most output in the market.
    c. elastic, as compared with the demand for the product of a monopoly producer.
    d. inelastic, as compared with the demand for the product of a monopoly producer.

4. As is also true in a perfectly competitive industry, in a monopolistically competitive industry,
    a. in the long run firms can easily enter the market in response to positive economic profits.
    b. in the short run the demand curve for each firm's product slopes downward.
    c. in the long run the price of each firm's output equals marginal cost.
    d. in the short run firms always earn positive economic profits.

5. As is also true of a monopoly, in a monopolistically competitive industry,
    a. in the long run more firms cannot enter the market in response to positive economic profits.
    b. in the short run each firm's marginal revenue declines as it increases its production and sales.
    c. in the short run the price of each firm's product is always less than marginal cost.
    d. in the long run the price of each firm's product equals average total cost.

6. For the monopolistic competitor, in the long run
    a. economic profits can be positive.
    b. output is too high, from society's point of view.
    c. the demand curve must be tangent to the ATC curve.
    d. output is produced to the right of the minimum ATC point.

7. The U.S. Patent and Trademark Office
    a. registers trademarks, which gives an owner the right to seek legal relief in the event proof it can prove misuse of the brand name by another party.
    b. acts as both judge and jury for determining whether a company has misused another firm's brand name and assessing fines on offending firms.
    c. creates all company trademarks, thereby determining the names of the brands that companies market to consumers via advertising.
    d. has its own police force, which seeks evidence of unauthorized uses of firms' brand names or false information about brands.

8. Advertising
   a. attempts to increase the demand for a firm's product.
   b. can provide more information to buyers.
   c. helps to differentiate a firm's product.
   d. All of the above

9. Persuasive advertising is
   a. most appropriate for search goods.
   b. aimed toward reducing the degree of product differentiation.
   c. designed to provide information about the main features of a good or service.
   d. intended to acquaint consumers with a taste or preference previously unknown to them.

10. Experience goods
    a. have qualities consumers can assess before purchase.
    b. must be consumed for buyers to evaluate their qualities.
    c. are most successfully marketed by way of informational advertising.
    d. are homogeneous items sold only in perfectly competitive industries.

11. In the United States, firms spend the majority of their advertising dollars on
    a. interactive marketing.
    b. direct marketing.
    c. mass marketing.
    d. none of the above.

12. For a firm that sells an information product, which one of the following pairs of cost curves *both* slope downward in the short run?
    a. AFC and ATC
    b. AVC and ATC
    c. MC and AVC
    d. MC and ATC

13. For a firm that sells an information product, which of the following costs are identical, constant, and relatively small over all ranges of output in the short run?
    a. AFC and ATC
    b. AVC and ATC
    c. MC and AVC
    d. MC and ATC

14. The term short-run economies of operations refers to decreasing
    a. marginal cost as more units of an information product are sold.
    b. average total cost as more units of an information product are sold.
    c. average fixed cost as more units of an information product are sold.
    d. marginal cost above the minimum point of the AVC curve for an information product.

15. If the producer of an information product faces a strictly enforced legal requirement that any units of output it produces and sells must be offered at a price equal to marginal cost, then
    a. the firm's desired output will be at the minimum point of the average total cost curve.
    b. the firm will earn positive economic profits.
    c. the firm's desired output will be zero units.
    d. the firm will earn zero economic profits.

16. In a long-run equilibrium for a profit-maximizing, monopolistically competitive producer of an information product,
   a. the firm's desired output will be at the minimum point of the average total cost curve.
   b. the firm will earn positive economic profits.
   c. the firm's desired output will be zero units.
   d. the firm will earn zero economic profits.

17. If a firm that manufactures and sells an information product sets the price of the product equal to marginal cost, it will earn
   a. total revenues equal to its total costs.
   b. an economic loss equal to its fixed costs.
   c. an economic loss equal to its variable costs.
   d. total revenues equal to its total fixed costs

18. In the short run, a monopolistically competitive firm that manufactures and sells an information product maximizes its economic profits by producing to the point at which
   a. price equals marginal cost.
   b. price equals average total cost.
   c. price equals average variable cost.
   d. marginal revenue equals marginal cost.

MATCHING

(1)

a. monopolistic competition
b. search good
c. information product
d. TV and radio advertisements
e. mail advertisements
f. experience good

(2)

g. direct marketing
h. informational advertising
i. persuasive advertising
j. product differentiation
k. short-run economies of operation
l. mass marketing

CHAPTER 25: MONOPOLISTIC COMPETITION

WORKING WITH GRAPHS

1. Use the graphs of a monopolistic competitor below to answer each of the following questions.

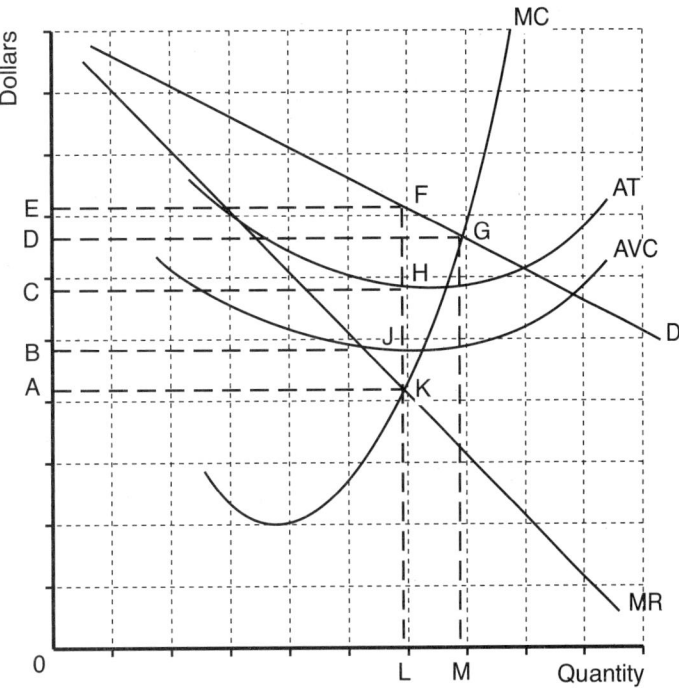

   a. At what level of output will this firm operate? _____
   b. What is marginal revenue at this level of output? _____
   c. What price will this firm charge for its product? _____
   d. The area of what rectangle is equal to total revenue? _____
   e. What is the firm's average cost in equilibrium? _____
   f. The area of what rectangle is equal to the firm's total cost? _____
   g. Is the firm making profits or incurring losses? _____
   h. The area of what rectangle is equal to profits or losses? _____

2. Use the graphs below to answer the questions that follow.

a. Which of the producers is a monopolistic competitor making positive economic profits? _____

b. Which of the producers appears to be in an industry that may have reached a long-run equilibrium? _____

c. Which of the producers is most likely to leave the industry in which it is currently operating? _____

d. Which of the producers is in an industry that is most likely to attract additional firms? _____

e. If all the firms in Producer C's industry are currently in a similar situation, what will most probably happen if there is a decrease in demand for the products of that industry? _____

f. Which producer(s) is/are incurring short-run losses? _____

PROBLEMS

1. Let PC = perfect competition, M = monopoly, and MC = monopolistic competition. Indicate by writing down the appropriate initials which of the following may be consistent with one, several, or all of those markets.
   _____ a. profit maximizer
   _____ b. advertising
   _____ c. long-run economic profits
   _____ d. social inefficiency
   _____ e. P > MC in equilibrium

_____ f. product differentiation
_____ g. large economies of scale relative to market demand
_____ h. long-run equilibrium at minimum ATC
_____ i. short-run economic profits
_____ j. easy entry
_____ k. ability to set price

ANSWERS TO CHAPTER 25

COMPLETION QUESTIONS

1. significant number of sellers; differentiated product; advertising; easy entry.
2. difficult; need not; a little
3. negatively; below
4. marginal revenue; marginal cost
5. greater than; inefficiency
6. equal to; greater than
7. demand for; differentiated
8. direct; mass; interactive
9. a search; an experience
10. informational; a search
11. persuasive; an experience
12. variable; total
13. variable; total variable; total fixed; negative
14. total; zero

TRUE-FALSE

1. T
2. F There are so many rivals, they can be ignored.
3. T
4. F Wheat is largely homogeneous.
5. T
6. F Social inefficiency exists because the monopolistic competitor's demand curve is negatively sloped; therefore, P > MC in equilibrium.
7. F Exclusively persuasive advertising is more likely to be used by the producer of an experience good.
8. T
9. T
10. F Heavy advertising expenses signals that a company intends to stay in business a long time and desires to develop a loyal customer base.
11. F In fact, producing an information product typically requires incurring relatively high fixed costs and relatively low marginal costs.
12. T
13. T
14. F In long-run equilibrium for an information-product firm in monopolistically competitive industry, price is equal to average total cost.

MULTIPLE CHOICE QUESTIONS

1.a; 2.c; 3.c; 4.a; 5.b; 6.c; 7.a; 8.d; 9.d; 10.b;
11.b; 12.a; 13.c; 14.b; 15.c; 16.d; 17.b; 18.d.

MATCHING

a and j; b and h; c and k; d and l; e and g; f and i

WORKING WITH GRAPHS

1. a. 0L; b. 0A; c. 0E; d. 0EFL; e. 0C; f. 0CHL; g. profits; h. CEFH
2. a. B; b. C; c. A; d. B; e. some firms will exit the industry; f. A

PROBLEMS

1. a. PC, M, MC; b. M, MC; c. M; d. M, MC; e. M, MC;
   f. MC; g. M; h. PC; i. PC, M, MC; j. PC, MC; k. M, MC.

GLOSSARY TO CHAPTER 25

Direct marketing: Advertising targeted at specific consumers, typically in the form of postal mailings, telephone calls, or e-mail messages.

Experience good: A product that an individual must consume before the product's quality can be established.

Information product: An item that is produced using information-intensive inputs at a relatively high fixed cost but distributed for sale at a relatively low marginal cost.

Informational advertising: Advertising that emphasizes the transmission of knowledge about the features of a product.

Interactive marketing: Advertising that permits a consumer to follow up directly by searching for more information and placing direct product orders.

Mass marketing: Advertising intended to reach as many consumers as possible, typically through television, newspaper, radio, or magazine ads.

Monopolistic competition A market situation in which a large number of firms produce similar but not identical products. Entry into the industry is relatively easy.

Persuasive advertising: Advertising that is intended to induce a consumer to try a product and discover a previously unknown taste for the item.

Product differentiation The distinguishing of products by brand name, color, and other minor attributes. Product differentiation occurs in other than perfectly competitive markets in which products are, in theory, homogeneous, such as wheat or corn.

Search good: A product with characteristics that enable an individual to evaluate the product's quality in advance of a purchase.

Short-run economies of operation: A distinguishing characteristic of an information product arising from declining short-run average total cost as more units of the product are sold.

CHAPTER 26
OLIGOPOLY AND STRATEGIC BEHAVIOR

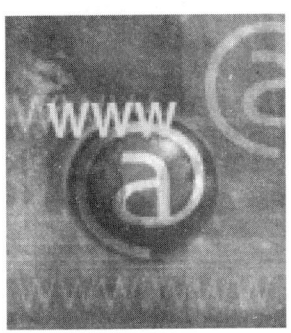

LEARNING OBJECTIVES

After you have studied this chapter you should be able to

1. list three reasons for the existence of oligopolies;

2. calculate concentration ratios and recognize their limitations;

3. distinguish between a cooperative and a noncooperative game;

4. answer questions concerning the essence of the kinked demand curve and enumerate criticisms of the kinked demand curve model;

5. distinguish among zero sum, positive sum, and negative sum games;

6. recognize three ways that existing oligopolists deter entry into the industry;

7. define network effects and explain how they can create positive or negative market feedback that can affect industry concentration;

8. compare the main features of perfect competition, monopoly, monopolistic competition, and oligopoly.

CHAPTER OUTLINE

1. *Oligopoly* is a market situation in which there are a very few sellers, each of which expects a reaction from its rivals to changes in its price and quantity; there are two major characteristics of oligopolies: a small number of firms and interdependence.

2. There are at least three reasons for the emergence of oligopolistic industries: economies of scale, barriers to entry, and merger (horizontal or vertical).
   a. Four- or eight-firm *concentration ratios* are often calculated to determine the extent to which an industry is "monopolized."
   b. Over time some industries experience drastic changes (up or down) in their concentration ratios; others show little change.

3. Before an oligopoly situation can be analyzed with respect to price and output, specific assumptions about rival *reactions* must be made; a different model arises with each assumption regarding the oligopolist's reaction function.

4. Because there is interdependence among oligopolistic competitors economists have developed an approach, called game theory, to describe how such firms interact rationally.
    a. If firms collude and form a cartel, the game is referred to as a cooperative game.
    b. If cartels are too expensive to form or enforce, then a noncooperative game is played among oligopolists.
    c. Games are classified as being zero sum, positive sum, or negative sum.

5. Oligopolistic decision makers derive a strategy, or rule used to make a choice; a dominant strategy is one that always yields the highest benefit, regardless of what the other oligopolists do.

6. The most famous example of game theory is called the prisoner's dilemma in which it can be shown that (under specified conditions) in situations in which there is more than one party to a crime, the dominant strategy for each prisoner is to confess.

7. A payoff matrix indicates the consequences of the strategies chosen by the players in the game.

8. Another oligopoly model results from assuming that rivals will match a price reduction, but ignore a price increase.
    a. In such a situation, for the oligopolist the price elasticity of demand above the current price will be very high, and the price elasticity of demand below the current price will be very low; the result is a kinked demand curve and a discontinuous marginal revenue curve.
    b. One implication of the kinked demand curve model is price rigidity; any change in marginal costs in the discontinuous gap of the marginal revenue curve will leave price unaltered.
    c. One criticism of this analysis is that it offers no explanation of how the current price was established; empirical evidence indicates that oligopolies tend to change price more frequently than do monopolies.

9. Sometimes even if no formal cartel arises among oligopolists, tacit collusion in the form of price leadership can occur; the largest firm announces its price and smaller competitors then follow this lead.

10. On occasion smaller rivals may set price too far below the price leader and a price war results.

11. Strategic decision making could lead to pricing or investing policies that deter entry by potential competitors; entry-deterrence strategies include threats of a price war, investment in excess capacity by existing firms, inducing governments to restrict entry, and raising switching costs to customers.

12. The limit-pricing model suggests that existing oligopolists collude to set the highest price they can without encouraging entry into the industry.

13. Network effects occur when the willingness of consumers to buy a product depends on how many other consumers purchase it.
    a. When network effects are an important feature of a product, an industry can experience positive market feedback, or a tendency for its product to come into favor with additional consumers because other consumers have chosen to purchase it; if a few firms can reap most of the benefits of positive market feedback, then the result can be greater concentration in the industry.

b. Network effects can also result in negative market feedback, which occurs if some consumers cut back on purchases of a product, causing it to fall out of favor with other consumers.

KEY TERMS

Oligopoly	Price war	Game theory
Concentration ratio	Payoff matrix	Noncooperative game
Horizontal merger	Vertical merger	Cooperative game
Reaction function	Network effect	Strategic dependence
Strategy		

KEY CONCEPTS

Zero sum game	Entry-deterrence strategy	Dominant strategies
Positive-sum game	Price leadership	Prisoner's dilemma
Negative-sum game	Limit pricing model	Opportunistic behavior
Tit-for-tat strategy behavior	Negative market feedback	Positive market feedback

COMPLETION QUESTIONS
Fill in the blank or circle the correct term.

1. Two key characteristics of oligopoly are _____ and _____.

2. Oligopolies may emerge because of _____, _____ _____, and _____.

3. Concentration ratios (fall, rise) as the definition of "industry" is narrowed, and they _____ as the definition is broadened.

4. Economists have developed an approach to analyze the interdependence among oligopolists called _____ theory.

5. If oligopolists collude and form a cartel this is a _____ game; if cartels are too expensive to form or enforce then oligopolists will play a _____ game.

6. Games are referred to as _____ sum if one player's benefit is exactly equal to the expense of the other, _____ sum if the sum of the players' benefit is positive, and _____ sum if the sum of the players' benefit is negative.

7. The most famous example of game theory is _____ in which the dominant strategy of prisoners (usually) is to (confess, not confess).

8. Assume that firm B is an oligopolist. If its rivals match its price reductions but ignore its price increases, firm B will have a _____ demand curve; its marginal revenue curve will be _____; firm B probably (will, will not) change its price very often. Because its demand curve is negatively sloped, in equilibrium firm B's (P = MC, P > MC, P < MC) and from society's point of view it will produce (too little, too much, just enough) and its price will be (too low, too high, just right).

9. Even if no formal cartel arises in an oligopolistic industry, tacit collusion in the form of _____ leadership may result; occasionally such a system breaks down and a price _____ results.

CHAPTER 26: OLIGOPOLY AND STRATEGIC BEHAVIOR

10. Existing oligopolists can use the following strategies to deter entry: _____, _____, and _____; the _____ model suggests that existing firms set the highest price they can without encouraging entry.

11. When a consumer's willingness to purchase a good or service is influenced by how many other consumers also purchase the item, there is a _____.

12. (Positive; Negative) market feedback arises when there is a tendency for a good or service to come into favor with additional consumers because other consumers have chosen to buy the item; (positive; negative) market feedback arises when there is tendency for a good or service to fall out of favor with more consumers because other consumers have stopped purchasing the item.

TRUE-FALSE QUESTIONS

Circle the **T** if the statement is true, the **F** if it is false. Explain to yourself why a statement is false.

T F 1. The main characteristic of the oligopoly market structure is that an oligopolist must consider the reaction of its rivals.

T F 2. Perhaps the strongest reason for the existence of oligopolies is economies of scale relative to market demand.

T F 3. Concentration ratios provide an accurate measure of the degree of monopoly power in an industry.

T F 4. If an oligopolist's rivals match all of its price changes, its demand curve will be kinked.

T F 5. Cartels are usually expensive to set up and enforce.

T F 6. A dominant strategy is one that is always preferred by a player, regardless of what other players do.

T F 7. Price wars result because all players are in a positive sum game.

T F 8. The limit-pricing model suggests that oligopolists set price at the highest price they can.

T F 9. Collusion may be found in both formal and tacit arrangements.

T F 10. Opportunistic behavior helps keep collusive agreements together.

T F 11. If a firm's strategy is to continue to cooperate with other firms in a collusive manner as long as other firms also do so, then it engages in tit-for-tat strategic behavior.

T F 12. The strongest element of the theory of the kinked demand curve is its ability to explain the current price and output decision of an oligopolist.

T F 13. A firm pursues an entry deterrence strategy if it engages in behavior designed to raise a potential competitor's cost of entering the industry.

T F 14. A network effect arises any time that one consumer's demand for an item is influenced by how many other consumers purchase the item.

T F 15. Positive market feedback can help explain why one firm can develop a position of dominance within an industry, but it cannot help explain why an entire industry might rapidly expand when the industry product is subject to network effects.

MULTIPLE CHOICE QUESTIONS
Circle the letter that corresponds to the best answer.

1. In which of the following will the players' sum of benefits be positive?
   a. negative sum game
   b. zero sum game
   c. positive sum game
   d. prisoner's dilemma

2. If oligopoly B's rivals ignore its price increases but match its price decreases, then B's demand curve will be
   a. discontinuous.
   b. kinked at the going price.
   c. below its marginal revenue curve.
   d. proportionate to the industry demand curve.

3. In long-run equilibrium for a profit-maximizing oligopolist,
   a. MR = MC.
   b. P > MR.
   c. economic profits can be greater than zero.
   d. All of the above

4. Which firms must have zero economic profits in the long run?
   a. monopolist, perfect competitor
   b. oligopolist, monopolistic competitor
   c. perfect competitor, monopolistic competitor
   d. perfect competitor, oligopolist

5. Of the following, the *best* explanation for the existence of oligopolies is
   a. no economies of scale exist.
   b. large economies of scale relative to market demand.
   c. advertising.
   d. one firm has exclusive ownership of an important raw material.

6. In an oligopolistic industry, entry will result if
   a. normal profits exist.
   b. the industry LAC curve is below the market demand curve.
   c. the industry LAC curve is above the market demand curve.
   d. advertising is permitted.

7. The kinked demand curve theory
   a. is supported by empirical evidence.
   b. requires that an oligopolist's rivals exactly match its price changes.
   c. predicts price rigidity.
   d. requires collusion.

8. Which of the following is a strategy to deter entry by potential competitors?
   a. raising switching costs to customers
   b. investment in excess capacity by existing firms
   c. limit-pricing strategy
   d. All of the above

9. The four-firm concentration ratio is
   a. the sum of the dollar sales of the four top-selling firms in an industry.
   b. the sum of the physical outputs of the top four producing firms in an industry.
   c. the percentage of total industry output produced by the leading four firms in an industry.
   d. the percentage of total industry dollar sales received by the leading four firms in an industry.

10. In the context of game theory, collusion is always a
    a. noncooperative game.
    b. negative-sum game.
    c. cooperative game.
    d. zero-sum game.

11. The strategy that always yields the highest benefit to a player in a game regardless of what other players may do is that player's
    a. dominant strategy.
    b. tit-for-tat strategy.
    c. positive-sum strategy.
    d. opportunistic strategy.

12. Price leadership
    a. is a form of implicit, or tacit, collusion among oligopolists.
    b. always results whenever there is a price war among oligopolists.
    c. always results whenever oligopolists engage in a noncooperative game.
    d. is a synonym for limit pricing intended to make market entry by other firms unprofitable.

13. Firms in an oligopolistic industry are more likely to be able to maintain a collusive agreement if
    a. their owners engage in opportunistic behavior.
    b. their collusive agreement is a zero-sum game.
    c. their collusive agreement is a positive-sum game.
    d. their collusive agreement is a negative-sum game.

14. A network effect exists for a product when
    a. the willingness of consumers to buy that product is influenced by how many other consumers purchase it.
    b. the willingness of consumers to buy that product is influenced by how many firms offer the item for sale.
    c. the willingness of firms to sell that product is influenced by how many consumers purchase the product.
    d. the willingness of firms to sell that product is influenced by how many other firms sell the product.

15. A situation in which a significant number of consumers have chosen to purchase more units of a good or service in response to purchases by other consumers, thereby causing an industry to experience surging sales, is an example of
    a. negative market feedback.
    b. positive market feedback.
    c. an outcome of limit pricing.
    d. an outcome of price leadership.

16. Which firm has the **LEAST** control over its price?
    a. monopolistic competitor
    b. perfect competitor
    c. monopolist
    d. oligopolist

17. In the United States, a good example of an oligopolistic industry is
    a. a single local power company.
    b. the college textbook industry.
    c. the roofing nail industry.
    d. the retail trade industry.

MATCHING
Choose the item in column (2) that best matches an item in column (1).

(1)	(2)
a. positive-sum game	g. a rule for making a choice
b. oligopoly	h. strategic dependence among a few firms
c. kinked demand curve	i. following the crowd to buy a hot product
d. cooperative game	j. all players benefit
e. strategy	k. discontinuous marginal revenue curve
f. positive market feedback	l. collusive behavior

164   CHAPTER 26: OLIGOPOLY AND STRATEGIC BEHAVIOR

WORKING WITH GRAPHS

1. Use the graphs of the oligopolist below to answer each of the questions that follow.

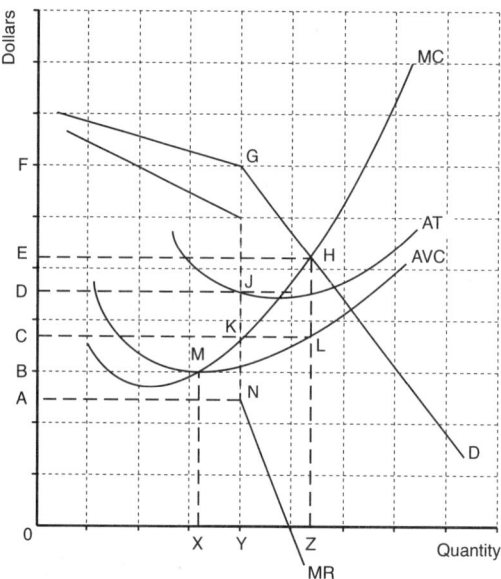

   a. At what level of output will this firm operate? _____
   b. What is the marginal cost at this level of output? _____
   c. What price will the firm charge for its product? _____
   d. The area of what rectangle equals total revenue? _____
   e. What is the firm's average cost? _____
   f. The area of what rectangle is equal to the firm's total cost? _____
   g. The area of what rectangle is equal to the firm's profit? _____
   h. Suppose the firm is operating at an output level of Y units. How low would marginal costs at Y units of output have to drop before the firm would lower its price? _____

PROBLEMS

1. Consider the table below, then answer the questions that follow. All information is for domestic firms.

Domestic Firms in Industry A	Annual Sales
1	$2,000,000
2	1,500,000
3	1,400,000
4	1,100,000
5	1,000,000
6	700,000
7	200,000
8	100,000
9-20 (remaining firms)	1,000,000

   a. What is the 4-firm concentration ratio?
   b. What is the 8-firm concentration ratio?

c. What would happen to the concentration ratios if industry B's product is a substitute for Industry A's product?
d. What would happen to the concentration ratios if the sales of imported goods in Industries A and B that are sold in domestic markets were included?

ANSWERS TO CHAPTER 26

COMPLETION QUESTIONS

1. small number of firms; interdependence
2. economies of scale; barriers to entry; product differentiation and advertising; merger
3. rise; fall
4. game
5. cooperative; noncooperative
6. zero; positive; negative
7. the prisoner's dilemma; confess
8. kinked; below its demand curve and discontinuous; will not; $P > MC$; too little; too high
9. price; war
10. threats of price wars; investment in excess capacity; get government to restrict entry; limit-pricing.
11. network effect
12. Positive; negative

TRUE-FALSE

1. T
2. T
3. F They are very inaccurate, if only because inter-industry competition exists; foreign competition exists too.
4. F Its demand curve will be proportionate to the industry demand curve.
5. T
6. T
7. F They result when price leadership strategies break down.
8. F They set price at the highest level that *will still discourage entry*.
9. T
10. F By definition, opportunistic behavior involves actions that ignore possible long-run benefits of cooperation.
11. T
12. F The theory of the kinked demand curve takes the current price and output of an oligopolist as given; it provides no explanation of how the firm has selected this price and output level.
13. T
14. T
15. F Positive market feedback can occur either for an individual firm or for an entire industry.

MULTIPLE CHOICE QUESTIONS

1.c; 2.b; 3.d; 4.c; 5.b; 6.b; 7.c; 8.d; 9.d; 10.c;
11.a; 12.a; 13.c; 14.a; 15.b; 16.b; 17.b.

MATCHING

a and j; b and h; c and k; d and l; e and g; f and i

CHAPTER 26: OLIGOPOLY AND STRATEGIC BEHAVIOR

WORKING WITH GRAPHS

1. a. 0Y; b. 0C; c. 0F; d. 0FGY; e. 0D; f. 0DJY; g. DFGJ; h. below 0A

PROBLEMS

1. a. 6/9 (or .67) b. 8/9 (or .89) c. They would fall. d. They would fall.

GLOSSARY TO CHAPTER 26

Concentration ratio The percentage of all sales contributed by the leading four or leading eight firms in an industry; sometimes called the *industry concentration ratio*.

Cooperative game A game in which the players explicitly cooperate to make themselves better off. As applied to firms, it involves companies colluding in order to make higher than competitive rates of return.

Dominant strategies Strategies that always yield the highest benefit. Regardless of what other players do, a dominant strategy will yield the most benefit for the player using it.

Entry-deterrence strategy Any strategy undertaken by firms in an industry, either individually or together, with the intent or effect of raising the cost of entry into the industry by a new firm.

Game theory A way of describing the various possible outcomes in any situation involving two or more interacting individuals when those individuals are aware of the interactive nature of their situation and plan accordingly. The plans made by these individuals are known as *game strategies*.

Horizontal merger The joining of firms that are producing or selling a similar product.

Limit-pricing model A model that hypothesizes that a group of colluding sellers will set the highest common price that they believe they can charge without new firms seeking to enter that industry in search of relatively high profits.

Negative market feedback A tendency for a good or service to fall out of favor with more consumers because other consumers have stopped purchasing the item.

Negative-sum game A game in which players as a group lose at the end of the game.

Network effect A situation in which a consumer's willingness to purchase a good or service is influenced by how many others also buy the item.

Noncooperative game A game in which the players neither negotiate nor cooperate in any way. As applied to firms in an industry, this is the common situation in which there are relatively few firms and each has some ability to change price.

Oligopoly A market situation in which there are very few sellers. Each seller knows that the other sellers will react to its changes in prices and quantities.

Opportunistic behavior Actions that ignore possible long-run benefits of cooperation and focus solely on short-run gains.

Payoff matrix A matrix of outcomes, or consequences, of the strategies chosen by players in a game.

Positive market feedback A tendency for a good or service to come into favor with additional consumers because other consumers have chosen to buy the item.

Positive-sum game A game in which players as a group are better off at the end of the game.

Price leadership A practice in many oligopolistic industries in which the largest firm publishes its price list ahead of its competitors, who then match those announced prices. Also called *parallel pricing*.

Price war A pricing campaign designed to capture additional market share by repeatedly cutting prices.

Prisoner's dilemma A famous strategic game in which two prisoners have a choice between confessing and not confessing to a crime. If neither confesses, they serve a minimum sentence. If both confess, they serve a longer sentence. If one confesses and the other doesn't, the one who confesses goes free. The dominant strategy is always to confess.

Reaction function The manner in which one oligopolist reacts to a change in price, output, or quality made by another oligopolist in the industry.

Strategic dependence A situation in which one firm's actions with respect to price, quality, advertising, and related changes may be strategically countered by one or more other firms in the industry. Such dependence can only exist when there are a limited number of major firms in an industry.

Strategy Any rule that is used to make a choice, such as "always pick heads."

Tit-for-tat strategic behavior In game theory, cooperation that continues so long as other players continue to cooperate.

Vertical merger The joining of a firm with another to which it sells an output or from which it buys an input.

Zero-sum game A game in which any gains within the group are exactly offset by equal losses by the end of the game.

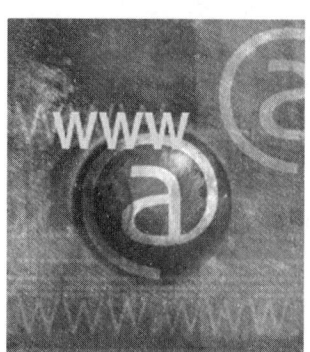

CHAPTER 27
REGULATION AND ANTITRUST POLICY IN A GLOBALIZED ECONOMY

LEARNING OBJECTIVES

After you have studied this chapter, you should be able to

1. define cost-of-service regulation, rate-of-return regulation, capture hypothesis, share-the-gains, share-the-pains theory, deregulation, theory of contestable markets, monopolization, market share test, and creative response;

2. indicate the problem with requiring a natural monopolist to engage in marginal cost pricing and list two ways to counter this problem;

3. distinguish between cost-of-service regulation and rate-of-return regulation, and answer questions that indicate an understanding of the difficulties involved with such regulation;

4. apply the regulator behavior model to predict the behavior of regulators;

5. recognize the essentials of the Supreme Court definition of monopolization;

6. enumerate the essential features of the major antitrust laws;

7. recognize the difficulties in applying the market share test in a world with multinational firms;

8. list four exemptions from the antitrust laws.

CHAPTER OUTLINE

1. A natural monopoly arises when there are large economies of scale relative to industry demand and one firm can produce at a lower cost than can be achieved by multiple firms.

2. When long-run average costs are falling, the long-run marginal cost curve is below the long-run average cost curve; the first firm to take advantage of decreasing costs can drive out all competitors by underpricing them.

a. If regulators force the natural monopolist to engage in marginal cost pricing, the firm will suffer economic losses and will shut down.
b. In such a situation, regulators might subsidize the natural monopolist to engage in marginal cost pricing.

3. There are three types of government regulation: regulation of natural monopolies, regulation of inherently competitive industries, and social regulation.
   a. Economic regulation typically concerns controlling prices that regulated enterprises are allowed to charge.
      i. Cost-of-service regulation allows regulated companies to charge in accordance with actual average costs.
      ii. Rate-of-return regulation allows regulated firms to earn a normal rate of return on their investment in the business.
   b. Regulators can control prices, but because quality is difficult to measure and control, regulated firms can change their price per constant-quality unit when forced to underprice services.
   c. Regulated firms engage in creative response, which is a response to a regulation that conforms to the letter of the law while undermining its spirit.

4. The regulator behavior model suggests that regulation benefits firms already in a regulated industry—not potential entrants or consumers.
   a. The capture hypothesis predicts that regulators will eventually be controlled by the special interests of the industry that is being regulated.
   b. The share-the-gains, share-the-pains theory maintains that regulators must take into account the demands of three groups: legislators, firms in the industry, and consumers of the regulated industry.

5. By some estimates, regulation costs our nation over $700 billion per year, or about 8 percent of yearly national income.

6. Deregulation can create costs and benefits.
   a. In the short run firms and workers can be hurt by deregulation, but the long-run effects are largely beneficial.
   b. The contestable market theory suggests that regulation should be concerned with ease of entry into an industry—and not with the current structure of an industry.

7. Antitrust policy attempts to prevent the emergence of monopoly and monopolistic behavior.
   a. In 1890 the Sherman Act was passed; it made illegal every contract and combination, in the form of a trust, that restrained trade.
   b. In 1914 the Clayton Act was passed; it made price discrimination and interlocking directorates illegal.
   c. The Federal Trade Commission Act of 1914 established that commission to prevent "unfair competition"; the 1938 Wheeler-Lea Act amended the 1914 act to allow the FTC to battle against false or misleading advertising.
   d. The Robinson-Patman Act of 1936 was aimed at preventing large producers from driving out small competitors by means of selective discriminatory price cuts.
   e. Numerous antitrust acts serve to exempt certain business (and union) practices from antitrust action.

8. The Sherman Act does not define monopoly, but the Supreme Court has defined the term monopolization as involving
   a. the possession of monopoly power in the relevant market, and
   b. the willful acquisition or maintenance of the power as distinguished from growth or development as a consequence of a superior product, business acumen, or historic accident.

9. In practice it is difficult to measure (and define) market power.

10. The relevant market consists of two elements: a relevant product market and a relevant geographic market. Defining both is increasingly difficult, because firms face increasing competition from abroad as well as within U.S. borders.

KEY TERMS
Cost-of-service regulation
Rate-of-return regulation

Deregulation

KEY CONCEPTS
Monopolization
Capture hypothesis
Share-the-gains, share-the-pains theory

Market share test
Theory of contestable markets
Creative response

COMPLETION QUESTIONS
Fill in the blank, or circle the correct term.

1. A natural monopoly arises when there are large _____ of scale relative to _____; in such a case the firm's average total costs persistently _____ and its marginal cost curve lies (below, above) its average cost curve; the first firm to expand will be able to offer a price that is _____ than those of its rivals and drive them out of business.

2. If a natural monopolist were forced to engage in marginal cost pricing for social efficiency, that firm would experience _____ economic profits; in order to counter that, regulators might _____ the natural monopolist.

3. The three types of government regulation are _____, _____, and _____.

4. Cost-of-service regulation requires firms to charge customers based on actual (marginal, average) costs; rate-of-return regulation permits regulated firms to earn _____ profits. Because price is easier to measure and regulate than quality, regulated firms can (lower, raise) the price per constant-quality unit, even if price is constant.

5. Regulated firms often try to avoid the effects of regulation, so they react to regulation by making a(n) _____ response; that is, they follow the letter, but not the spirit, of a regulation.

6. The regulator behavior model suggests that much regulation is for the benefit of (consumers, firms already in the industry); two such theories are _____ and _____.

7. Monopolization is the possession of monopoly power in the _____ market, and the _____ acquisition or maintenance of the power, as distinguished from growth as a consequence of _____, _____, or _____.

8. One predictable short-run result of deregulation is _____; long-run results include _____ and _____.

9. The Sherman Act makes illegal those contracts or trusts that act to _____ trade; the provisions of this act are (vague, clear); the Clayton Act makes price _____ illegal if it substantially lessens competition.

10. The Federal Trade Commission (FTC) Act attempts to prevent _____ competition; the Wheeler-Lea Act amended the FTC Act and permits the FTC to battle against false or misleading _____. The FTC Act was formed to protect _____, while the Wheeler-Lea Act attempts to protect _____.

11. The _____ Act is aimed at preventing producers from driving out competitors by means of selected discriminatory price cuts; it is commonly referred to as the _____ act.

12. Four exemptions to antitrust laws are _____, _____, _____ and _____.

13. The primary measure of monopoly is the _____ test, which is determined by the _____ of a market that a firm controls.

14. The contestable markets theory suggests that regulation should be more concerned with the _____ into an industry and not the current _____ of the industry.

TRUE-FALSE QUESTIONS
Circle the **T** if the statement is true, the **F** if it is false. Explain to yourself why a statement is false.

T F 1. Natural monopolies arise mainly due to large economies of scale.

T F 2. If a natural monopolist is required to engage in marginal cost pricing, it will earn abnormal profits.

T F 3. Everyone benefits from deregulation.

T F 4. Traditionally in the United States inherently competitive industries have not been regulated.

T F 5. Regulated firms often follow the letter of a rule but violate its spirit.

T F 6. Regulators can easily regulate the price per constant-quality unit of regulated firms.

T F 7. According to the regulator behavior theory, regulators are mostly concerned with the well-being of consumers.

T F 8. Monopolization, according to the Supreme Court, requires a willful act.

T F 9. One predictable result of deregulation is bankruptcy for the less efficient firms.

T F 10. The Wheeler-Lea Act attempts to protect small competitors, while the FTC Act attempts to protect consumers.

T F 11. The Robinson-Patman Act was aimed at preventing producers from driving out smaller competitors by means of selected discriminatory price cuts.

T F 12. Labor unions are exempted from antitrust laws, even if their actions restrain trade.

T F 13. Monopolization requires a willful acquisition of monopoly power in the relevant market.

MULTIPLE CHOICE QUESTIONS
Circle the letter that corresponds to the best answer.

1. A natural monopoly results because
   a. of large economies of scale.
   b. of persisting declining average and marginal costs.
   c. the largest firm can underprice its competitors.
   d. All of the above

2. If the natural monopolist were forced to price at marginal cost, it would earn
   a. abnormal profits.
   b. economic profits.
   c. economic losses.
   d. zero economic profit.

3. If an industry were to be deregulated,
   a. short-run costs to some existing producers would be significant.
   b. all producers would be hurt.
   c. all consumers would be helped.
   d. All of the above

4. Which of the following is **NOT** a recognized type of government regulation?
   a. regulation of natural monopolies
   b. regulation for the benefit of Congress
   c. regulation of inherently competitive industries
   d. regulation for public welfare across all industries

5. Which of the following is probably the most difficult to regulate?
   a. price
   b. output
   c. quality
   d. profit

6. Which of the following is **NOT** consistent with the regulator behavior model?
   a. Regulators are concerned with benefiting themselves.
   b. Regulators are concerned with benefiting vocal customers.
   c. Regulators are concerned with benefiting firms already in the industry.
   d. Regulators are concerned with benefiting potential entrants into an industry.

7. Which of the following is a predictable consequence of deregulation?
   a. increased bankruptcies in the short run
   b. long-run abnormal profits
   c. a long-run price that is even greater than MC
   d. short-run misallocation of resources

8. Which action is considered monopolization?
   a. willful acquisition of monopoly power
   b. producing a superior product
   c. business acumen
   d. historic accident

9. Which of the following are **NOT** exempt from antitrust laws?
   a. labor unions
   b. professional sports
   c. suppliers of military equipment
   d. all unincorporated businesses

10. The contestable markets theory maintains that regulators should be primarily concerned with
    a. the degree to which entry into an industry is possible.
    b. concentration ratios.
    c. profits today.
    d. past profits.

MATCHING
Choose the item in column (2) that best matches an item in column (1).

(1)	(2)
a. contestable markets	f. willful acquisition of monopoly power
b. monopolization	g. persistent fall in long-run AC
c. natural monopoly	h. behavior of regulated firms
d. creative response	i. behavior of regulators
e. capture hypothesis	j. ease of entry into industry

WORKING WITH GRAPHS

1. Suppose you are an analyst for a regulatory board that is in charge of the regulation of local monopolies. Given the information in the graph that follows, answer the list of questions submitted by your supervisor.

a. If this monopolist is not regulated, what will be the level of output? Price? Total revenue? Total costs? Profit or loss?

b. If this monopolist is regulated by marginal cost pricing, what will be the level of output? Price? Total revenue? Total costs? Profits or loss? Will the monopoly need a subsidy? If so, how much?

c. If cost-of-service regulation is imposed on this monopolist, what will be the level of output? Price? Total revenue? Total costs? Profit or loss?

ANSWERS TO CHAPTER 27

COMPLETION QUESTIONS

1. economies; industry demand; fall; below; lower
2. negative; subsidize
3. regulation of natural monopolies; regulation of inherently competitive industries; social regulation
4. average; normal; raise
5. creative
6. firms already in the industry; capture theory; share-the-gains, share-the-pains theory
7. relevant; willful; a superior product; business acumen; historic accident
8. increased bankruptcies; prices closer to marginal cost; smaller abnormal profits
9. restrain; vague; discrimination
10. unfair; advertising; small competitors; consumers
11. Robinson-Patman; chain store
12. any of the following: labor unions; public utilities; professional baseball; cooperative acts among U.S. exporters; hospitals; public transit and water systems; suppliers of military equipment; joint publishing arrangements by two or more newspapers in a single city
13. market share; percentage
14. degree to which entry is permitted; market structure

TRUE-FALSE QUESTIONS

1. T
2. F It will realize losses.
3. F Some firms and workers are hurt in the short run.
4. F Inherently competitive industries such as trucking and airlines have been regulated.
5. T
6. F It is difficult to regulate quality.
7. F They, like the rest of us, are assumed to be concerned with their own well-being.
8. T
9. T
10. F Just the opposite.
11. T
12. T
13. T

MULTIPLE CHOICE QUESTIONS

1.d;   2.c;   3.a;   4.b;   5.c;   6.d;   7.a;   8.a;   9.d;   10.a.

MATCHING

a and j;   b and f;   c and g;   d and h;   e and i

WORKING WITH GRAPHS

1. a. 1700 units, $3.50, $5950, $5440 (or 1700 x $3.20), profit of $510 (**note**: dollar figures are approximations.)
   b. 3000 units, $1.50, $4500, $7500, loss of $3000, yes, $3000
   c. 2000, $3, $6000, $6000, $0

GLOSSARY TO CHAPTER 27

Capture hypothesis   A theory of regulatory behavior that predicts that the regulators will eventually be captured by the special interests of the industry being regulated.

Cost-of-service regulation   Regulation based on allowing prices to reflect only the actual cost of production and no monopoly profits.

Creative response   Behavior on the part of a firm that allows it to comply with the letter of the law but violates the spirit, significantly lessening the law's effects.

Deregulation   The elimination or phasing out of past regulations on economic activity.

Market share test   The percentage of a market that a particular firm supplies, used as the primary measure of monopoly power.

Monopolization   The possession of market power in the relevant market and the willful acquisition or maintenance of that power, as distinguished from growth or development as a consequence of a superior product, business acumen, or historic accident.

Rate-of-return regulation   Regulation that seeks to keep the rate of return in the industry at a competitive level by not allowing excessive prices to be charged.

Share-the-gains, share-the-pains theory   A theory of regulatory behavior in which the regulators must take account of the demands of three groups: legislators, who established and who oversee the regulatory agency; members of the regulated industry; and consumers of the regulated industry's products or services.

Theory of contestable markets   A hypothesis concerning pricing behavior that holds that even though there are only a few firms in the industry, they are forced to price their products more or less competitively because of the ease of entry by outsiders. The key aspect of a contestable market is relatively costless entry into and exit from the industry.

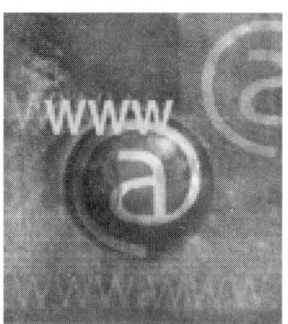

CHAPTER 28
LABOR DEMAND AND SUPPLY

LEARNING OBJECTIVES

After you have studied this chapter you should be able to

1. define marginal factor cost, marginal physical product of labor, derived demand, marginal revenue product, labor market, efficiency wages, and insider-outsider theory;

2. determine the profit-maximizing quantity of labor to hire for a firm that is a perfect competitor in both the product and the labor market;

3. determine the profit-maximizing quantity of labor to hire for a firm that is a perfect competitor in the labor market and a monopolist in the product market;

4. distinguish between the MRP of labor curve for a perfect competitor and the MRP of labor curve for a monopolist;

5. determine the equilibrium wage rate, given the supply of labor and the demand for labor;

6. list four determinants of the price elasticity of demand for an input;

7. recognize how workers can actually earn wages above the equilibrium wage rate;

8. list three factors that cause the total demand curve for labor to shift;

9. list two factors that cause the total supply of labor curve to shift;

10. recognize the minimum total cost condition for producing a given rate of output.

CHAPTER OUTLINE

1. What is the profit-maximizing quantity of labor to hire for a firm that is a perfect competitor in both the labor market and the product market?
    a. The marginal physical product of labor is the change in total output accounted for by hiring one worker, holding all other factors of production constant.

b. Because of the law of diminishing returns, the marginal physical product of labor eventually declines.
c. Because this firm is in a competitive labor market, it is a price taker; it can hire as much labor as it wants to hire at the going wage rate.
d. The marginal benefit from hiring one more unit of labor is that laborer's marginal physical product multiplied by the firm's constant product selling price, or the marginal revenue product (MRP).
e. The profit maximizing rule for hiring is to hire laborers up to the point where the wage rate equals the MRP of labor.

2. The demand for labor is a derived demand; laborers (or other inputs) are desired only because they can be used to produce products that are expected to be sold at a profit.

3. The market demand for labor curve is negatively sloped.

4. There are four principal determinants of the price elasticity of demand for an input. The price elasticity of demand for a variable input will be greater
   a. the greater the price elasticity of demand for the final product.
   b. the easier it is to substitute for that variable input.
   c. the larger the proportion of total costs accounted for by a particular variable input.
   d. the longer the time period being considered.

5. The industry supply of labor curve is upward sloping from left to right.
   a. As wage rates rise in an industry, more laborers are willing to accept jobs there.
   b. Nevertheless, the individual firm faces a horizontal supply curve at the going wage rate.

6. The equilibrium market wage rate is determined where the industry demand for labor curve intersects the industry supply of labor curve.

7. There are two alternative theories of wage determination.
   a. Some workers may earn efficiency wages (above equilibrium) due to
      i. firms trying to reduce turnover costs.
      ii. firms attempting to attract higher quality workers.
      iii. firms encouraging existing workers to work harder in order to keep relatively high-paying jobs.
   b. The insider-outsider theory predicts that wages may remain above equilibrium for insiders even though outsiders may be willing to work for lower wages because the firm would have to incur costs by replacing insiders with outsiders.

8. When nonwage determinants of the supply of and the demand for labor change, those curves shift.
   a. The labor demand curve shifts if there is a change in (1) the demand for the final product, (2) labor productivity, or (3) the price of related factors of production.
   b. The labor supply curve shifts if there is a change in the (1) alternative wage rate offered in other industries, or (2) nonmonetary aspects of the occupation under study.

9. What is the profit-maximizing quantity of labor to hire for a firm that is a perfect competitor in the labor market but a monopolist in the product market?
   a. Such a firm's demand for labor (or any other input) is negatively sloped because (1) the marginal physical product falls and (2) the price (and, therefore, MR) falls as output increases.
   b. Such a firm's labor demand curve is its MRP curve, which equals labor's marginal physical product multiplied by the firm's MR; thus MRP = MR × MPP.

c. Given the going market wage rate, this firm hires up to the point where MRP equals the wage rate.
d. The monopolist hires fewer workers than a perfectly competitive producer would, other things being constant.

10. How much of *each* variable factor should the firm use when combining those factors to produce a given output?
    a. The firm will hire all variable inputs up to the point where each input's MRP equals its price.
    b. In order to minimize the total cost of producing a given output, the firm should equate the ratios of each factor's marginal physical product to its respective price; this condition is referred to as the *least-cost combination of resources*.

KEY TERMS
Marginal physical product (MPP) of Labor   Marginal revenue product (MRP)
Marginal factor cost (MFC)

KEY CONCEPTS
Derived demand   Insider-outsider theory
Efficiency wages

COMPLETION QUESTIONS
Fill in the blank or circle the correct term.

1. To a firm that is a perfect competitor in both the labor and the product market, the marginal benefit from hiring labor equals labor's _____ times _____, or MRP.

2. A competitive firm's MRP curve is negatively sloped because labor's _____ falls, due to the law of _____.

3. To such a competitive firm, the marginal cost of hiring labor is the _____, which (falls, rises, remains constant) as the firm hires more laborers; in the labor market, such a firm is a price (taker, maker).

4. The competitive firm hires labor up to the point where _____ equals _____; at that point it is maximizing _____.

5. The demand for labor is a _____ demand; therefore if the product's selling price increases, the competitive firm's demand for labor curve will shift to the _____; the market demand curve for labor will be _____ sloped.

6. Determinants of the price elasticity of demand for an input include _____, _____, _____, and _____.

7. The supply of labor to a competitive firm is _____ elastic, therefore its labor supply curve is (vertical, horizontal); the supply of labor curve for the industry, however, is _____ sloped.

8. Workers may earn wages above equilibrium, or _____ wages, because firms _____ _____, or _____.

9. The industry demand for labor curve shifts if there is a change in the _____, _____, or _____; the industry supply curve shifts if there is a change in _____ or _____.

10. Assume a firm is a perfect competitor in the labor market but a monopolist in the product market. Its marginal benefit from hiring labor equals _____ times _____, or MRP of labor. This firm's MRP curve is negatively sloped because _____ falls due to the law of _____ and because _____ falls due to the fact that this firm must reduce its _____ as it produces more. This firm will hire labor up to the point where _____ equals _____.

11. If a competitive firm hires more than one variable input, its equilibrium condition is that _____; stated alternatively, it can minimize the total cost of producing a given output by equating _____.

12. The insider-outsider theory maintains that insiders will earn (less, more) than equilibrium wages because firms incur costs such as _____, and _____ if they replace insiders with outsiders.

TRUE-FALSE QUESTIONS
Circle the **T** if the statement is true, the **F** if it is false. Explain to yourself why a statement is false.

T F 1. A firm that is a competitor in all markets will discover that its demand for labor curve is horizontal at the going wage rate.

T F 2. A competitive firm will hire labor up to the point where MRP equals the going wage rate.

T F 3. The marginal physical product of labor declines due to diseconomies of scale.

T F 4. Because the demand for labor is a derived demand, it shifts when wage rates change.

T F 5. The price elasticity of demand for labor will be higher the lower is the price elasticity of demand for the final good.

T F 6. A competitive firm's supply of labor curve is perfectly elastic, but the entire industry supply of labor curve is upward sloping.

T F 7. Existing workers can earn efficiency wages because employers are generous.

T F 8. If labor productivity rises, the demand for labor increases.

T F 9. A firm that is a competitor in the labor market but a monopolist in the product market hires labor up to the point where the MRP of labor equals the going wage rate.

T F 10. If a firm suddenly monopolizes a perfectly competitive industry, more workers will be hired.

T F 11. If a competitive firm hires two factors of production it will hire up to the point where the MRP of one factor divided by that factor's price equals the MRP of the other factor divided by that factor's price.

T F 12. Outsiders cause wage rates to be lower than equilibrium for insiders.

MULTIPLE CHOICE QUESTIONS
Circle the letter that corresponds to the best answer.

1. Which of the following is **NOT** true about a firm that is a perfect competitor in all markets?
    a. Its supply of labor curve is perfectly elastic.
    b. Its demand for labor curve is downward sloping.
    c. Its price falls as it produces more output.
    d. Its marginal physical product of labor falls as it hires more labor.

2. For a firm that is a perfect competitor in all markets, the profit-maximizing quantity of labor to hire occurs where
    a. a falling MRP equals a rising wage rate.
    b. a rising MRP equals a rising wage rate.
    c. a falling MRP equals a falling wage rate.
    d. a falling MRP equals a constant wage rate.

3. A firm that is a perfect competitor in all markets finds that its MRP for labor falls because as it hires more labor
    a. the marginal physical product of labor falls.
    b. the price of output falls as output increases.
    c. Both of the above
    d. None of the above

4. The marginal factor cost of labor
    a. equals the going wage rate to a competitive firm.
    b. equals the change in wage rates divided by the change in labor.
    c. rises for the competitive firm.
    d. equals the change in total cost divided by the change in wage rates.

5. The demand for labor
    a. is a derived demand.
    b. shifts as selling price of the good produced changes.
    c. shifts to the right if labor productivity increases.
    d. All of the above

6. Which of the following will **NOT** lead to a relatively high price elasticity of demand for labor?
    a. high price elasticity of demand for the final product
    b. no good substitutes for the labor skill in question
    c. high ratio of labor to total costs
    d. a very long period of time after the wage change

7. The supply of labor
    a. to a perfect competitor is positively sloped.
    b. for the entire industry is perfectly elastic.
    c. is positively sloped for the industry.
    d. depends on labor's marginal physical product.

8. Efficiency wages
   a. are greater than MRP.
   b. are profitable for employers.
   c. reduce turnover costs, attract higher quality workers, and encourage workers to be more productive.
   d. all of the above

9. The insider-outsider theory maintains that
   a. outsider competition reduces insider wages.
   b. insiders set up entry barriers to outsiders.
   c. insiders earn wage rates below equilibrium.
   d. employers are altruistic.

10. Which of the following will **NOT** lead to an increase in the demand for labor?
    a. price of labor falls
    b. increase in the productivity of labor
    c. increase in the price of a labor substitute input
    d. increase in the demand for the final product

11. If firm B is a competitor in the labor market and a monopolist in the product market, then
    a. its demand for labor is negatively sloped.
    b. its supply of labor is positively sloped.
    c. its selling price is a constant.
    d. its wage rates rise as it hires more labor.

12. If firm B is a competitor in the labor market and a monopolist in the product market, then
    a. its supply of labor curve is perfectly elastic at the going wage rate.
    b. it hires labor up to the point where MRP of labor equals the going wage rate.
    c. its MRP curve falls because the marginal product of labor falls and its selling price falls.
    d. All of the above

13. The monopolist in the product market finds that its MRP for labor falls as it hires labor because
    a. the MPP of labor falls and output price is constant.
    b. the MPP of labor falls and output price falls.
    c. the MPP of labor is constant and output price falls.
    d. the MPP of labor rises but output price falls faster.

14. If a perfectly competitive market is suddenly monopolized, the amount of labor hired will
    a. remain constant.
    b. fall.
    c. rise.
    d. fall in the short run, rise in the long run.

15. If a firm hires two variable inputs, A and B, it is minimizing costs when
    a. MPP of A/price of A = MPP of B/price of B.
    b. MPP of A/price of B = MPP of B/price of A.
    c. MRP of A/MPP of B = MRP of B/MPP of A.
    d. MRP of A/price of B = MRP of B/price of A.

MATCHING

Choose the item in column (2) that best matches an item in column (1).

(1)

a. MPP
b. MPP × MR
c. MPP × price
d. least cost combination
e. derived demand
f. wage rate above MRP

(2)

g. insider-outsider theory
h. MRP of competitive firm
i. MRP of monopolistic firm
j. labor demand curve
k. change in output for a unit input change
l. equate MPP/price of all factor inputs

WORKING WITH GRAPHS

1. Analyze the diagram below, then answer the questions that follow. Assume that a union bargains for a wage rate equal to $22.50 per hour.

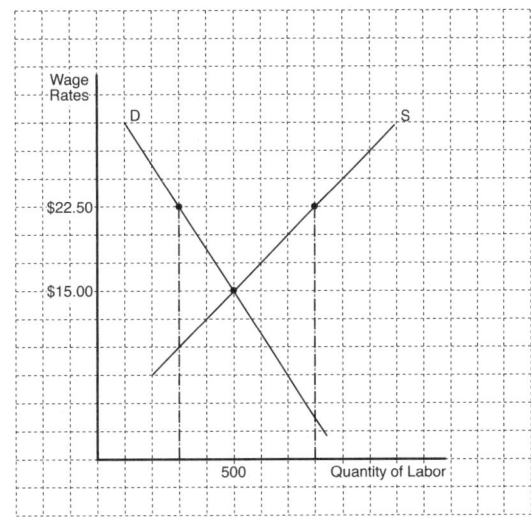

a. What is the equilibrium wage rate in this market?

b. What is the quantity supplied of labor at the wage rate negotiated by the union?

c. What is the quantity demanded for labor at the union-negotiated wage rate?

d. What market situation exists at the union-negotiated wage rate?

e. How many workers were laid off, due to the union-negotiated wage rate?

f. How many workers entered the labor force, seeking a job, due to the union-negotiated wage rate?

g. Are workers in this industry better off or worse off as a result of this union-negotiated wage?

h. Which workers are more likely to be laid off?

PROBLEMS

1. In the following table you are given information about a firm operating in a competitive market. Consider all factors of production fixed at the moment, with the exception of labor services. The other factors of production cost the firm $50 per day, which may be thought of as a fixed cost. Assume that the firm maximizes economic profits.

Labor input (workers per day)	Total physical product (units per day)	Marginal physical product (units per day)	Marginal revenue product ($ per worker)
0	0		
1	22	_____	_____
2	40	_____	_____
3	56	_____	_____
4	70	_____	_____
5	82	_____	_____
6	92	_____	_____
7	100	_____	_____
8	106	_____	_____

   a. Assume that the firm sells its output at $3 per unit. Complete the last two columns in the table above.

   b. If the going market wage is $36 per day, the firm will hire _____ workers per day and produce _____ units of output.

   c. Given your answer to part b, the firm will have total revenues of _____ per day and total costs of _____ per day.

   d. The above will result in a (profit, loss) of _____ per day.

2. Suppose you work for a firm that sells its output in a monopoly market. Answer the following questions.

   a. If you hire an additional worker, output goes up by 50 units to 125 units per day. If you wish to sell the additional 50 units, you must lower your price from $3 per unit to $2 per unit. What is the maximum wage you would be willing to pay the additional worker?

   b. Assume you hired the worker from part a and output now stands at 125 units per day. If another worker is hired, output rises to 165 units per day. Given the demand curve for your product, you know that in order to sell the additional output, price will have to be dropped from $2 per unit to $1 per unit. What is the maximum wage you would be willing to pay this additional worker?

ANSWERS TO CHAPTER 28

COMPLETION QUESTIONS

1. marginal physical product; price
2. marginal physical product; diminishing returns
3. wage rate; remains constant; taker
4. MRP of labor; wage rate; total profits
5. derived; right; negatively
6. price elasticity of demand for final good; ease with which other inputs can substitute for this input; proportion of total costs accounted for by the input in question; length of time period being considered
7. perfectly; horizontal; positively
8. efficiency; try to reduce turnover costs; attempt to attract higher quality labor; encourage existing workers to work harder in order to keep their jobs.
9. demand for final good; labor productivity; price of related factors; wage rate in other industries; nonmoney job aspects
10. marginal physical product of labor; MR; marginal physical product; diminishing returns; MR; price; MRP; the wage rate
11. the ratio of MRP to price of factor is equated for all factors; the ratio of marginal physical product to factor price for all factors.
12. more; termination wages; litigation expenses.

TRUE-FALSE QUESTIONS

1. F Its demand for labor curve is negatively sloped.
2. T
3. F It declines due to the law of diminishing returns.
4. F If wage rates change, we move along a given labor demand curve.
5. F It will be lower.
6. T
7. F Employers may find it profitable to offer efficiency wages because they could reduce turnover costs, among other things.
8. T
9. T
10. F Fewer workers will be hired, because output falls.
11. T
12. F Insiders can reduce outsider competition by increasing entry barriers.

MULTIPLE CHOICE QUESTIONS

1.c; 2.d; 3.a; 4.a; 5.d; 6.b; 7.c; 8.d; 9.b; 10.a;
11.a; 12.d; 13.b; 14.b; 15.a.

MATCHING

a and k; b and i; c and h; d and l; e and j; f and g.

WORKING WITH GRAPHS

1. a. $15.00
   b. 800
   c. 300
   d. surplus, or excess quantity supplied of labor

e. 200
f. 300
g. Those who kept their jobs are better off; those who became unemployed are worse off. Group income fell from $7,500 to $6,750.
h. younger, lower income—lower productivity workers.

PROBLEMS

1. a. MPP: 22, 18, 16, 14, 12, 10, 8, 6
      MRP: 66, 54, 48, 42, 36, 30, 24, 18
   b. 5, 82
   c. $246, (5 × $36) + $50 = $230
   d. profit, $16

2. a. $25 per day since MRP = $25
   b. A negative wage, because the price decrease necessary to sell the additional output causes total revenues to decline (MR < 0), MRP for this worker is negative, and the firm must be paid to hire another unit of labor.

GLOSSARY TO CHAPTER 28

Derived demand Input factor demand derived from demand for the final product being produced.

Efficiency wages Wages set above competitive wages to increase labor productivity and profits by enhancing the efficiency of the firm through lower turnover, ease of attracting higher-quality workers, and better on-the-job efforts by workers.

Insider-outsider theory A theory of labor markets in which workers who are already employed have an influence on wage bargaining in such a way that outsiders who are willing to work for lower real wages cannot get a job.

Marginal factor cost (MFC) The cost of using an additional unit of an input. For example, if a firm can hire all the workers it wants at the going wage rate, the marginal factor cost of labor is the wage rate.

Marginal physical product (MPP) of labor The change in output resulting from the addition of one more worker. The MPP of the worker equals the change in total output accounted for by hiring the worker, holding all other factors of production constant.

Marginal revenue product (MRP) The marginal physical product (MPP) times marginal revenue (MR). The MRP gives the additional revenue obtained from a one-unit change in labor input.

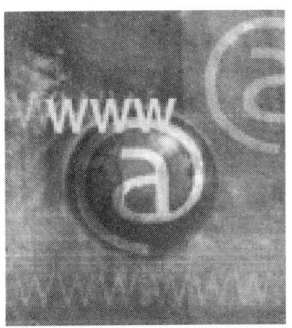

CHAPTER 29
UNIONS AND LABOR MARKET MONOPOLY POWER

LEARNING OBJECTIVES

After you have studied this chapter, you should be able to

1. define labor unions, craft unions, collective bargaining, industrial unions, right-to-work laws, closed shop, union shop, jurisdictional dispute, sympathy strike, secondary boycott, featherbedding, monopsonist, monopsonistic exploitation, strikebreakers, and bilateral monopoly;

2. identify the key provisions of major legislation dealing with unions;

3. distinguish between craft unions and industrial unions;

4. list three possible union goals and predict the quantity of labor that will be employed under each union strategy;

5. show how unions can redistribute income from low-seniority to high-seniority workers;

6. predict the quantity of labor hired and the wage rate that will result, given a market structure in which a firm is a perfect competitor in the product market and a monopsonist in the labor market;

7. predict the quantity of labor hired and the wage rate that will result, given a firm that is a monopolist in the product market and a monopsonist in the labor market.

CHAPTER OUTLINE

1. Unions are workers' organizations that usually seek to secure economic improvements for their members.
   a. The U.S. labor movement started with craft unions, which are composed of workers who engage in a particular skill or trade.
   b. The American Federation of Labor (AFL), a craft union, was formed by Samuel Gompers in 1886; its membership growth flourished until World War I, when government withdrew its support.

c. The Great Depression brought the National Recovery Act in 1933, which attempted to raise wages to predepression levels; its key provision was to guarantee the right of labor to bargain collectively.
d. The Wagner Act also guaranteed collective bargaining and granted workers the right to form unions.
e. In 1938 John L. Lewis formed the Congress of Industrial Organizations (CIO), which was composed of industrial unions, that is, unions with membership from an entire industry.
f. The Taft-Hartley Act was enacted to stem union power; it allows individual states to pass right-to-work laws, which make illegal the requirement of union membership for continued employment. It also bans the closed shop everywhere and the union shop in states with right-to-work laws, and outlaws jurisdictional disputes, sympathy strikes, and secondary boycotts.
g. The percentage of the labor force that is unionized has fallen because of the higher percentage of women who are in the labor force, persistent illegal immigration, and the increasing number of white collar workers in the service sector relative to the number of blue collar manufacturing workers.

2. Unions can be analyzed as setters of minimum wages; the strike is the ultimate bargaining tool for unions.

3. It is not clear what unions wish to maximize. Unions can either set wage rates or select the quantity of its membership that will be employed; they can't do both.
   a. To the extent that unions set wage rates above equilibrium, they create a surplus of labor, or a shortage of jobs that they ration.
   b. If unions wish to employ all members, they must accept a relatively low wage rate.
   c. If unions wish to maximize total wages, they set wage rates at the point at which the price elasticity of demand equals 1; some members will be unemployed.
   d. If unions maximize wage rates for a given number of workers—presumably high-seniority workers—low-seniority workers will become unemployed because wage rates probably will be set above equilibrium.
   e. One union strategy is to limit total union membership to the original quantity; over time, if demand increases, wage rates will rise.
   f. Unions can raise wage rates for members by (a) limiting membership, and (b) increasing union labor productivity, thereby increasing the demand for union labor relative to nonunion labor.

4. It is not apparent that unions have raised *overall* wage rates; on average, unions redistribute income within unions from low- to high-seniority workers.

5. Recent studies indicate that unions can both (a) act as monopolies that redistribute income from low-seniority to high-seniority members and (b) increase labor productivity.

6. Consider a firm that is a perfect competitor in the product market and a monopsonist in the labor market.
   a. That firm faces an upward-sloping supply of labor curve; before it can hire more labor it must raise wage rates for *all* of its employees.
   b. As a consequence, the marginal factor cost of hiring labor to that firm exceeds the wage rate; the MFC curve is that firm's additional cost of hiring labor, and it rises as the firm hires more labor.
   c. The marginal benefit of hiring labor to such a firm is its MRP curve, which falls (due to declining marginal product of labor) as it hires more labor.
   d. The profit-maximizing employment level occurs at the point at which the decreasing MRP curve intersects the rising MFC curve; the wage rate is set on the supply curve, consistent with that quantity of labor.

e. In such a situation, monopsonistic exploitation of labor results because the wage rate is below the MRP of labor.

7. A summary of monopoly, monopsony, and perfectly competitive situations is presented in Figure 29-8.

KEY TERMS
Craft unions
Collective bargaining
Right-to-work laws
Jurisdictional dispute
Monopsonist
Labor unions
Strikebreakers
Industrial unions

KEY CONCEPTS
Featherbedding
Closed shop
Monopsonistic exploitation
Union shop
Sympathy strike
Marginal factor cost (MFC)
Bilateral monopoly
Secondary boycott

COMPLETION QUESTIONS
Fill in the blank, or circle the correct term.

1. The U.S. labor movement started with local _____ unions, which are comprised of workers in a particular _____; the other major type of union is the _____ union, which consists of workers from a particular _____

2. The Great Depression generated legislation that (helped, hurt) the union movement.

3. The Taft-Hartley Act of 1947 (is, is not) considered pro–labor union; it allows states to pass _____ laws. The act makes illegal the following union practices: _____, _____, _____ strikes, and _____ boycotts.

4. The original craft unions were the _____.

5. The ultimate bargaining tool for the union is the _____.

6. If a union sets wage rates above market clearing levels, it creates a(n) _____ of labor; viewed alternatively, it creates a(n) _____ of jobs, which it must then ration to workers.

7. If a union chooses to employ all of its members, it (must, need not) accept a lower wage rate; if the union wants to maximize the value of total wages, it sets the wage rate at the point at which the price elasticity of demand for labor equals the number _____; if the union wants to set relatively high wages for its high-seniority members, its _____ members will be laid off.

8. Assume that a firm is a perfect competitor in the product market and a monopsonist in the labor market. The marginal benefit of hiring labor for such a firm is its _____ curve, which is (horizontal, negatively sloped, positively sloped), due to the law of _____; the marginal cost of hiring labor for such a firm is its _____ curve, which is (horizontal, positively sloped, negatively sloped). The firm's MFC curve rises because as it hires more labor, wage rates (fall, rise, remain constant) since the industry supply

of labor curve is _____ sloping; the firm's MFC is (equal to, greater than, less than) the wage rate.

9. Assume a firm is a monopolist in the product market and a monopsonist in the labor market. The marginal benefit of hiring labor for that firm is its _____ curve, which falls due to _____ and _____ as output increases. The marginal cost of hiring labor is that firm's _____ curve, which rises because in order to hire more labor, that firm must _____ wage rates of _____ employees; this is because the firm's supply of labor curve is _____ sloping.

10. A firm maximizes total profits by hiring labor up to the point at which the marginal benefit (exceeds, equals, is less than) the marginal cost from doing so. Suppose Firm A is a perfect competitor in the product market and a monopsonist in the labor market. Firm A will hire labor up to the point at which a downward-sloping _____ curve intersects an upward-sloping _____ curve; given that quantity of labor, the wage rate will be set at that level consistent with the (supply, demand) curve of labor.

11. Firm B is a monopolist in the product market and a monopsonist in the labor market. If it wants to maximize total profits, it will hire labor up to the point at which a downward-sloping _____ curve intersects an upward-sloping _____ curve.

12. When a resource is paid less than its _____, monopsonistic exploitation exists.

TRUE-FALSE QUESTIONS
Circle the T if the statement is true, the F if it is false. Explain to yourself why a statement is false.

T F 1. The growth rate of unions and the extent to which unions are effective has depended on government support.

T F 2. The Wagner Act increases union power, but the Taft-Hartley Act reduces it.

T F 3. Union power was decreased during the Great Depression.

T F 4. In recent years, public employee union membership has increased significantly.

T F 5. Unions tend to create a shortage of labor and a surplus of jobs.

T F 6. In the United States, unions can set wage rates or determine the quantity of labor hired, but they can't do both.

T F 7. If a union wants to maximize the value of total wages, it sets wage rates as high as it possibly can.

T F 8. If a union can restrict the total quantity of laborers to a fixed number, its members will earn higher wages in the future.

T F 9. Recent studies indicate that unions do not increase labor's productivity.

T F 10. A profit-maximizing firm that is a perfect competitor in the product market but a monopsonist in the labor market will hire labor up to the point at which MRP of labor equals the going wage rate.

T F 11. A firm that is a monopolist in the product market and a monopsonist in the labor market maximizes total profit by hiring labor up to the point at which the MRP of labor equals the MFC of labor.

T F 12. Monopsonistic exploitation exists when workers receive a wage below their MRP.

MULTIPLE CHOICE QUESTIONS
Circle the letter that corresponds to the best answer.

1. Which of the following is **NOT** associated with a craft union?
   a. United Auto Workers
   b. AFL
   c. Knights of Labor
   d. Pipefitters Union

2. Which of the following acts is **NOT** pro–labor union?
   a. National Industrial Recovery Act
   b. Wagner Act
   c. Taft-Hartley Act
   d. National Labor Relations Act

3. Which of the following is legal in **NON**-right-to-work states?
   a. closed shop
   b. union shop
   c. sympathy strike
   d. secondary boycott

4. Which of the following is true about the union movement?
   a. The growth and effectiveness of unions depends in part on the extent of government help.
   b. Since 1968 private-employee union membership has risen.
   c. Since 1968 public-employee union membership has fallen dramatically.
   d. All of the above

5. Unions tend to
   a. set minimum wages for members above the market clearing level.
   b. create unemployment for low-seniority members.
   c. create surpluses of labor and shortages of union jobs.
   d. All of the above

6. If a union sets wage rates above market clearing levels, then
   a. jobs must be rationed among union members.
   b. a surplus of jobs is created.
   c. a shortage of labor is created.
   d. high-seniority members will complain.

7. Which of the following is inconsistent with the others?
   a. surplus of labor
   b. shortage of jobs
   c. wage rate above the market clearing level
   d. wage rate below the market clearing level

8. If unions want to maximize the value of total wages, they set wage rates
   a. as high as they can.
   b. as low as they can.
   c. at the point at which the price elasticity of demand for labor equals 1.
   d. in the inelastic range of the product demand curve.

9. If unions maximize the wage rate of high-seniority workers, then
   a. low-seniority workers will become laid off.
   b. all union members will remain employed.
   c. they violate the Wagner Act.
   d. they violate the Taft-Hartley Act.

10. Which of the following statements probably best describes the impact of unions on wage rates?
    a. Unions have increased all wage rates in the economy.
    b. Unions have increased all union worker wage rates.
    c. Unions increase the wage rates of some workers at the expense of other workers.
    d. Unions cannot raise wage rates for their members.

11. Unions
    a. can set wage rates but not employment levels.
    b. can set wage rates and employment levels.
    c. can set neither wage rates nor employment levels.
    d. can set either wage rates or employment levels, but not both.

12. If Firm B is a monopsonist in the labor market and a perfect competitor in the product market, then
    a. it faces a horizontal supply of labor curve.
    b. it faces a horizontal demand for labor curve.
    c. its wage rate equals its MFC.
    d. its marginal benefit from hiring labor equals the MRP of labor.

13. Firm B, in the previous question (No. 12), can maximize total profits by hiring labor up to the point at which
    a. a decreasing MRP of labor curve intersects a decreasing MFC of labor curve.
    b. a decreasing MRP of labor curve intersects a rising MFC of labor curve.
    c. a decreasing MRP of labor curve intersects a horizontal supply of labor curve, at the going wage rate.
    d. a horizontal MRP of labor curve is intersected by a rising MFC of labor curve.

14. Firm B, in questions 12 and 13, faces
    a. a rising MFC of labor.
    b. a declining labor MRP.
    c. an upward-sloping supply of labor curve.
    d. All of the above

15. If Firm A is a monopolist in the product market and a monopsonist in the labor market, then
    a. it faces a horizontal labor supply and a horizontal labor demand curve.
    b. it faces a downward-sloping supply of labor curve.
    c. the marginal revenue product of labor falls and the marginal factor cost of labor rises.
    d. the marginal revenue product of labor is constant and the marginal factor cost of labor rises.

16. Firm A, in the previous question (No. 15), can maximize total profits by hiring labor up to the point at which
    a. a downward-sloping MRP of labor curve intersects an upward-sloping MFC of labor curve.
    b. an-upward sloping MRP of labor equals a constant wage rate.
    c. a constant MRP of labor curve equals a falling MFC of labor.
    d. a horizontal MRP of labor curve is intersected by a rising supply of labor curve.

17. Firm A in question 17
    a. observes a MFC that exceeds the wage rate.
    b. observes a selling price that exceeds the marginal revenue of an extra unit of output.
    c. maximizes profits by hiring to the point at which MRP of labor = MFC of labor.
    d. All of the above

18. Which of the following is probably an example of monopsony exploitation, as defined in this text?
    a. A low-skilled laborer is paid $1 per hour in a competitive labor market.
    b. A professional athlete gets paid $1 million per year but his MRP is $1.5 million per year.
    c. Mr. Smith can earn $35,000 per year as a plumber but chooses to work as a high school teacher for $20,000 per year.
    d. Mrs. Calvo has a Ph.D. in English, but only earns $10,000 per semester teaching university English because there are so many qualified teachers in that area.

19. Monopsonistic exploitation equals
    a. marginal physical product of labor minus the wage rate.
    b. marginal revenue product of labor minus the wage rate.
    c. marginal physical product of labor minus marginal revenue product of labor.
    d. marginal factor cost of labor minus marginal physical product.

WORKING WITH GRAPHS

1. Suppose you are given the following graphical representation for a monopsonist selling its output in a competitive market. Answer the following questions.

   a. Given the market conditions that exist in the above graph, the monopsonist will hire _____ workers per day at a wage of _____ per hour.

   b. Suppose that the government (or a labor union) initiates a minimum wage of $12.50 per hour in this particular market. As a result, the monopsonist will (increase, decrease) its employment rate to _____ workers per day at a wage of _____ per hour.

2. Use the graph below to answer the following questions. Note: define monopolistic exploitation as being equal to the difference between VMP (or price times the marginal product of labor) and MRP—as defined in the text. (Note: VMP is not defined in your text; therefore this is a difficult question. It is purely optional.)

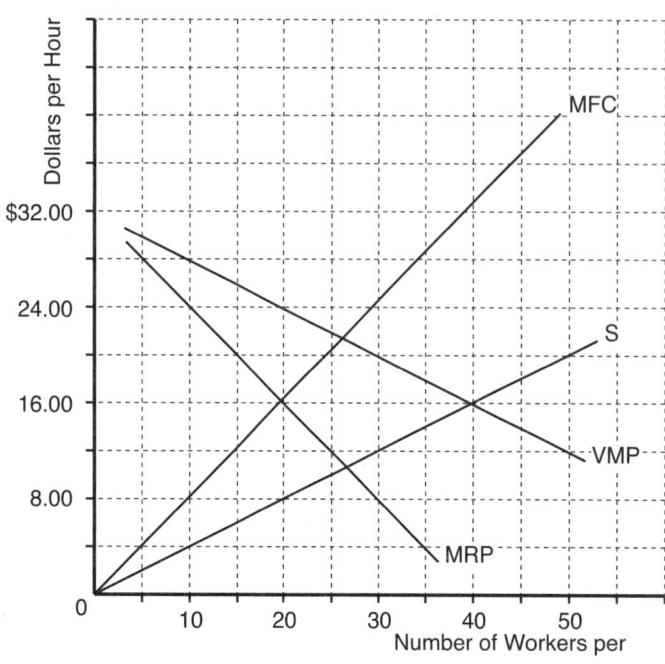

a. This monopolist-monopsonist will hire _____ workers per day and pay a wage of _____ per hour.

b. At this rate of employment, the value of marginal product of labor (VMP) is _____ per hour.

c. With no outside intervention in this market, we will observe (monopsonistic, monopolistic, both monopsonistic and monopolistic) exploitation.

d. The level of monopsonistic exploitation is _____ per hour, and the level of monopolistic exploitation is _____ per hour.

e. The total level of exploitation is _____ per hour, represented by the difference between the _____ and the _____.

ANSWERS TO CHAPTER 29

COMPLETION QUESTIONS

1. craft; skill or trade; industrial; industry
2. helped
3. is not; right-to-work; closed shop (union shop in right-to-work states); jurisdictional disputes; sympathy; secondary
4. European merchant guilds
5. strike
6. surplus; shortage
7. must; 1; low-seniority
8. MRP of labor; negatively sloped; diminishing returns; MFC of labor; positively sloped; rise; upward; greater than
9. MRP of labor; diminishing marginal physical product of labor; decreasing product price; MFC of labor; raise; all; upward
10. equals; MRP of labor; MFC of labor; supply
11. MRP of labor; MFC of labor
12. marginal revenue product

TRUE-FALSE QUESTIONS

1. T
2. T
3. F   It was increased by President Roosevelt.
4. T
5. F   They create a surplus of labor and a shortage of jobs.
6. T
7. F   It set the wage rate at the point at which the price elasticity of demand equals 1.
8. F   Not necessarily; demand may fall dramatically.
9. F   They may increase productivity by creating a safer and more secure environment.
10. F   It hires up to the point at which MRP = MFC of labor.
11. T
12. T

MULTIPLE CHOICE QUESTIONS

1.a; 2.c; 3.b; 4.a; 5.d; 6.a; 7.d; 8.c; 9.a; 10.c;
11.d; 12.d; 13.b; 14.d; 15.c; 16.a; 17.d; 18.b; 19.b.

WORKING WITH GRAPHS

1. a. 20, $10; b. increase, 25, $12.50
2. a. 20, $8; b. $24; c. both monopsonistic and monopolistic; d. $8, $8;
   e. $16, VMP of $24 per hour, wage of $8 per hour

GLOSSARY FOR CHAPTER 29

Bilateral monopoly A market structure consisting of a monopolist and a monopsonist.

Closed shop A business enterprise in which employees must belong to the union before they can be employed and must remain in the union after they are hired.

Collective bargaining Bargaining between the management of a company or of a group of companies and the management of a union or a group of unions for the purpose of setting a mutually agreeable contract on wages, fringe benefits, and working conditions for all employees in the unions involved.

Craft unions Labor unions composed of workers who engage in a particular trade or skill, such as baking, carpentry, or plumbing.

Featherbedding Any practice that forces employers to use more labor than they would otherwise or to use existing labor in an inefficient manner.

Industrial unions Labor unions that consist of workers from a particular industry, such as automobile manufacturing or steel manufacturing.

Jurisdictional dispute A dispute involving two or more unions over which should have control of a particular jurisdiction, such as over a particular craft or skill or over a particular firm or industry.

Labor unions Workers' organizations that usually seek to secure economic improvements for their members; they also seek to improve the safety, health, and other benefits (such as job security) of their members.

Monopsonist The only buyer in a market.

Monopsonistic exploitation Paying a price for the variable input that is less than its marginal revenue product; the difference between marginal revenue product and the wage rate.

Right-to-work laws Laws that make it illegal to require union membership as a condition of continuing employment in a particular firm.

Secondary boycott A boycott of companies or products sold by companies that are dealing with a company being struck.

Strikebreakers Temporary or permanent workers hired by a company to replace union members who are striking.

Sympathy strike A strike by a union in sympathy with another union's strike or cause.

Union shop A business enterprise that allows the hiring of nonunion members, conditional on their joining the union by some specified date after employment begins.

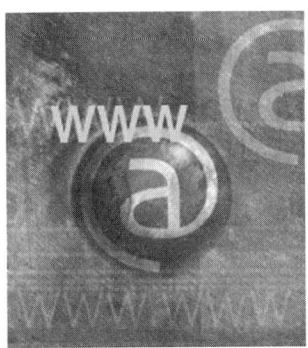

CHAPTER 30
INCOME, POVERTY, AND HEALTH CARE

LEARNING OBJECTIVES

After you have studied this chapter, you should be able to

1. define distribution of income, Lorenz curve, income in kind, comparable-worth doctrine, age-earnings cycle, third parties, and medical savings accounts (MSAs);

2. list criticisms of using the Lorenz curve as an indicator of the degree of income inequality in a country;

3. distinguish between income and wealth;

4. recognize facts concerning income distribution and poverty in the United States;

5. list three determinants of income differences;

6. list two normative standards of income distribution and distinguish between them;

7. describe the situation of poverty in the U.S.;

8. list ways poverty is reduced in the U.S.;

9. relate third-party payment systems to the moral hazard problem;

10. enumerate costs associated with forcing more income equality in a nation;

11. enumerate three reasons that explain why medical costs have risen rapidly in the U.S;

12. list benefits and costs to using medical savings accounts to counter the moral hazard problem in the health care industry.

CHAPTER 30: INCOME, POVERTY, AND HEALTH CARE

CHAPTER OUTLINE

1. This chapter attempts to define distribution of income and present theories of why income is unevenly distributed across the population.

2. The Lorenz curve is a geometric representation of the distribution of income.
   a. There are some criticisms of using the Lorenz curve to measure the degree of income inequality in a nation.
      i. The curve does not take into account income in kind.
      ii. It does not account for differences in family size and effort.
      iii. It does not account for age differences.
      iv. It measures pretax money income.
      v. It does not measure underground economy earnings.
   b. Since World War II the distribution of money income in the United States has not changed very much.
   c. The distribution of total income, which includes in-kind transfers, has become more equal in the U.S. since 1962.

3. Wealth and income are not synonymous.
   a. Wealth is a stock concept, and income is a flow concept.
   b. A stock is evaluated at a given moment in time; a flow is evaluated during a period of time.
   c. Each of us inherits a different endowment, including human attributes and nonhuman wealth, which strongly affects our ability to earn income in the marketplace.

4. There are numerous determinants of income differences.
   a. The wage-earnings cycle typically shows that at a young age income is low; it builds gradually to a peak at around age 50, and then gradually curves down until it approaches zero at retirement age.
   b. In competitive markets, workers can expect to earn, approximately, their marginal revenue product (MRP).
   c. Determinants of an individual's marginal productivity include innate abilities and attributes, experience, and training.

5. Inheritance is also a determinant of income differences.

6. Discrimination undoubtedly contributes somewhat to income differences.
   a. White families earn higher median incomes than black families.
   b. Males earn higher median incomes than females.

7. The comparable-worth doctrine contends that females (or minorities) should receive the same wages as males if the levels of skills and responsibility in their different jobs are equal. Skill and responsibility levels, in practice, are difficult to define and arbitrariness inevitably results in setting such wage rates.

8. There are normative standards of income distribution: equality and productivity.

9. Western nations have sustained enough economic growth over the last several hundred years so that mass poverty has disappeared.

10. If poverty is measured in absolute terms, it will be eliminated by economic growth. If poverty is defined in relative terms, it will be mathematically impossible to eliminate it, unless everyone has the same income—an improbable event. If we correct poverty rates for in-kind transfers, they fall dramatically in the United States.

11. There is a variety of income-maintenance programs designed to help the poor: They include social insurance, Supplemental Security Income, Temporary Assistance to Needy Families, food stamps, and the Earned Income Tax Credit program.

12. In spite of the numerous programs designed to reduce poverty, officially defined poverty rates have shown no long-run tendency to drop since their relatively dramatic decline through 1973.

13. In recent years the price of health care services and health care insurance have increased dramatically in the United States; U.S. citizens have been spending higher and higher percentages of their income on health care.

14. There are several explanations as to why health care costs have risen rapidly in the United States.
    a. Our population is, on average, getting older and the elderly are the main users of health care.
    b. Technological advances in medicine have spawned expensive machinery that everyone wants to use (both suppliers and demanders).
    c. The third-party payment system has created a situation in which physicians and hospitals have no incentive to keep health care costs down.
        i. Because health care is subsidized by government, people want more than they would otherwise; thus, a moral hazard exists.
        ii. Both government and private-provided health care insurance create a situation in which third parties (insurers) pay most of the costs of medical services; hence people want more health care than if they were paying for it themselves.

15. There have been numerous suggestions for altering the U.S. health care system.
    a. Some have suggested a national health care plan to replace the private insurance system that the U.S. has; an essential ingredient of such a system is price ceilings on physicians' fees and hospital costs.
    b. Others have suggested a national health insurance plan which, presumably, would be offered only to lower-income groups.
    c. A recent suggestion is the medical savings account, in which people save money in tax-exempt accounts on which they can draw to pay for health care; what is not spent belongs to the individual.

KEY TERMS
Lorenz curve

KEY CONCEPTS
Distribution of income
Age-earnings cycle
Comparable-worth doctrine
Income in kind
Third parties
Medical savings accounts (MSAs)

COMPLETION QUESTIONS
Fill in the blank, or circle the correct term.

1. A Lorenz curve shows what portion of total money income is accounted for by different _____ of a nation's households; if it is a 45 degree line, then _____ income inequality exists.

2. The Lorenz curve as a representation of income inequality has been criticized because it does not _____, or account for _____, _____, _____, and _____.

3. Since World War II, the lowest 20 percent of the income distribution in the United States had a combined money income of _____ percent of the total money income of the entire population; however, if income in kind is taken into account, income inequality has (decreased, increased) relative to the period immediately following World War II.

4. (Wealth, Income) is a stock concept, while _____ is a flow concept.

5. One determinant of income inequality is age; the age-earnings cycle indicates that teenagers' incomes are relatively (low, high). Incomes rise gradually to a peak at around age _____, and then gradually fall toward zero as people approach _____. People earn different amounts over their lifetime because age is related to a worker's _____.

6. If a worker's MRP exceeds her wage rate, chances are that she will (change jobs, be laid off); if a worker's wage rate is greater than her MRP, then chances are she will be _____. As long as it is costly to obtain information about a specific worker's MRP, there (will, will not) be some difference between a worker's wage and her MRP.

7. Four determinants of an individual's marginal productivity are _____, _____, and _____; other than differences in marginal productivity, income differences are also due to _____ and _____.

8. Two theories of normative standards of income distribution are _____ and _____.

9. (Absolute, Relative) poverty will automatically be eliminated by economic growth, but _____ poverty can never be eliminated, in practice.

10. In the United States there are several income-maintenance programs aimed at eliminating poverty. The best known is _____ Security, which in effect is an intergenerational income transfer; another is SSI, which establishes a nationwide _____ income for the aged, the blind, and the disabled; the TANF program is for families who are _____ in need.

11. In the United States since 1973 there (has, has not) been a long-run trend toward reduced officially defined poverty.

12. Many economists believe that the major cost to increased income equality is _____; hence a trade-off exists.

13. In recent years the percent of total income spent on medical care has (decreased, increased) dramatically because (1) our population, on average, is getting (younger, older), (2) technological advances in medical equipment have caused (a decrease, an increase) in the demand for medical services, (3) third-party billing has (decreased, increased) due to health insurance, and (4) physicians and hospitals have (few, strong) incentives to keep costs down.

14. Most national health care plans incorporate a system to put a (floor, ceiling) on medical fees and services; this will create (surpluses, shortages) eventually.

CHAPTER 30: INCOME, POVERTY, AND HEALTH CARE

TRUE-FALSE QUESTIONS

Circle the T if the statement is true, the F if it false. Explain to yourself why a statement is false.

T F 1. In the real world, no country has a linear (straight-line) Lorenz curve.

T F 2. Third-party paying avoids the moral hazard problem that exists in the health care system.

T F 3. When in-kind transfers are considered, measured income inequality in the U.S. rises and poverty levels fall.

T F 4. Not considering income-in-kind, the bottom 20 percent of U.S. income earners earn about 5% of total U.S. income.

T F 5. Income and wealth are unrelated.

T F 6. The comparable-worth doctrine accepts the notion that workers should be paid their MRP, as determined by markets.

T F 7. In the United States, over time, income inequality has increased dramatically.

T F 8. An age-earnings cycle exists because age and marginal productivity are related.

T F 9. In a competitive economy, workers tend to get paid their marginal revenue product.

T F 10. In the United States, inheritance and discrimination are more important determinants of income differences than are marginal productivity differences.

T F 11. In the United States the return to investment in human capital is significantly higher than it is for other investments.

T F 12. Mass poverty is still a problem for even the advanced Western economies.

T F 13. Economic growth will eventually eliminate relative poverty.

T F 14. Despite massive sums of money devoted to income redistribution programs in the United States, officially measured poverty has remained roughly unchanged since 1973.

T F 15. All economists agree that more income equality in the United States is desirable.

T F 16. Because health care is usually paid for by third parties, buyers are largely insensitive to price increases.

T F 17. Physicians and hospitals, like other service providers, have an incentive to keep costs down.

T F 18. Medical savings accounts can help to avoid the moral hazard problem.

MULTIPLE CHOICE QUESTIONS
Circle the letter that corresponds to the best answer.

1. The Lorenz curve
    a. gives a numerical measure of a nation's degree of income inequality.
    b. is a straight line in modern, industrial societies.
    c. is a straight line in socialist countries.
    d. overstates the true degree of income inequality, as it is currently measured.

2. Which of the following states about the Lorenz curve is correct?
    a. It accounts for age differences.
    b. It considers income-in-kind transfers.
    c. It considers pretax income.
    d. It considers income earned in the underground economy.

3. In 2002, in the United States, the lowest 20 percent of income earning families had a combined income of about _____ percent of the total money income of the entire population.
    a. 5
    b. 10
    c. 15
    d. 20

4. Which of the following statements is **FALSE**?
    a. The U.S. population, on average, is getting older.
    b. Technological advances in medicine have reduced health care costs.
    c. Much of health care is subsidized by governments.
    d. Most health care is paid for by third parties.

5. Analogy: Income is to flow as _____ is to stock.
    a. wealth
    b. poverty
    c. consumption
    d. investment

6. Total economic wealth
    a. is a flow concept.
    b. includes human attributes.
    c. excludes nonhuman wealth.
    d. is zero for most people in the United States.

7. In the United States the long-run trend shows
    a. increased poverty.
    b. increased income inequality.
    c. little change in officially measured poverty.
    d. increased poverty once income-in-kind adjustments are made.

8. In the United States, over the age-earnings cycle,
    a. productivity changes.
    b. income peaks at about age 65.
    c. income rises with age, throughout.
    d. income first falls with age, then rises with age.

9. In the United States an age-earnings cycle exists because
   a. age is unrelated to income.
   b. age and income are related by law.
   c. productivity and age are related.
   d. of minimum wage laws.

10. Which of the following is probably the **MOST** important determinant of income differences in the United States?
    a. differences in marginal productivity
    b. inheritance of nonhuman wealth
    c. discrimination
    d. income assistance programs

11. Which is **LEAST** like the others, with respect to productivity?
    a. innate abilities and attributes
    b. experience
    c. education and training
    d. inheritance of nonhuman wealth

12. Medical savings accounts
    a. are currently illegal.
    b. reduce the moral hazard problem.
    c. are likely to increase health care costs.
    d. decrease consumer price elasticity of demand.

13. Which of the following does **NOT** occur with economic growth?
    a. elimination of absolute poverty
    b. elimination of relative poverty
    c. increasing living standards
    d. increasing life expectancy

14. In recent years, in the United States,
    a. health care costs have increased as a percentage of national income.
    b. the population, on average, has been getting younger.
    c. technological discoveries have reduced the cost of medical care.
    d. health care costs have risen, but national income has risen more rapidly.

15. The Earned Income Tax Credit program (EITC) creates
    a. incentives for those taxed to work.
    b. disincentives for its recipients to work.
    c. incentives for its recipients to increase MRP.
    d. neither incentives nor disincentives for anyone to work.

16. We have to worry about greatly increasing Medicare expenditures because
    a. the U.S. population is getting older.
    b. there is a moral hazard issue with respect to Medicare.
    c. Congress keeps adding to eligible expenses for Medicare repayment.
    d. All of the above

17. The optimal amount of income inequality
    a. is zero.
    b. is a positive economics concept.
    c. is a normative economics concept.
    d. is agreed on by all economists.

18. In a nation in which complete income equality has been achieved,
    a. economic incentives would be reduced dramatically.
    b. economic freedom would be curtailed dramatically.
    c. national output and national income would fall dramatically.
    d. All of the above

MATCHING
Choose the item in column (2) that best matches an item in column (1).

(1)	(2)
a. Lorenz curve	g. equal pay for equal work
b. moral hazard	h. inherited traits or MRP
c. comparable-worth doctrine	i. stock
d. determinant of income inequality	j. third-party payments
e. wealth	k. flow
f. income	l. geometric measure of income distribution

WORKING WITH GRAPHS

1. Use the table below and the grid provided to construct a Lorenz curve.

Cumulative percent of population	Cumulative percent of income
20	5
40	10
60	30
80	70
100	100

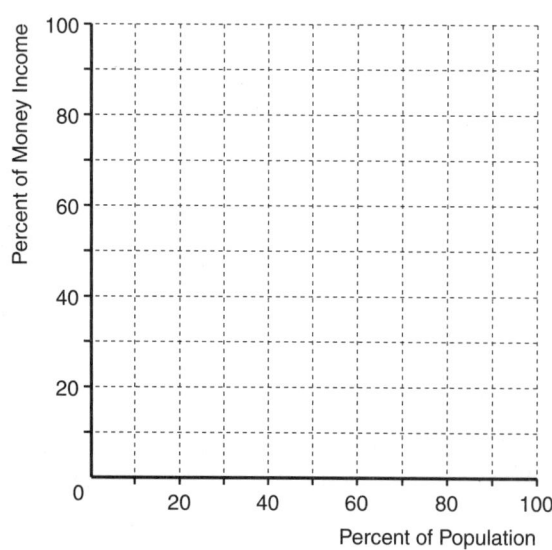

2. Below are income figures for two countries. Plot the Lorenz curve for both countries on the grid provided.

Percent of population	Percent of Income Country A	Country B
20	5	10
40	20	20
60	40	30
80	60	50
100	100	100

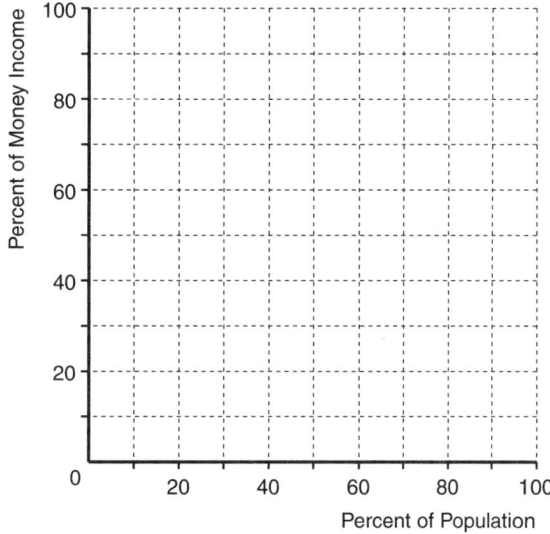

Which of the two countries has the more equal distribution?

PROBLEM

1. In your text you learned that income and wealth are different concepts. But they can be related via the discounting technique that you learned in Chapter 29. How?

ANSWERS TO CHAPTER 30

COMPLETION QUESTIONS

1. proportions; zero
2. include income in kind; differences in family size and effort; age; taxes; underground economy earnings
3. about 5; decreased
4. Wealth; income
5. low; 50; retirement; productivity
6. change jobs; laid off; will
7. age; innate abilities and attributes; experience or training; inheritance; discrimination
8. equality; productivity
9. Absolute; relative
10. Social; minimum; temporarily
11. has not
12. less economic efficiency
13. increased; older; an increase; increased; few
14. ceiling; shortages

TRUE-FALSE QUESTIONS

1. T
2. F Third-party paying causes a moral hazard problem.
3. F Income inequality and poverty both fall.
4. T
5. F The present value of income equals "human" wealth; see the problem section.
6. F It rejects MRP and substitutes an entirely different approach.
7. F It has remained constant, or fallen somewhat.
8. T
9. T
10. F Marginal productivity differences are the most important.
11. F The rate of return is about the same.
12. F Economic growth has eliminated it.
13. F Relative poverty can never be eliminated.
14. T
15. F Many believe it undesirable; almost all recognize its costs.
16. T
17. F No, such a lack of incentive is one reason costs have risen.
18. T

MULTIPLE CHOICE QUESTIONS

1.d; 2.c; 3.a; 4.b; 5.a; 6.b; 7.c; 8.a; 9.c; 10.a;
11.d; 12.b; 13.b; 14.a; 15.b; 16.d; 17.c; 18.d

MATCHING

a and l; b and j; c and g; d and h; e and i; f and k

WORKING WITH GRAPHS

1. See graphs below.

2. See graphs below. Country A has a more equal distribution of income.

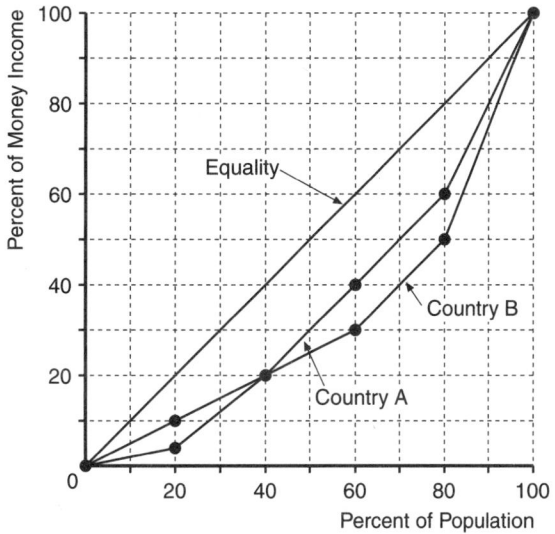

PROBLEMS

1. The value of "human" wealth can be considered as being the present value of the (net) income stream that a person earns over his or her work life.

GLOSSARY TO CHAPTER 30

Age-earnings cycle The regular earnings profile of an individual throughout his or her lifetime. The age-earnings cycle usually starts with a low income, builds gradually to a peak at around age 50, and then gradually curves down until it approaches zero at retirement.

Comparable-worth doctrine The belief that women should receive the same wages as men if the levels of skill and responsibility in their jobs are equivalent.

Distribution of income The way income is allocated among the population.

Income in kind Income received in the form of goods and services, such as housing or medical care; to be contrasted with money income, which is simply income in dollars or general purchasing power that can be used to buy any goods and services.

Lorenz curve A geometric representation of the distribution of income. A Lorenz curve that is perfectly straight represents perfect income equality. The more bowed a Lorenz curve, the more unequally income is distributed.

Medical savings accounts (MSAs) A tax-exempt health care account into which individuals would pay on a regular basis and out of which medical care expenses could be paid.

Third parties Parties who are not directly involved in a given activity or transaction. For example, in the relationship between caregivers and patients, fees may be paid by third parties (insurance companies, government).

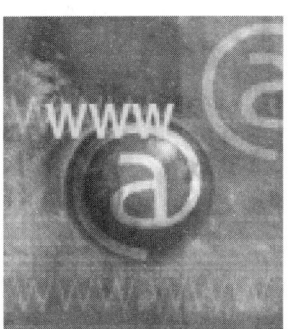

CHAPTER 31
ENVIRONMENTAL ECONOMICS

LEARNING OBJECTIVES

After you have studied this chapter, you should be able to

1. define private costs, social costs, externality, optimal quantity of pollution, private property rights, common property, transaction costs, and recycling;

2. distinguish between private costs and social costs;

3. recognize how common property and species extinction are related;

4. list three choices that businesses must make if they are charged to pollute;

5. determine the optimal quantity of pollution, when given sufficient information;

6. distinguish between private property rights and common property, and predict how rational economic agents behave under each;

7. list various ways to reduce pollution toward the optimal quantity;

8. recognize how to test whether or not a resource is becoming scarcer;

9. recognize how voluntary exchange can solve the externality problem.

CHAPTER OUTLINE

1. It is important to distinguish between private costs and social costs.
   a. Private costs are those incurred by individuals when they use scarce resources.
   b. Social costs include private costs plus the cost of actions borne by people other than those who commit those actions; social costs embody the full opportunity cost of a resource-using action.
   c. When people use resources in production or consumption, pollution may be an unwanted by-product; if so, the social costs of consuming and producing will exceed the private costs of doing so.

2. An externality exists when a private cost or benefit diverges from a social cost or benefit; if an externality exists, the costs or benefits of an action are not fully borne by the two parties engaged in an exchange, or by an individual using resources.

3. In theory, it is possible to change the signals in an economy so that individuals can be forced to take into account all the costs of their actions.
   a. If polluters are charged to pollute, they will (i) install pollution-abatement equipment, (ii) reduce pollution-causing activities, or (iii) pay the price to pollute.
   b. In general, charging a uniform price to pollute is inefficient because a given physical quantity of pollution has different social costs in different places.

4. Ultimately, the optimal quantity of pollution is a normative, not a positive, economics concept.
   a. The waste-disposing capacity of our ecosystem is a scarce resource that can be analyzed like any other resource; the marginal benefit curve for a cleaner environment declines, and the marginal cost curve for a cleaner environment rises.
   b. The optimal quantity of pollution occurs where the declining marginal benefit curve intersects the rising marginal cost curve; in general, the optimal quantity of pollution will exceed zero.

5. Common property is owned by everyone; hence private property rights, which allow the use, transfer, and exchange of property, do not exist for common property.
   a. If a resource is scarce and it is common property, it will be wasted; certain species will become extinct if people value them but property rights do not exist.
   b. A resource that is scarce, but is not common property, can be used efficiently under certain conditions.
   c. Externalities can be internalized via voluntary contracting, even when property rights do not exist,
      i. if the transaction costs associated with making, reaching, and enforcing agreements are low relative to the expected benefits of reaching an agreement, and
      ii. if the number of individuals involved is small.
   d. Private property rights can be assigned (through governments) so that an externality can be internalized.

6. Recycling has the potential to save scarce resources and reduce pollution; unfortunately the existing state of the art is such that recycling processes are costly and create pollution themselves.

KEY TERMS
Private costs
Social costs

Transaction costs

KEY CONCEPTS
Externality
Recycling
Common property

Optimal quantity of pollution
Private property rights

COMPLETION QUESTIONS
Fill in the blank, or circle the correct term.

1. Costs incurred by individuals when they use scarce resources are called _____ costs; _____ costs include private costs and external costs and represent the full cost that society bears when a resource-using action occurs.

2. When we add external costs to internal costs, we get _____ costs; an externality exists if there is a divergence between _____ and _____.

3. In theory, decision makers can be made to take into account all of the costs of their actions if people who impose costs on others are (taxed, subsidized).

4. If polluters are charged to pollute, they have the following three options: _____, _____, and _____.

5. A uniform tax on polluters will not be economically efficient if a given physical quantity of pollution imposes different _____ costs in different places.

6. As more and more pollution is reduced, then the marginal benefit (falls, rises) and the marginal cost _____; the optimal quantity of pollution occurs where _____.

7. If at a zero price the quantity demanded of a resource _____ its quantity supplied, that resource is scarce; if a scarce resource is common property, it probably (will, will not) be wasted.

8. Sheep, cows, and other species are not in danger of extinction because they are valued and _____ rights exist; other species are becoming extinct because they are _____ property.

9. If a businessperson/environmentalist treats pollution voluntarily, he or she will be at a competitive (advantage, disadvantage) in the marketplace.

10. Externalities can be internalized if _____ costs are low and if the number of parties involved is (small, large).

11. Recycling, in theory, can save scarce resources; however it is very _____ and itself creates _____.

12. Many people feel that the world is running out of resources; but the evidence is that the inflation-adjusted price of most resources has (fallen, increased) historically.

TRUE-FALSE QUESTIONS
Circle the **T** if the statement is true, the **F** if it is false. Explain to yourself why a statement is false.

T F 1. Social costs do not include private costs.

T F 2. Private costs do not include external costs.

T F 3. If social costs exceed private costs, too much of the good normally will be produced.

T F 4. Pollution is an example of a social cost.

T F 5. The optimal quantity of pollution is zero.

T F 6. Air pollution is a problem because air is common property.

T F 7. A given quantity of physical pollution causes the same amount of economic damage everywhere.

T F 8. If polluters are charged to pollute, we may end up with less pollution.

T F 9. If a specific firm pays to reduce its output of pollution, it may be at a competitive disadvantage.

T F 10. If private property rights don't exist, the private sector cannot internalize externalities.

T F 11. Externalities may be internalized if the government assigns private property rights.

T F 12. Private property rights to sheep exist; therefore they are not in danger of extinction.

T F 13. Attempts to protect one species may well impose costs on humans.

T F 14. Recycling is always a good idea.

T F 15. The inflation-adjusted price of most resources has fallen, historically.

MULTIPLE CHOICE QUESTIONS
Circle the letter that corresponds to the best answer.

1. Social costs
    a. exclude internal costs.
    b. exclude external costs.
    c. exclude both internal and external costs.
    d. include both internal and external costs.

2. Air pollution
    a. is an internal cost to firms.
    b. is an external cost to firms.
    c. exists because air is a privately owned resource.
    d. has the same costs to society everywhere.

3. A misallocation of resources may result if
    a. social costs exceed private costs.
    b. social benefits exceed private benefits.
    c. a scarce resource is communally owned.
    d. All of the above

4. If polluters are charged to pollute, then
    a. pollution will disappear.
    b. the environment will be damaged severely.
    c. less pollution is a probable result.
    d. less voluntary pollution abatement will result.

CHAPTER 31: ENVIRONMENTAL ECONOMICS   **213**

5. Which of the following will **NOT** help to reduce the problem that exists when social costs exceed social benefits?
    a. subsidize polluters
    b. subsidize parties damaged by pollution
    c. charge polluters to pollute
    d. internalize external costs

6. If polluters are charged to pollute, efficiency requires that
    a. they be charged according to the economic damages they create.
    b. they be charged the same amount.
    c. they be charged according to the physical quantity of pollution they generate.
    d. nonpolluters be charged also.

7. The optimal quantity of pollution exists when the
    a. rising marginal benefit of pollution abatement equals the falling marginal cost.
    b. rising marginal cost of pollution abatement equals the falling marginal benefit.
    c. constant marginal cost of pollution abatement equals the falling marginal benefit.
    d. constant marginal benefit of pollution abatement equals the rising marginal cost.

8. Externalities can be internalized by the private sector if
    a. transaction costs of doing so are low.
    b. benefits of doing so are high.
    c. the number of people involved is small.
    d. All of the above

9. Which statement is **NOT** true?
    a. Recycling can be costly and can add to pollution.
    b. Attempts to protect one species often harm landowners and consumers.
    c. The evidence is that most natural resources are becoming scarcer.
    d. The inflation-adjusted price of landfills has been falling in the U.S.

10. Recycling
    a. may save resources.
    b. can be very costly.
    c. can create its own pollution problems.
    d. All of the above

11. Which one of the following gives people an economic incentive to actively assist in repopulating an endangered species?
    a. Making hunting of the endangered species illegal
    b. Legalizing trading in the hides, bones, or other body parts of members of the endangered species
    c. Allowing people to own the endangered species and to charge the public to view them in nature displays, safaris, and the like
    d. Completely separating the endangered species from people, perhaps by placing members of the species in compounds that few humans can visit

WORKING WITH GRAPHS

1. Use the graphs below to answer the questions that follow. Note that S represents the industry supply curve and SS represents the marginal costs to society—which include marginal private costs and external costs. Assume that no positive externalities exist.

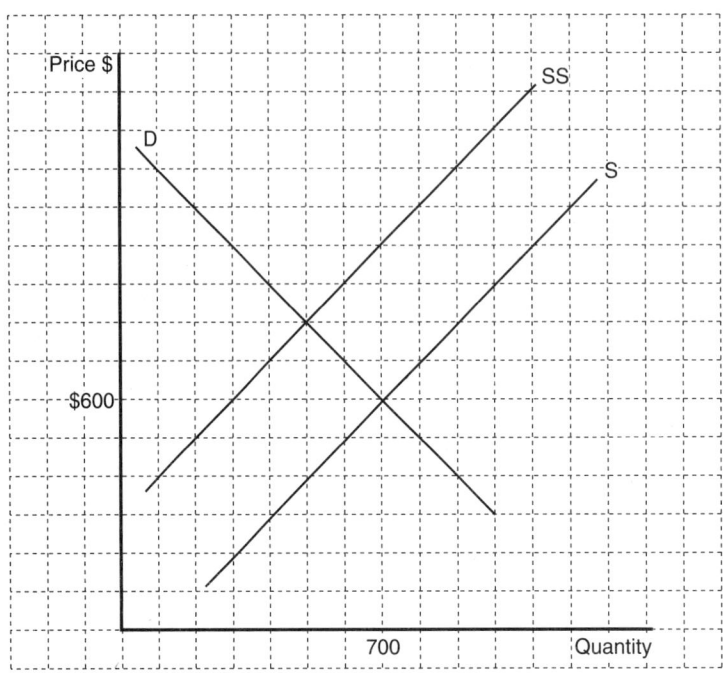

   a. Which curve represents the marginal private costs of producing the good in question?

   b. Which curve reflects the marginal social costs of producing this good?

   c. Which curve represents both the marginal private benefits and the marginal social benefits of this good?

   d. How many units of this good will be produced by the private sector? What is the value of the marginal social cost of that quantity? the value of the marginal social benefits?

   e. What is the optimal quantity of this good, from society's point of view? Why?

2. Suppose you are given the following graph for the demand and supply of fertilizer per week. As a by-product of fertilizer production, the fertilizer plant dumps harmful chemicals into local streams. A local agency has determined that if fertilizer production were limited to 2 tons per week, the local streams would be able to handle the by-products without harm. The agency has decided to impose a tax on the fertilizer plant. What tax per unit of output is necessary to achieve the agency's goal of no harm to the local streams? Can we conclude that if the agency charges this tax that society is better off? Why or why not?

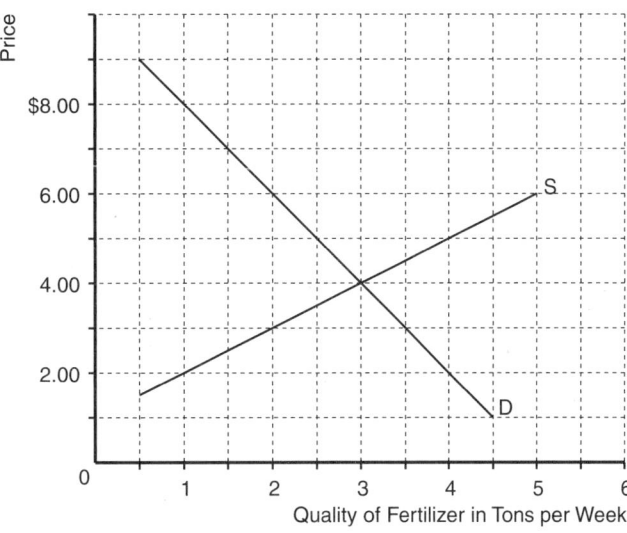

PROBLEMS

1. Suppose you live in a small town with a privately owned solid-waste disposal facility (garbage dump) just west of town that services a larger city about 30 miles away. Because of the prevailing westerly wind, your town suffers from an unpleasant odor generated at the dump. The more garbage that arrives at the dump in a given week, the more unpleasant the odor. A study is undertaken, and the results are partially summarized in the table that follows.

(1) Garbage processed in tons per week	(2) Dump's marginal cost	(3) Consumers' valuation of disposal services	(4) External costs due to odor	(5) Marginal social cost
5	$4.00	$8.00	$0.00	$4.00
10	4.25	7.60	0.20	4.45
15	4.50	6.60	0.50	5.00
20	4.80	5.80	1.00	_____
25	5.20	5.20	1.75	_____
30	5.80	4.80	2.75	_____

Column 1 represents the quantity of garbage disposed of at the dump in tons per week.

Column 2 is the private marginal cost of disposing of various quantities of garbage—the supply of disposal services.

Column 3 represents the demand (willingness to pay) for various quantities of garbage disposal by the consumers of the service in the city to the west.

Column 4 is the external costs that are imposed on residents in your town by the dumping of various quantities of garbage.

Column 5 is the marginal social cost of the dumping services, which includes both private and external costs.

a. Under present conditions, with the disposal plant ignoring external cost, what is the equilibrium price and quantity of disposal services in the market?

b. Complete column 5.

c. Using your answers from a and b, can you tell what is happening in this market at the present?

d. If the disposal plant were forced to internalize all the relevant costs of operation, what would be the equilibrium price and quantity in this market?

ANSWERS TO CHAPTER 31

COMPLETION QUESTIONS

1. private; social
2. social; social costs and private costs or social benefits and private benefits.
3. taxed
4. install pollution-abatement equipment; reduce pollution-causing activity; pay the price to pollute
5. social
6. falls; rises; MB = MC of pollution reduction
7. exceeds; will
8. private property; common
9. disadvantage
10. transaction; small
11. expensive; pollution
12. fallen

TRUE-FALSE QUESTIONS

1. F They are the sum of private costs and negative externalities (if any).
2. T
3. T
4. T
5. F It is a positive amount because it costs society resources to have a cleaner environment.
6. T
7. F The next unit of air pollution causes more economic damage in New York City than it does in a small town in Arizona.
8. T
9. T
10. F The private sector, throughout history, has sometimes been able to do so, when transaction costs are low.
11. T
12. T
13. T
14. F Sometimes recycling is too costly, or it creates pollution itself.
15. T

MULTIPLE CHOICE QUESTIONS

1.d; 2.b; 3.d; 4.c; 5.a; 6.a; 7.b; 8.d; 9.c; 10.d;
11. c.

WORKING WITH GRAPHS

1. a. curve S
   b. curve SS
   c. curve D
   d. 700; $1000; $600
   e. 500; that is where the MB to society equals the MC to society

2. $3 per ton of fertilizer; No. We are given no information about how much society values unharmed streams in the area, so we are not justified in concluding that the tax has made society better off.

PROBLEMS

1. a. $5.20, 25 tons per week
   b. Marginal social cost: $5.80, $6.95, $8.55
   c. With the external costs being ignored, the disposal plant's marginal cost at the equilibrium level is below the true marginal social cost.
   d. $5.80, 20 tons per week

GLOSSARY TO CHAPTER 31

Common property Property that is owned by everyone and therefore by no one. Air and water are examples of common property resources.

Externality A situation in which a private cost (or benefit) diverges from a social cost (or benefit); a situation in which the costs (or benefits) of an action are not fully borne (or gained) by the two parties engaged in exchange or by an individual engaging in a scarce-resource-using activity.

Optimal quantity of pollution That level of pollution for which the marginal benefit of one additional unit of clean air just equals the marginal cost of that additional unit of clean air.

Private costs Costs borne directly by the individuals who incur them. Also called *internal costs*.

Private property rights Exclusive rights of ownership that allow the use, transfer, and exchange of property.

Recycling The reuse of raw materials from used manufactured products.

Social costs The full costs borne by society whenever a resource use occurs. Social costs can be measured by adding private, or internal, costs to external costs.

Transaction costs All costs associated with making, reaching, and enforcing agreements.

CHAPTER 32
COMPARATIVE ADVANTAGE AND THE OPEN ECONOMY

LEARNING OBJECTIVES

After you have studied this chapter, you should be able to

1. define absolute advantage, comparative advantage, quota system, dumping, infant industry argument, General Agreement on Tariffs and Trade (GATT), World Trade Organization (WTO), voluntary import expansion (VIE), and voluntary restraint agreement (VRA);

2. explain how nation pays for its imports;

3. distinguish between absolute advantage and comparative advantage and determine each for nations, given sufficient information;

4. interpret a graph that shows the effect of an import quota;

5. interpret a graph that shows the effect of a tariff;

6. relate comparative advantage to opportunity cost;

7. list reasons why trade arises between nations;

8. list potential costs of international trade;

9. identify the pros and cons of arguments against free trade among nations;

10. contrast and compare the results of import quotas and tariffs.

CHAPTER OUTLINE

1. The proportion of GDP accounted for by trade varies greatly among individual nations, but if trade were curtailed, even such nations as the United States would be affected significantly.

a. A nation ultimately pays for its imports by exports; thus restrictions on imports ultimately reduce exports.
b. If trade is voluntary, then both nations participating in an exchange benefit.

2. A nation has an absolute advantage in the production of good A if it can produce more units of good A than other nations can, from a given quantity of inputs; a nation has a comparative advantage in producing good A if out of all the goods it can produce, good A has the lowest opportunity cost.

3. Opportunity costs, and hence comparative advantages, differ among nations.

4. There are numerous arguments that have been presented as being anti–free trade. Such arguments include the infant industry argument, protecting domestic jobs, countering foreign subsidies and dumping, protecting the environment, and national defense concerns. Some of these arguments are simply wrong, and others emphasize costs to the neglect of benefits.

5. There are numerous methods that nations have used to restrict foreign trade.
a. Some nations place import quotas on foreign goods.
b. Some nations place taxes or tariffs on foreign goods.
c. Both quotas and tariffs raise prices to domestic consumers and reduce the quantity of goods traded.

KEY TERMS
General Agreement on Tariffs and Trade (GATT)
Infant industry argument

Quota system
World Trade Organization (WTO)

KEY CONCEPTS
Comparative advantage
Absolute advantage
Dumping

Voluntary import expansion (VIE)
Voluntary restraint agreement (VRA)

COMPLETION QUESTIONS
Fill in the blank, or circle the correct term.

1. A nation ultimately pays for imports by _____.

2. If world trade ceased to exist, all trade-related jobs (would, would not) be lost in the long run; instead nations would simply _____. Nevertheless, worldwide living standards would (fall, rise) significantly.

3. International trade permits each nation to specialize in the production of those goods for which it has a(n) _____ advantage; each nation specializes in the production of goods for which its opportunity costs are the (lowest, highest).

4. Nations have an incentive to specialize and trade because they have different collective tastes and because different nations will always have different _____ costs to producing goods.

5. There are numerous arguments against free trade; they include the _____ industry argument, the argument that trade may impede _____ protection, and the contention that trade may interfere with national _____ efforts.

6. Two ways to restrict foreign trade analyzed in the text are _____ on imports and _____ on imported goods.

7. Most restrictions on international trade have one major element in common: they interfere with nations' specializing in the production of goods for which they have a(n) _____ advantage. Therefore they are economically (inefficient, efficient).

8. Because a nation ultimately pays for imports with its _____, restricting imports to save jobs destroys jobs in the _____ sector of the economy; hence, on net, import restrictions (do, do not) save jobs.

TRUE-FALSE QUESTIONS
Circle the **T** if the statement is true, the **F** if it is false. Explain to yourself why a statement is false.

T F 1. If all world trade ceased, import sector jobs and export sector jobs would be permanently destroyed.

T F 2. Because international trade is voluntary in the private sector, both nations benefit from trade that is continued.

T F 3. Imports are paid for by exports.

T F 4. In effect, a tariff makes the supply of the good in question a vertical line at a level below the original equilibrium quantity.

T F 5. A U.S. tariff on Japanese-made goods will lead to an increase in the demand for U.S. goods that are substitutes for those Japanese-made goods.

T F 6. Import quotas harm domestic consumers but help domestic producers of those goods on which quotas are placed.

T F 7. Tariffs harm domestic consumers and harm domestic producers of goods that compete with the goods on which tariffs are placed.

T F 8. A tariff on good X will cause a leftward shift of the supply curve for good X in the foreign country, and a rightward shift of the demand curve for good X in the country that imposed the tariff.

T F 9. In a two-country world, it is possible for both countries to have a comparative advantage in the production of a specific good.

T F 10. If the United States has a comparative advantage in producing wheat, it must be true that the opportunity cost for producing wheat in the United States is below that opportunity cost in other nations.

T F 11. Because in the real world nations have different resource endowments and different collective tastes, trade will always be advantageous.

T F 12. It is easy to determine the industries to which the infant industry argument applies.

T F 13. If a nation imposes anti-dumping laws, its consumers will pay lower prices for goods.

CHAPTER 32: COMPARATIVE ADVANTAGE AND THE OPEN ECONOMY

T   F   14. Free trade may increase a nation's instability in the short run, because over time a nation's comparative advantage can change.

T   F   15. When a nation restricts imports to protect jobs, it in effect preserves less productive employment at the expense of more productive employment.

T   F   16. One difference between the economic effects of quotas versus tariffs is that tariffs lead to a higher price to consumers but quotas do not.

MULTIPLE CHOICE QUESTIONS
Circle the letter that corresponds to the best answer.

1. In the long run, a nation pays for its imports by
   a. exporting.
   b. creating money.
   c. extending credit to the exporting nation.
   d. All of the above

2. The U.S. ratio of imports to GDP is about _____ percent.
   a. 5
   b. 10
   c. 15
   d. 20

3. If trade between two nations is voluntary and continued, then
   a. both nations benefit.
   b. one nation could benefit more than the other.
   c. living standards are higher in both nations than if trade were not permitted.
   d. All of the above

4. Country A can produce both wheat and oranges using fewer resources than country B. Which of the following statements is true?
   a. Country A has a comparative advantage in producing both goods.
   b. Country A has an absolute advantage in producing both goods.
   c. Country B has no comparative advantage.
   d. Country B must have an absolute advantage in producing one of the goods.

5. If Country C has a comparative advantage in producing wheat, then its opportunity cost of producing wheat
   a. is maximized.
   b. equals the opportunity cost of producing other goods.
   c. cannot be determined.
   d. is lowest among its trading partners.

6. Nations find it advantageous to trade because they
   a. have different resource endowments.
   b. have different collective tastes.
   c. have different comparative advantages.
   d. All of the above

7. Which of the following is **NOT** an argument used against free trade?
   a. Free trade makes nations more interdependent.
   b. Free trade leads nations to specialize in production.
   c. Free trade increases average and total worldwide incomes.
   d. Imports may destroy some domestic jobs.

8. Which of the following is most **UNLIKE** the others?
   a. import quota
   b. tariff
   c. free trade
   d. anti-dumping laws

9. Concerning import quotas and tariffs, which of the following statements is true?
   a. Both lead to lower prices for consumers.
   b. Both lead to more imports.
   c. Tariffs lead to higher prices, but quotas do not.
   d. Quotas directly restrain imports, while tariffs induce people to choose fewer imports.

10. Which statement is **NOT** true, concerning the use of import restrictions to save jobs?
    a. The cost to consumers often exceeds the value of the jobs saved.
    b. Some jobs are destroyed in the export sector.
    c. In the long run they do not save jobs in those industries in which a nation has lost its comparative advantage.
    d. They are the most efficient way to help domestic workers threatened by foreign competition.

MATCHING

Choose the item in column (2) that best matches an item in column (1).

(1)	(2)
a. anti-dumping law	e. minimum opportunity cost of production
b. tariff	f. trade restriction
c. comparative advantage	g. tax on foreign-produced goods
d. absolute advantage	h. producing at a lower cost

WORKING WITH GRAPHS

1. Analyze the graphs below, then answer the questions that follow. They deal with an import quota set on foreign-made sugar. Start at point A.

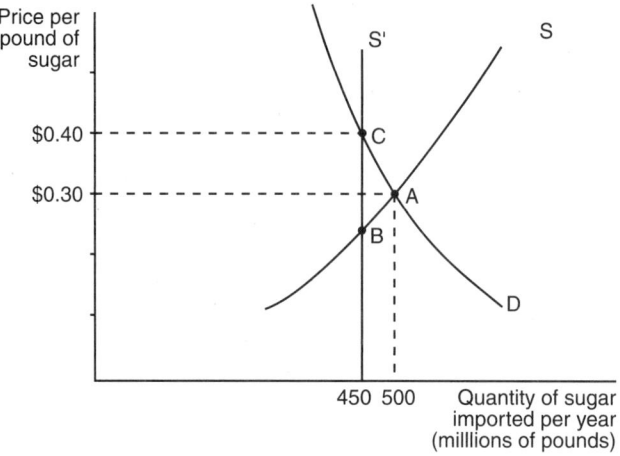

   a. What is the price of sugar in this country, without the import quota?
   b. What is the maximum amount of imported sugar given the quota?
   c. What is the price of sugar, given the import quota?
   d. What is the effective import supply curve, given the quota?

2. Analyze the graphs below, which deal with a U.S. tariff placed on Japanese-made autos, then answer the questions that follow. Start with point A.

   a. What is the price of U.S.- and Japanese-made autos in the U.S., without the tariff?
   b. Which curve represents the supply of Japanese-made autos into the U.S., after the tariff?
   c. Which curve shows the demand for U.S.-made autos in the U.S., after the tariff?
   d. What is the price of autos in the United States, after the tariff is imposed?

PROBLEMS

1. Suppose that Germany and the United States are both experiencing full employment and can produce the following amounts of wine and beer per week. Use this information to answer the following questions.

	Wine (gallons)	Beer (gallons)
Germany	600	1200
United States	400	1600

    a. Germany has a comparative advantage in the production of _____, whereas the United States has a comparative advantage in the production of _____.

    b. What is the cost of wine in terms of beer in Germany? What is the cost of wine in terms of beer in the United States?

2. Let us assume we are again in a two-country world, with the countries being Germany and the United States. Again, to simplify, let us assume that there are only two goods produced, coal and steel. In the table that follows, you will find the production possibilities of both countries. Assume that each country is currently operating at combination B on its production possibilities schedule. Use this information to answer the following questions. (Hint: Remember that movements along production possibilities curves involve opportunity costs and that comparative advantage and trade depend on opportunity costs.) Entries are in thousands of tons per week.

		A	B	C	D
Germany:	Coal	0	24	48	72
	Steel	18	12	6	0
United States:	Coal	0	36	72	108
	Steel	36	24	12	0

    a. Which country has an absolute advantage in the production of coal? Steel?

    b. Which country has a comparative advantage in the production of coal? Steel?

    c. What is the cost of coal in terms of steel in Germany? What is the cost of coal in terms of steel in the United States?

    (Remember that these are opportunity costs as determined by production possibilities.)

    d. What is the current world production of coal and steel?
    e. If both countries specialize in the production of goods in which they have a comparative advantage, Germany will produce _____ thousand tons of _____, the United States will produce _____ thousand tons of _____, and the world output of coal will increase by _____ thousand tons.

ANSWERS TO CHAPTER 32

COMPLETION QUESTIONS

1. exporting
2. would not; produce the goods themselves; fall
3. comparative; lowest
4. opportunity
5. infant; environmental; defense
6. quotas; tariffs
7. comparative; inefficient
8. exports; export; do not

TRUE-FALSE QUESTIONS

1. F Eventually each nation will produce its own goods—but at a higher cost and (perhaps) lower quality.
2. T
3. T
4. F That describes the effect of an import quota.
5. T
6. T
7. F They help domestic producers of such goods.
8. T
9. F Not for a *specific* good.
10. T
11. T
12. F In practice it is difficult to predict which industries will eventually be successful without aid.
13. F Consumers will pay higher prices.
14. T
15. T
16. F Both lead to higher prices for consumers.

MULTIPLE CHOICE QUESTIONS

1.a;   2.c;   3.d;   4.b;   5.d;   6.d;   7.c;   8.c;   9.d;   10.d.

MATCHING

a and f;   b and g;   c and e;   d and h

WORKING WITH GRAPHS

1. a. 30 cents per pound
   b. 450 million pounds
   c. 40 cents per pound
   d. The same as the regular supply curve up to 450 million pounds; vertical from that point on.

2. a. $30,000 per auto
   b. S_2
   c. D_2
   d. $40,000 per auto

CHAPTER 32: COMPARATIVE ADVANTAGE AND THE OPEN ECONOMY

PROBLEMS

1. a. wine; beer
   b. 1 gallon wine = 2 gallons beer; 1 gallon wine = 4 gallons beer
2. a. United States; United States
   b. Germany; United States
   c. 4000 tons coal = 1000 tons steel; 3000 tons coal = 1000 tons steel
   d. 60,000 tons coal; 36,000 tons steel
   e. 72; coal, 36; steel; 12

GLOSSARY TO CHAPTER 32

Absolute advantage The ability to produce more output from given inputs of resources than other producers can.

Comparative advantage The ability to produce a good or service at a lower opportunity cost than other producers.

Dumping Selling a good or service abroad at a price below the price charged in the home market or at a price below its cost of production.

General Agreement on Tariffs and Trade (GATT) An international agreement established in 1947 to further world trade by reducing barriers and tariffs. GATT was replaced by the World Trade Organization in 1995.

Infant industry argument The contention that tariffs should be imposed to protect from import competition an industry that is trying to get started. Presumably, after the industry becomes technologically efficient, the tariff can be lifted.

Quota system A government-imposed restriction on the quantity of a specific good that another country is allowed to sell in the United States. In other words, quotas are restrictions on imports. These restrictions are usually applied to one or several specific countries.

Voluntary import expansion (VIE) An official agreement with another country in which it agrees to import more from the United States.

Voluntary restraint agreement (VRA) An official agreement with another country that "voluntarily" restricts the quantity of its exports to the United States.

World Trade Organization (WTO) The successor organization to GATT that handles trade disputes among its member nations.

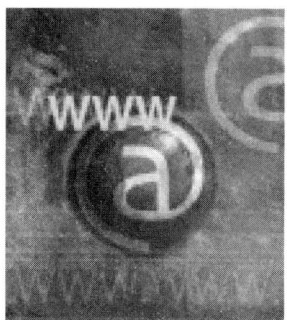

CHAPTER 33
EXCHANGE RATES AND THE BALANCE OF PAYMENTS

LEARNING OBJECTIVES

After you have studied this chapter, you should be able to

1. define foreign exchange rate, accounting identities, foreign exchange market, flexible exchange rates, appreciation, depreciation, gold standard, balance of trade, balance of payments, special drawing rights (SDRs), International Monetary Fund (IMF), dirty float, and par value;

2. distinguish among the balance of trade, the balance on current account, the balance on capital account, and the balance of payments;

3. list three factors that affect a nation's balance of payments;

4. enumerate official reserve account transactions;

5. list transactions that lead to an increase in the supply of a domestic country's currency and an increase in the demand for foreign currency, and distinguish such transactions from transactions that lead to a demand for a domestic country's currency and a supply of a foreign country's currency;

6. recognize the equilibrium exchange rate from graphs, and predict how specific events will change the exchange rate;

7. distinguish between a gold standard international payments system and a flexible exchange rate international payments system.

CHAPTER OUTLINE

1. A balance of trade reflects the difference between the value of a nation's merchandise exports and its merchandise imports; the balance of payments reflects all economic transactions between a nation and the rest of the world.
    a. The current account balance equals the sum of (1) the balance of trade, (2) the balance of services, and (3) net unilateral transfers (private gifts and government grants). If the current

CHAPTER 33: EXCHANGE RATES AND THE BALANCE OF PAYMENTS   229

   account balance is negative, a current account deficit exists; if it is positive, a current account surplus exists.
   b. Capital account transactions consist of direct investment purchases in financial assets among countries and loans to and from foreigners. If the capital account is a negative number, a capital account deficit exists; if it is positive, a capital account surplus exists.
   c. If the sum of a nation's current account and its capital account is negative, that nation has an international payments disequilibrium (deficit) that must be financed by official (government) reserve account transactions; of course, another nation must have an international payments surplus.
      i. Official reserve account transactions include sales or purchases of foreign currencies, gold, special drawing rights, the reserve position in the International Monetary Fund, and financial assets held by official government agencies.
      ii. Official transactions must exactly equal (but be of opposite sign to) the balance of payments.

2. Under a flexible exchange rate system of international payments, exchange rates between nations are determined by the forces of supply and demand.
   a. When U.S. residents import a foreign good or service, this leads to a supply of dollars and a demand for foreign currency on foreign exchange markets.
   b. When U.S. residents export goods and services to a foreign country, this leads to a supply of foreign currency and a demand for dollars.
   c. The equilibrium exchange rate is determined in the same way that the equilibrium price for anything is established.
      i. The U.S. demand curve for (say) Japanese yen is negatively sloped; as the dollar price of the yen falls—it takes fewer dollars to purchase a given quantity of yen—the quantity demanded for yen, by U.S. residents, rises.
      ii. The U.S. demand for yen is a derived demand; we demand Japanese yen because we demand Japanese goods and services.
      iii. The Japanese supply yen because they want (say) U.S. goods and services; as the dollar price of yen rises—it takes fewer yen to purchase one dollar—Japanese residents will increase their quantity supplied of yen in order to purchase more U.S. goods.
      iv. The equilibrium dollar price per yen is established at the intersection of the U.S. demand for yen curve and the Japanese supply of yen curve; the equilibrium yen price per dollar is automatically determined thereby.
   d. If U.S. residents experience a change in tastes in favor of Japanese goods, the demand for yen will increase. The dollar price of yen rises and the yen price of dollars falls; the dollar depreciates and the yen appreciates.
   e. Other determinants of exchange rates include (relative) changes in real interest rates, changes in productivity, changes in tastes, and perceptions of economic stability.

3. Under a gold standard, each nation fixes its exchange rate in terms of gold; therefore all exchange rates are fixed. Under the pure gold standard, each nation would have to abandon an independent monetary policy; each nation's money supply would automatically change whenever a balance of payments disequilibrium occurred.

4. In 1944 representatives of the world's capitalist nations met in Bretton Woods to create a new international payments system to replace the gold standard that had collapsed in the 1930s.
   a. The International Monetary Fund (IMF) was established in 1944; the IMF established a system of fixed exchange rates and a means to lend foreign exchange to deficit nations.
   b. Member governments were obligated to intervene in foreign exchange markets, to maintain the values of their currencies within 1 percent of the declared par value.
   c. In 1971, the United States ended the connection between the value of the dollar and gold, and in 1973 the Bretton Woods system ended.

5. To fix a nation's exchange rate, a central bank must influence the demand for its nation's currency in the foreign exchange market.
   a. To do this, the central bank must buy or sell foreign exchange reserves; if the central bank must persistently sell reserves of foreign currencies to keep the value of its currency at a pegged level, then the exchange rate can remain fixed only as long as the central bank's foreign exchange reserves last.
   b. A key rationale for fixing the exchange rate is to limit foreign exchange risks so that a nation's residents do not have to hedge against losses from fluctuations in exchange rates.
   c. Between a flexible exchange rate system and a fixed exchange rate is a "dirty float," or a managed exchange rate system, in which governments (through their central banks) intervene in foreign exchange markets in order to affect the price of currencies; this is the approach used by most developed nations today.
   d. Some countries have "split the difference" between fixed and floating exchange rates by using a crawling peg, in which the target value of a nation's currency automatically changes over time, or by adopting a target zone, which is an allowed range of permitted exchange rate variations between upper and lower exchange rate bands.

KEY TERMS
Crawling peg
Flexible exchange rates
Foreign exchange market
Foreign exchange rate
Appreciation
Depreciation

Dirty float
International Monetary Fund (IMF)
Gold standard
Balance of trade
Balance of payments
Special drawing rights (SDRs)

KEY CONCEPTS
Accounting identities
Bretton Woods system
Current account

Capital account
Gold standard
Par value

COMPLETION QUESTIONS
Fill in the blank, or circle the correct term.

1. When U.S. residents wish to import Japanese-made goods, they supply _____ to the foreign exchange market and demand _____ on that market; when the Japanese wish to import U.S.-made goods, they supply _____ and demand _____ on the foreign exchange market.

2. In a flexible exchange rate system, exchange rates are determined by (governments, supply and demand); if the exchange rate goes from $0.010 per yen to $0.012 per yen, the dollar has (appreciated, depreciated) and the yen has _____.

3. If the Japanese yen depreciates, it takes (fewer, more) yen to purchase a dollar; this leads to (an increase, a decrease) in the quantity demanded of yen by U.S. residents and (an increase, a decrease) in the quantity supplied of yen by Japanese residents.

4. If U.S. tastes move in favor of European goods, there will be a(n) _____ in the demand for euros; other things being constant, the euro will (appreciate, depreciate) on the foreign exchange market. This eventually will induce U.S. residents to export (less, more) to Europe and import _____ from Europe.

5. Under a pure gold standard, exchange rates (float, are fixed).

6. If the value of U.S. imports exceeds the value of its exports, the U.S. balance of trade will be a (negative, positive) number, and another country's balance of trade must be a(n) _____ number. The United States then is said to have a trade (deficit, surplus), while the other nation has a trade _____.

7. If governments do not intervene, by definition the sum of a nation's balance on current account plus its balance on capital account will equal _____; if governments intervene in the balance of payments process, then the sum of a nation's balance on current account plus its balance on capital account must exactly _____, but be of opposite sign to, its official transactions.

8. Official reserve account transactions involve the following assets of individual countries: _____, _____, _____, _____, and _____.

9. A nation's balance of payments is affected by, among other things, relative changes in that nation's _____ and _____.

10. If the value of a nation's exports is less than the value of its imports, it is running a trade _____; its currency will (depreciate, appreciate) under a flexible exchange rate system.

11. When nations intervene in foreign exchange markets in order to affect exchange rates, a freely floating exchange rate system becomes a(n) _____ float.

12. An automatically adjusting target for a nation's exchange rate is a(n) _____.

13. The possibility that people may incur losses as a result of unexpected variations in the value of a nation's currency in foreign exchange markets is called _____.

TRUE-FALSE QUESTIONS
Circle the **T** if the statement is true, the **F** if it is false. Explain to yourself why a statement is false.

T F 1. If you wish to buy German goods, you ultimately offer dollars and demand euros.

T F 2. If you wish to send money to your relatives in England, you ultimately offer dollars and demand English currency.

T F 3. In a flexible exchange rate system, gold flows lead to international payments equilibrium.

T F 4. If French tastes move in favor of U.S. goods, the supply of dollars on the foreign exchange market rises relative to the demand for dollars.

T F 5. The U.S. demand for British pounds rises if the British inflation rate exceeds the U.S. inflation rate.

T F 6. In a flexible exchange rate system, if Canadian tastes move away from U.S. goods (other things being constant), both the U.S. dollar and the Canadian dollar will depreciate.

T F 7. The gold standard is one form of a fixed exchange rate system.

T F 8. Under the gold standard, if disequilibrium exists in the world's balance of payments, gold will flow from one nation to another until payments equilibrium is restored.

T F 9. Under a flexible exchange rate system, if disequilibrium exists in the world's balance of payments, exchange rates will change until payments equilibrium is restored.

T F 10. Under a flexible exchange rate system, each nation must give up control over its own monetary policy.

T F 11. In today's world, the sum of a nation's current account balance plus its capital account balance must be zero.

T F 12. If one nation has a current account deficit, another nation must have a current account surplus.

T F 13. A nation can finance a current account deficit with a capital account surplus.

T F 14. A dirty float results because nations do not want to pay the price of adjusting to a balance of payments disequilibrium.

T F 15. Under a flexible exchange rate system, payments equilibrium is brought about by a change in the exchange rate; under a gold standard, national price levels change to restore payments equilibrium.

T F 16. To fix, or peg, the exchange rate for its nation's currency, a central bank must buy or sell domestic securities such as bonds issued by the nation's government.

T F 17. Under a target zone approach to managing the exchange rate, a central bank intervenes to keep the exchange rate above an upper band or below a lower band.

MULTIPLE CHOICE QUESTIONS
Circle the letter that corresponds to the best answer.

1. If the foreign exchange rate is that $1 is equivalent to 4 Polish zlotys, then 1 zloty is worth
    a. $4.
    b. 40 cents.
    c. 25 cents.
    d. 4 cents.

2. The demand schedule for yen on the foreign exchange market
    a. is derived partially from foreign demand for Japanese goods.
    b. reflects the fact that Japanese residents want to import goods and services.
    c. shows the quantity of yen demanded at different income levels.
    d. is unimportant if Japan is on a fixed exchange rate system.

3. Which of the following does **NOT** lead to an increase in the demand for Mexican pesos?
    a. A worldwide change in tastes in favor of Mexican goods occurs.
    b. The Mexican inflation rate exceeds the world inflation rate.
    c. Mexico's interest rate rises relative to world rates.
    d. World real income rises.

4. Which of the following leads to an increase in the demand for the U.S. dollar on the foreign exchange market?
   a. an increase in U.S. exports
   b. an increase in foreign investment in the United States
   c. an increase in gifts from foreigners to U.S. residents
   d. All of the above

5. If a nation has an international payments surplus in a flexible exchange rate system, then
   a. its currency will appreciate.
   b. its price level will rise.
   c. gold will flow from it to nations with a payments surplus.
   d. All of the above

6. Which of the following statements is **NOT** true?
   a. Under flexible exchange rates, international payments equilibrium is restored through changes in exchange rates.
   b. Under a gold standard, international payments equilibrium is restored through changes in national price levels.
   c. Under a flexible exchange rate system, a nation cannot pursue a monetary policy that is independent of its trading partners.
   d. Under the gold standard, international payments disequilibrium leads to gold flows, which restore equilibrium.

7. If Thailand has a payments deficit, payments equilibrium can be restored if Thailand's
   a. price level rises relative to the world's.
   b. interest rate rises relative to the world's.
   c. real national income rises relative to the world's.
   d. money supply rises relative to the world's.

8. A nation can finance a deficit on its current account with
   a. a surplus on its capital account.
   b. a deficit on its capital account.
   c. official purchases of foreign currencies with its own currency.
   d. purchases of gold from foreign countries with its own currency.

9. If a nation has a deficit on both its current account and its capital account, then
   a. it is in a balance of payments equilibrium.
   b. the world must be on a flexible exchange rate system.
   c. it must have official transactions that are identical to (but opposite in sign to) the sum of those two deficits.
   d. it will experience gold inflows.

10. A nation's balance of payments is affected by its relative
    a. interest rate.
    b. political stability.
    c. inflation rate.
    d. All of the above

11. The dirty float
    a. has emerged in recent years because nations want less flexible exchange rates.
    b. makes fixed exchange rates more flexible.
    c. is common under a gold standard.
    d. is favored over a pure float by people who want their nation to have a monetary policy independent of its trading partners.

234 CHAPTER 33: EXCHANGE RATES AND THE BALANCE OF PAYMENTS

MATCHING

Choose the item in column (2) that best matches an item in column (1).

(1)	(2)
a. appreciation	f. rise in one currency's value relative to another's
b. depreciation	g. fall in one currency's value relative to another's
c. fixed exchange rate system	h. balance of payments settlements
d. special drawing right	i. gold standard
e. trade deficit	j. value of imports exceeds value of exports

WORKING WITH GRAPHS

1. Consider a situation in which exchange rates are flexible. Consumers in the United States wish to import a good from Germany, a nation that is part of the European Monetary Union.
   a. Calculate the U.S. price of this good, given the German price of the good and the different exchange rates that might prevail as listed in the table below, and place these calculations in the appropriate column. Calculate the quantity of euros demanded by U.S. consumers in order to purchase the import good at different exchange rates. Enter these numbers in the last column.

Exchange rate ($/euro)	German price of the good	U.S. price of the good	Quantity demanded	Total U.S. euro expenditures
0.80/1	1 euro	____	90	____
0.85/1	1 euro	____	80	____
0.90/1	1 euro	____	70	____
0.95/1	1 euro	____	60	____
1.00/1	1 euro	____	50	____

   By looking at the table above, one can conclude that as it takes more dollars to purchase one euro, the dollar price of the import good will _____.

   b. In the table above, you are given the quantity of the import good at different prices. Graph the demand for euros on the grid provided below.

   c. Let us now assume that people in Germany wish to import from the United States some good that costs $1 per unit. Calculate the German price of the good given the U.S. price and the different exchange rates that might prevail, as listed in the table below, and place these numbers in the appropriate column.

Exchange rate ($/euro)	U.S. price of the good	German price of the good	Quantity demanded	Total German $ expenditures
0.80/1	$1	_____	24.0	_____
0.85/1	$1	_____	42.5	_____
0.90/1	$1	_____	63.0	_____
0.95/1	$1	_____	85.5	_____
1.00/1	$1	_____	110.0	_____

By looking at the above table, one can conclude that as it takes more dollars to purchase 1 euro, the euro price of the good will _____.

d. In the last table, you are given the quantity of the import good that German consumers wish to purchase at different German prices. Use this information to calculate the quantity of euros that German consumers will be willing to supply at different exchange rates in order to import the U.S. good. (Note: Round off to the nearest whole number.) Enter these numbers in the last column. Graph the supply of German euros on the same grid as your graph of part b.

e. Assume for simplicity that the only trade between the United States and Germany involves the two goods discussed above. Under this assumption, the equilibrium exchange rate will be approximately _____ dollars per euro or _____ euros per dollar.

f. Suppose that now U.S. consumers undergo a change in tastes and preferences for the German import good. As a result, the U.S. demand for the import good increases as shown in the table below.

Exchange rate ($/euro)	German price of the good	U.S. price of the good	Quantity demanded	Total U.S. euro expenditures
0.80/1	1 euro	_____	120	_____
0.85/1	1 euro	_____	110	_____
0.90/1	1 euro	_____	100	_____
0.95/1	1 euro	_____	90	_____
1.00/1	1 euro	_____	80	_____

Enter in the last column the quantity of euros now demanded by U.S. consumers for use in purchasing the German import good. (Note: Round off to the nearest whole number.) Graph the new demand for euros on the same grid provided for part b.

The new equilibrium exchange rate will be approximately _____ dollars per euro, or _____ euros per dollar. As a result of the increase in the U.S. demand for German imports, with all else constant, the dollar will _____ and the euro will _____.

g. Now consider the above problem assuming that the exchange rate was fixed at $0.90/euro. When the U.S. demand for German goods increased, the United States would have purchased _____ units and paid a total of $_____ for German imports. German residents would have bought _____ units from the United States and paid a total of $_____ for U.S. exports. As a result, the United States would have lost $_____, or approximately _____ euros, in foreign exchange.

2. The figure below shows the supply of, and the demand for, British pounds, as a function of the exchange rate—expressed in U.S. dollars per pound. Assume that Britain and the United States are the only two countries in the world.

   a. How might the shift from D to D' be accounted for?

   b. Given the shift from D to D', what exists at $1.60 = 1 pound?

   c. Will the pound now appreciate or depreciate?

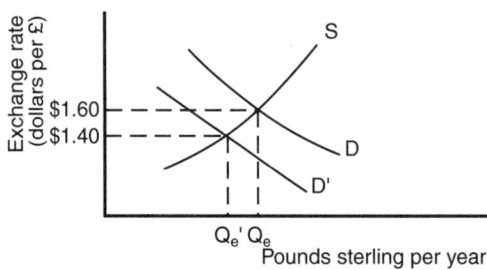

PROBLEMS

1. Below are balance of payments figures for North Shore during 2004. (All figures are in billions of dollars.

Allocations of special drawing rights	$ 710
Balance on the capital account	-3507
Foreign official assets	10475
Errors and omissions	-1879
Balance on the current account	-5795
North Shore official assets	-4

   a. The official reserve transactions balance was (+/-) _____ $_____.

   b. The official reserve transactions were

      (1) the sum of $_____, _____, and _____

      (2) totaled (+/-) _____ $_____

2. Suppose both Canada and the United States had been on a pure gold standard; and the Canadian government had been willing to buy and sell gold at a price of 53.85 Canadian dollars for an ounce of gold, and the U.S. government had been willing to buy and sell gold at a price of $35 an ounce. In the foreign exchange markets, the price of a Canadian dollar would have been _____ U.S. dollars and the price of a U.S. dollar would have been _____ Canadian dollars.

CHAPTER 33: EXCHANGE RATES AND THE BALANCE OF PAYMENTS   **237**

3. Below are hypothetical demand and supply schedules for the European Monetary Union's euro during a week. (The quantities of euros demanded and supplied are measured in millions, and the exchange rate for the euro is measured in dollars.)

Quantity Demanded	Exchange Rate	Quantity Supplied
100	$0.98	570
200	0.97	520
300	0.96	460
400	0.95	400
500	0.94	330
600	0.93	260
700	0.92	180

a. The equilibrium exchange rate for the euro is $_____; and at this equilibrium the rate of exchange for the dollar is _____ euros.

b. At the equilibrium exchange rate,

   (1) _____ million euros are demanded and supplied each week;

   (2) _____ million dollars are bought and sold each week.

c. If the European Central Bank wished to peg the exchange rate for the euro at

   (1) $0.96, it would have to (buy/sell) (how many) _____ million euros for dollars each week;

   (2) $0.94, it would have to (buy/sell) (how many) _____ million euros for dollars each week.

4. Which of the following will cause the yen to appreciate?

   a. U.S. real incomes increase relative to Japanese real incomes.

   b. It is expected that in the future the yen will depreciate relative to the dollar.

   c. The U.S. inflation rate rises relative to the Japanese inflation rate.

   d. The after-tax, risk-adjusted real interest rate in the United States rises relative to that in Japan.

   e. U.S. tastes change in favor of Japanese-made goods.

ANSWERS TO CHAPTER 33

COMPLETION QUESTIONS

1. dollars; yen; yen; dollars
2. supply and demand; depreciated; appreciated
3. more; an increase; a decrease
4. increase; appreciate; more; less
5. are fixed
6. negative; positive; deficit; surplus
7. zero; equal
8. foreign currencies; gold; SDRs; reserve position in the IMF; any financial asset held by an official government agency
9. inflation rate; political stability
10. deficit; depreciate;
11. dirty
12. crawling peg
13. foreign exchange risk

TRUE-FALSE QUESTIONS

1. T
2. T
3. F   Changes in exchange rates lead to payments equilibrium.
4. F   The demand for dollars rises relative to the supply of dollars, because the French want to buy relatively more U.S. goods.
5. F   U.S. residents will demand fewer pounds because British goods are now relatively higher priced.
6. F   The U.S. dollar will depreciate relative to the Canadian dollar; the Canadian dollar therefore must appreciate relative to the U.S. dollar.
7. T
8. T
9. T
10. F   Floating exchange rate systems permit an independent monetary policy.
11. F   In today's world, nations intervene in exchange markets; hence international settlements among governments are necessary.
12. T
13. T
14. T
15. T
16. F   The central bank must buy or sell foreign exchange reserves.
17. F   Interventions would keep the exchange rate between the upper and lower band, or within the target zone.

MULTIPLE CHOICE QUESTIONS

1.c; 2.a; 3.b; 4.d; 5.a; 6.c; 7.b; 8.a; 9.c; 10.d; 11.a.

MATCHING

a and f; b and g; c and i; d and h; e and j

WORKING WITH GRAPHS

1. a. U.S. prices of the good: 0.80, 0.85, 0.90, 0.95, 1.00. Total U.S. euro expenditures: 90, 80, 70, 60, 50; rise
   b. See graph below.
   c. German prices of the good: 1.250, 1.176, 1.111, 1.053, 1.00; Total German dollar expenditures: 24.00, 42.50, 63.00, 85.50, 110.00; fall
   d. Total German expenditures in euros: 30, 50, 70, 90, 110. See graph below.
   e. 0.90, 1.11
   f. Total U.S. euro expenditures: 120, 110, 100, 90, 80. See graph below. 0.95; 1.53; depreciate; appreciate
   g. 100; 111.10; 63, 63.00; 48.10 (or $111.10 - $63.00), 53 (48.1 ÷ $0.90 = 53.44).

2. a. A decrease in the demand for British pounds will occur if world tastes change away from British-made goods, the British price level rises relative to the world's, world income falls relative to British income, and/or British interest rates fall relative to world interest rates, among other reasons.
   b. A surplus of British pounds, and a British balance of payments deficit.
   c. depreciate

PROBLEMS

1. a. -, 11181;   b. (1) 710, 10475, -4 (any order) (2) +, 11181
2. 0.65, 1.538
3. a. 0.95, 1.053; b. (1) 400 (2) 421.05;   c. (1) buy, 160 (2) sell, 170
4. a, c, and e

GLOSSARY TO CHAPTER 33

Accounting identities Values that are equivalent by definition.

Appreciation An increase in the exchange value of one nation's currency in terms of the currency of another nation.

Balance of payments A system of accounts that measures transactions of goods, services, income, and financial assets between domestic households, businesses, and governments and residents of the rest of the world during a specific time period.

Balance of trade The difference between exports and imports of goods.

Capital account A category of balance of payments transactions that measures flows of real and financial assets.

Crawling peg An exchange rate arrangement in which a country pegs the value of its currency to the exchange value of another nation's currency but allows the par value to change at regular intervals.

Current account A category of balance of payments transactions that measures the exchange of merchandise, the exchange of services, and unilateral transfers.

Depreciation A decrease in the exchange value of one nation's currency in terms of the currency of another nation

Dirty float Active management of a floating exchange rate on the part of a country's government, often in cooperation with other nations.

Exchange rate The price of one nation's currency in terms of the currency of another country.

Flexible exchange rates Exchange rates that are allowed to fluctuate in the open market in response to changes in supply and demand. Sometimes called *floating exchange rates*.

Foreign exchange market A market in which households, firms, and governments buy and sell national currencies.

Foreign exchange risk The possibility that changes in the value of a nation's currency will result in variations in the market value of assets.

Hedge A financial strategy that reduces the chance of suffering losses arising from foreign exchange risks.

International Monetary Fund A multinational organization that aims to promote world economic growth through more financial stability.

Par value The officially determined value of a currency.

Special drawing rights (SDRs) Reserve assets created by the International Monetary Fund for countries to use in settling international payment obligations.

Target zone A range of permitted exchange rate variations between upper and lower exchange rate bands that a central bank defends by selling or buying foreign exchange reserves.